The Internet Says It's True

Stories that Sound Made Up–But Aren't

by Michael Kent

Copyright © 2025 by KentMagic Productions, LLC

All rights reserved.

No portion of this book may be reproduced in any form without written permission from the publisher or author, except as permitted by U.S. copyright law.

This publication is designed to provide accurate and authoritative information in regard to the subject matter covered. It is sold with the understanding that neither the author nor the publisher is engaged in rendering legal, investment, accounting or other professional services. While the publisher and author have used their best efforts in preparing this book, they make no representations or warranties with respect to the accuracy or completeness of the contents of this book and specifically disclaim any implied warranties of merchantability or fitness for a particular purpose.

KentMagic Productions, LLC
Hilliard, OH 43026
michaelkentlive.com

Cover Design by Michael Kent
Copy Editing by Erik Hane

For Alison, who puts up with me spending four hours in the basement every Sunday recording and editing podcasts and is the reason why it's so sweet to come upstairs.

Special Thanks to TISITORS: Eugene Anderson, Jim & Joanne Martin, Kicktraq, Jake Schneider, Matthew Dillon, Nicholas Decker & Shaun Brown. Additional thank you to WCBE and all of the amazing guests I've been fortunate to have on my show.

Table of Contents

Introduction 7
The Pepsi Cola Navy 8
The Challenger Disaster and Big Bird 13
The Man Who Invented Pringles Was Buried inside a Pringles Can 18
The Time We Almost Nuked South Carolina 21
The Vulcan Salute: The Power of a Feminine God 27
The Confederados: The Confederate Flag Flies in Brazil 31
Mind Your Business: Our First Minted Coin 36
Polio Outbreak: The Illicit Lemonade Stand 41
The Most Kissed Girl in the World 45
Ted Slauson: The Man Who Beat The Price is Right 50
Adobe Flash and the Demise of a Chinese Railroad 56
Dung Beetles: Crappy Celestial Travelers 60
Overthrowing the Government: The Insurrection in Wilmington ... 64
Stupid Contagion: The Limping Ladies of London 71
Evel Knievel: The Naming of a Legend 75
Human Sacrifice and Mexican Food 80
The Nebraska Miracle: The West End Baptist Church Explosion 85
A Titanic Hero at Dunkirk: Charles Lightoller 90
The Hartlepool Monkey Hangers 95
Measuring Misfortune: The Pirate Who Stole America's Metric System 100
Crowd Sourcing World War II: The Normandy Photo Contest 107
Pablo Escobar's Cocaine Hippos 113
Nazis in America: The Madison Square Garden Rally 119

Stuart Little and the Hungarian Masterpiece 127
The Vexing Vampires of Venice 132
The Dublin Whiskey Fire: Why Thirteen People Died 137
Poisoned: 344 Meals and a Miracle 142
Inglorious Bruin: Wojtek the Soldier Bear 148
The Woman Who Fell from the Sky and Lived 154
The Battle of Los Angeles: Real Bullets and Imaginary Targets.... 159
Edgar Allan Poe and the Cabin Boy, Richard Parker 164
Real-Life Jaws: The 1916 New Jersey Shark Attacks 170
Bat Bombs: A Crazy Military Idea That ALMOST Happened .. 178
Real or Fake? Palisade, Nevada's "Wild" West 185
The Amazing Pearl Harbor Prediction of Billy Mitchell 190
Bamber Bridge: American Racial Tension in the UK 195
Dumbest Civil Unrest Ever: The Straw Hat Riots 203
Eternal Neighbors: Nick Beef and Lee Harvey Oswald 209
22 Caliber Surgery: George's Horrible, Awful OCD Cure 217
Al Capone's Altruism and Spoiled Milk 223
Peter the Eagle: The U.S. Mint's Unofficial Pet Bird 229
Malicious Compliance: The Car Company That Sabotaged the Nazis.. 233
Cobra Invasion: The Springfield Snake Scare of 1953 239
Why Are Pencils Yellow? 246
The Immovable Ladder and the Status Quo 252
Puffin Patrol: Throwing Puffins off a Cliff 257
William Rankin: The Man Who Fell through a Cloud 262
Self-Surgery: Leonid Rogozov Removed His Own Appendix . 267
The Amazing Story behind the Bluetooth Logo 274
London Bridge is Falling Down (and Coming to America) 279
Running Out of Bullets: Greeks and Turks 284

Tarrare: The Man Who Ate Everything 289

Swindled in Wichita Falls: The World's Littlest Skyscraper.....295

The Explosion at Black Tom Island 301

Nub City: The Worst Kind of Insurance Fraud..........................307

The Awful Reason There Aren't More Mummies......................314

The Boston Molasses Flood 319

Thirteen Months: The Kodak Calendar Experiment 324

Abraham Lincoln Invented the Chokeslam 332

About the Author 337

Introduction

"Well the Internet says it's true, so it must be!" You'll only hear this statement used in conversation sarcastically. No one trusts "The Internet" as a source. Even saying "Wikipedia says so" isn't reliable enough for schoolteachers grading essays to accept. People discount fact-checking websites like Snopes and Politifact as biased or inaccurate. But their sources—those links listed at the bottom of the page—that's where the real truth of the Internet lies. That's where you find the news articles, the peer-reviewed journals, the firsthand accounts, and the experts. And the stories in this book are all well-sourced and researched. For every story, we scoured and searched through old newspaper articles, watched TV news reports, read books, viewed documentaries, and tried our best to represent the information accurately.

"The Internet Says It's True" started as a podcast in September of 2020 when my career performing comedy magic shows on the road turned into a career performing magic shows for a camera in my basement due to the COVID-19 pandemic. I had all the gear, I had the idea to make a non-magic podcast, and I had this fascination with the concept that no matter how smart we get, there are always new stories, facts, and bits of history to learn. The stories in this book are taken from stories I covered on the podcast over the past few years. If you'd like to "listen along," I've placed a QR code at the end of every story. It will lead you to the accompanying podcast episode. In addition to hearing the story, you'll also get to hear me discuss the topic with a guest!

I hope you tell these stories at parties.

The Pepsi Cola Navy

In the summer of 1959, American Vice President Richard Nixon and Soviet First Secretary Nikita Khrushchev met inside a home in Moscow. They were followed by countless press secretaries and aides, and multiple television cameras who would broadcast their meeting in color.

The home wasn't real. It was an exhibition set up in Sokolniki Park to show off the American way of living to the Soviets. In addition to the model home, more than 450 American companies had set up trade-show booths to show off their products. Plans for a similar exhibition in New York City would be made to show Americans the Soviet way of living. It was all part of the American National Exhibition, an effort to improve relations between the U.S. and the Soviet Union in a time when things were heating up between the two countries. The intercontinental ballistic missile had just been invented.

The two countries had very different ways of living, two very different forms of government and economy, and—in addition to bringing in three million visitors who would marvel at the exhibit in Solkoniki Park—it would be the site of what became known as the "Kitchen Debate" between Nixon and Khrushchev.

In front of television cameras, the two men walked around the American-style model home and debated the merits of capitalism versus communism. America was already becoming wary of the Soviets and their way of life. For the last decade the House Unamerican Activities Committee had been seeking out and blacklisting people in Hollywood with purported ties to communism.

During the Kitchen Debate, Khrushchev condemned the Americans' use of gadgets in the home, like the handheld lemon juicer. After some amount of bickering, the two men decided they should find areas where they agreed.

This is where we meet one of the key figures in our story: Donald Kendall. Kendall was the head of the Pepsi Cola Company's International Operations, and he was in the right place at the right time. As the debate between Nixon and Khrushchev was heating up, he helped to cool the tensions with a cold cup of Pepsi. Each of the men sipped the Pepsi, and this led to an exchange about how Pepsi tasted just as good when made with water from Russia. Khrushchev loved the drink and a seed was planted.

At this point in the telling of the story, we have to skip forward a bit, which is hard because a LOT happened right after the American National Exhibition: Kennedy becomes President, the Cuban Missile Crisis, Kennedy is assassinated, Johnson becomes President, the War in Vietnam, USSR invades Czechoslovakia. We can't get into all of that because for this story, we need to jump to 1972.

When Nixon became President, he was looking for ways to improve relations with the Soviets. At this point, the Soviet leader was Leonid Brezhnev and the two countries came up with a deal to open twenty Pepsi Bottling plants in the Soviet Union. It would be the very first American product manufactured there. Part of the deal was that their rival, Coca Cola, couldn't be marketed in the USSR.

Pepsi would ship over all the supplies needed to make cola with Russian water supplies and in return, well—the Soviet currency wasn't worth anything outside of Russia. There weren't enough American dollars in the Soviet Union to pay for their end of the trade deal. So what they came up with was something creative. Stolichnaya Vodka was a company that was owned and controlled by the Soviet government. Pepsi was granted exclusive rights to import and market Stolichnaya in the United States. The Soviets get Pepsi; the Americans get vodka. Seems like a good deal. And it *was* for a while. But then geopolitical tensions got in the way again.

The USSR had invaded Afghanistan. The Americans helped the Afghans defend themselves. Now President Ronald Reagan and Soviet Leader Mikhail Gorbachev had been working to improve relations once again, but for the American public, the damage had been done. Many Americans refused to buy Soviet products, including Stolichnaya Vodka. As Reagan left office and George Bush became President, Pepsi wanted to build twenty-six more bottling plants in the Soviet Union, but the Pepsi for Vodka deal was no longer working. They needed to figure out another solution. And that brings us to one of the weirdest trade deals in history.

The Soviet Union's invasion of Afghanistan had turned many Americans against buying Soviet-made products. So as a result, no one was buying enough Stolichnaya

Vodka to account for the amount of Pepsi being sent to Russia.

It was 1989 and there was one thing that Gorbachev's government had a lot of: surplus military equipment. Pepsi's Donald Kendall was still involved. He was retired but still serving on the Board of Directors for PepsiCo. The deal that Gorbachev's government came up with was to give Pepsi seventeen diesel-powered attack submarines, a cruiser, a destroyer, a frigate, and a few oil tankers, around twenty ships in all. Pepsi accepted. This raised more than a few red flags with the American government.

But here's the thing: these ships were pretty much all obsolete. These loud diesel submarines had been replaced by quieter nuclear-powered subs. The ships were old, rusty and hardly usable. Even so, the government didn't like the idea of a corporation holding such a large naval fleet. That's where we get this amazing quote from none other than Pepsi's Donald Kendall. He said to the Pentagon, "I'm dismantling the Soviet Union faster than you are."

The ships weren't sea-worthy. Most of them listed to one side. They were only valuable for scrap. So as soon as they could, Pepsi sold the ships to a Swedish company for recycling, and used that money to fund their shipping and bottling operations in the Soviet Union. But here's the punchline, and this is 100 percent true: For a short time, from the time they received the ships to the time they sold them, the Pepsi Cola Company was the sixth largest naval military in the world.

The Challenger Disaster and Big Bird

Like so many of Jim Henson's creations, Big Bird started as a simple sketch. He was creating characters for a new television show, *Sesame Street*. The producers of the show had asked that Henson create some of his muppets for the show that would interact with the human characters on *Sesame Street*. The original sketch of Big Bird is nothing but a pencil drawing of a man with the big bird outline around him holding his arm straight above his head to make the mouth of the tall figure talk. There's also a color drawing of what he thought Big Bird looked like, and it ended up being pretty similar to the character that we now know.

The muppets' chief puppet creator, Kermit Love, built the Big Bird costume as a larger-than-life, eight-foot-two-inch creation. The right arm of the person inside would control the mouth and face and the left arm would control Big

Bird's left wing. There wasn't a spot for holes to see out, so a small camera would lead to a tiny television inside the costume. Kermit Love was particularly proud of the fact that Big Bird was created to occasionally shed a yellow feather or two as he moved around. Love compared this to a tall tree dropping the occasional leaf.

The rest of Big Bird is all due to the man who is synonymous with the character: Carol Spinney. Spinney gave Big Bird his voice, his mannerisms, and his child-like demeanor, which he's described as perpetually six years old. Carol had worked with Jim Henson for the last seven years after the two met at a puppeteering convention. He played both the parts of Big Bird and Oscar the Grouch on *Sesame Street,* and worked on the show for forty-nine years. One of the ways that Big Bird taught children was through frequently misunderstanding things—the same types of things that a six-year-old might misunderstand—and that presented a brilliant way for the children to learn along with Big Bird.

Since he first appeared on the very first episode of *Sesame Street* on November 10th, 1969, Big Bird rose to huge popularity and fame and became a symbol for educational television. He's met with many famous guests. Big Bird appeared with every first lady from Pat Nixon to Dr. Jill Biden, with the only exceptions being Nancy Reagan and Melania Trump.

Jim Henson died on May 16, 1990. And at his memorial service, Big Bird sang a song that will go down in history. A tear-jerking rendition of "It's Not Easy Being Green," a song that Henson had made famous through his signature "Kermit the Frog" character. Carol Spinney continued playing Big Bird until 2018, and while neither Jim Henson nor Carol Spinney are with us today, the character of Big Bird continues on—still six years old.

The second story is one of which I have a really strong memory. Picture this with me. I'm in Miss Hayes's first grade class at East Elementary in Urbana, Ohio. They've wheeled a television cart into the classroom so we could take part in a special event: the Challenger Space Shuttle liftoff. We were so excited. My first-grade teacher, Miss Hayes, was so excited for us to witness the launch. Not many people know this, but the Challenger liftoff was not watched live by that many Americans. A lot of people have a sort of Mandela effect that they remember watching it live at home, but in reality, NASA Space Shuttle missions had become fairly commonplace and weren't seen as particularly noteworthy by the late 80s. It was broadcast live on CNN, but people weren't watching cable news around the clock like they do now. Most people who remember watching it actually witnessed it when the news replayed the event after it happened. Even so, a survey was conducted that concluded 85 percent of Americans knew about within an hour. But for people my age—people in grade school at the time—it WAS noteworthy and was shown in every classroom because of a special guest on the shuttle.

Christa McAuliffe was a thirty-seven-year-old social studies schoolteacher from New Hampshire who was going to be the first teacher in space. She was selected from more than 11,000 applicants. The Teacher in Space program had been announced by Ronald Reagan in 1984 to inspire students and increase interest in math, science, and space exploration. For that reason, the launch of the Challenger for its mission STS-51-L was shown live in classrooms across America on January 28, 1986.

McAuliffe was a civilian but had trained with NASA for a year after being chosen. She was among the six other NASA crew members on board that day and, as many know, one minute and thirteen seconds after liftoff, disaster struck. The shuttle broke apart on its ascent and onlookers watching from the ground saw the solid stream of white smoke break apart into several swirling patterns and clouds.

No one survived the disaster. The Teacher in Space program was cancelled soon after. After lengthy investigations, it was determined that a rubber gasket in the solid rocket booster had weakened due to the freezing temperatures before the launch. NASA knew about this weakness, but this particular mission had been delayed so many times that they pushed to launch anyway.

So back to that first-grade classroom. The image of that craft breaking apart on television still remains with me. I remember turning around to see Miss Hayes crying.

The third story is where stories one and two come together. Before Christa McAuliffe, before the 11,000 applicants, even before the Teacher in Space program, another idea was proposed. It was a priority to get kids interested in space and math and science. They knew they wanted to use the Space Shuttle missions to do that.

So in the early 1980s, Carol Spinney got a letter. He had been invited to go up in the Challenger Space Shuttle. Carol Spinney, as Big Bird, would be the first American civilian in space. Millions of American school children would get to see one of their childhood friends, Big Bird, fly into space. Spinney would have to undergo testing and training, but it never got to that point.

The big bird costume was big. It weighed ten pounds, but it took up a LOT of area. They couldn't figure out how they would stow the Big Bird suit in the tight quarters of the Challenger.

After it was decided that Big Bird wouldn't be able to do the mission, they decided that Big Bird's teddy bear,

Radar, would be on the mission. This idea would eventually be scrapped with the development of the Teacher in Space concept.

Big Bird never went to space. It wasn't meant to be. The Challenger space shuttle disaster was a horrible tragedy. And it would have been one that would have absolutely devastated children just as much if their beloved friend Big Bird had been one of those souls lost on board.

Today, Big Bird continues to delight and educate children. He received a star on the Hollywood Walk of Fame, one of just a few fictional characters to receive the honor. He's appeared in movies, television shows, *Saturday Night Live,* and *The Tonight Show,* and has never stopped that original mission of educating kids from their level—just like he's done for fifty-two years.

The Man Who Invented Pringles Was Buried inside a Pringles Can

This story goes back to Cincinnati, Ohio, in 1956. Proctor & Gamble, a company that started by selling candles but which was famous for Tide detergent, Ivory soap, and Crest toothpaste, wanted to offer a potato chip product that addressed common complaints about chips. They wanted a product that wouldn't break, wasn't greasy, and didn't come in a bag filled with air. They gave this job to Fredric J. Baur, a chemist.

Baur was an organic chemist who received a master's and PhD from The Ohio State University, my alma mater. He was an aviation physiologist in the Navy and had invented various frying oils in addition to Freeze-Dried Ice Cream— side note, I love that stuff, so thanks Fred.

He spent two years developing the saddle-shaped product. The shape is called a hyperbolic paraboloid; the claim is that the unique shape of the chip provides an aerodynamic profile that keeps it in place during packaging and because they are stacked manufactured in a consistent shape and stacked tightly, they don't break as much.

Putting them in a cylinder-style packaging container was Fred Baur's idea. The tube worked together with the shape of the chip to allow them to stack without coming apart from each other during shipping. The whole point was to keep the chips fresh and keep them from breaking.

There are various theories on why the chips were called Pringles. One story is that they wanted the chips to have a family appeal, so they chose a name out of a phone book. Another story says they chose the name out of a hat. A slightly more plausible theory comes from the fact that two Proctor & Gamble advertising execs lived on Pringle Drive in a Cincinnati suburb. But maybe the most likely is that they were named as an homage to a man named Mark Pringle, who filed a potato chip processing patent that was cited in their own patent.

The flavor of the chips was created by a man named Alexander Liepa. The machine that made them was invented by Gene Wolfe, who was a mechanical engineer but was better known as a science-fiction author.

So in 1968, Pringles were finally unveiled to the public in Indiana, and were so popular that they were available across the U.S. by the mid 1970s and available internationally in the early 1990s.

Now owned by Kellogg's, Pringles are available now in twenty-one flavors in the U.S. and other flavors internationally. In the UK, you can get Prawn Cocktail

Pringles and in Asia they've offered grilled shrimp and seaweed flavors. Gross.

Frederic Baur passed away at the age of eighty-nine. Sadly he died of Alzheimers in 2008. Two months later, *Time Magazine* ran a story about the peculiar way in which he was buried.

Baur had thought of the idea of being buried in the Pringles can he designed in the 1980s and joked with his kids about it. But they soon realized he was serious. He was cremated and, on the way to pick up his remains, his children stopped at a nearby Walgreens and bought a can of original-flavor Pringles. They put part of his ashes in the can and buried this Pringles can below his headstone in Arlington Memorial Gardens in Cincinnati. If you visited the grave, you'd never know that six feet below the earth, there is a Pringles can full of the ashes of the man who invented it.

The Time We Almost Nuked South Carolina

Remember that movie *Broken Arrow*? John Travolta and Christian Slater as a couple Air Force pilots whose job it is to locate some missing dropped nuclear warheads? Fun film. Well it turns out "Broken Arrow" is the official term the military uses for an accident involving nuclear weapons. And in the 76 years since the invention of nuclear weapons in 1945, we've had at least 32 Broken Arrow scenarios.

For this story, we're just going to be talking about one particular aircraft: the Boeing B-47 Stratojet. Even before the end of World War Two, the Air Force had asked manufacturers to start drawing up plans for a long-range jet-powered bomber. Remember, the airplane that really ended World War Two by dropping atomic bombs in

Japan was the B-29, a propeller aircraft. The United States never did put any jet aircraft into combat in that war. It was still very early in the development of jet-powered flight.

The B-47 was finally put into service in 1951. It was a swept-wing sleek-looking bomber aircraft with 6 engines carried under its wings. And if I had to describe the problem with these aircraft, it would be that they suffered from growing pains.

There were the growing pains of jet-propelled flight itself. While the aircraft was incredibly fast and powerful, it took a very long time to accelerate. The newly designed swept wing caused structural issues. New design elements like the sweep wings and power elements like jet engines were being put on an aircraft essentially using outdated metallurgy and construction techniques. And there were a lot of limits on its capability. It was a difficult plane to fly for airmen who were used to a ten-man crew. The B-47 flew with only three. So every moment of flight—every issue, every warning—was happening faster and with fewer men to tend to it. The slightest lapse in attention could now be catastrophic. Then there were the growing pains of a quickly growing air force. Ramping up mass production on the aircraft led to a few manufacturing issues. By the time they were produced, the existing refueling infrastructure didn't meet the demands of these new long-range bombers.

They started retiring the B-47 just eighteen years after it was introduced. To give you a frame of reference, the B-52 Bomber was introduced in 1955 and has yet to be retired from service 66 years later. So the B-47 Stratojet was a short-lived bomber designed to face a very real and serious threat of nuclear war. It was designed to carry nuclear bombs and could fly all the way to the Soviet Union with them.

There were just over 2,000 Stratojets manufactured. And a staggering 10 percent of them—203 to be exact—were lost in crashes. And when you look at the timeline of when this aircraft was in its peak duty, it coincides with the time when aircraft started carrying nuclear weapons. That leads to the horrible events of 1957 and 1958 that we'll get to in just a moment.

The reason we spent so much time learning about the B-47 is that out of the thirty-two Broken Arrow events in history, nine of them involved this aircraft. Now think back to what we learned about how short-lived this airplane's operational lifespan was; this gives you a pretty good idea of how dangerous it really was. And it's even crazier than that. Those nine potential nuclear accidents happened in a period of just three years, from 1956 to 1958. And in 1957 and 1958, 49 of these aircraft crashed, killing a total of 122 airmen. As many problems as there were with the B-47, neither of the two stories we're going to talk about were the fault of the aircraft.

In the dark early morning of February 5 of 1958, a B-47 Crew commanded by Air Force Colonel Howard Richardson left from Homestead Air Force Base in Florida to conducted a simulated combat mission for training. It was carrying a 7,600-pound Mark 15 nuclear bomb. In airspace nearby, Air Force Lt. Clarence Stewart was piloting his F-86 fighter jet. He didn't see the B-47 on his radar and at approximately 2 a.m., the two aircrafts collided. With the wing missing from his small fighter jet, Lt. Stewart ejected and parachuted to safety in a swamp. For the B-47 bomber, their fuel tanks had been heavily damaged and were leaking fuel. Colonel Richardson didn't know if he could land the bomber without the nuclear bomb detaching and detonating. He made the choice to ditch the bomb in the waters off Tybee Island in Georgia. He was able to land the plane safely at Hunter Air Base in Savannah. But that bomb landed in the Atlantic Ocean near Wassaw Sound. And as far as we know...that's where the bomb rests, undetonated, today.

Just over one month later, on March 11 of 1958, it was the middle of the afternoon in Mars Buff, South Carolina, when six-year-old Helen and nine-year-old Frances Gregg were playing in their yard with their cousin Ella. Suddenly, there was a whistle from the sky followed by a ground-shaking explosion.

Here's what happened: Captain Earl Koehler was piloting a B-47E Stratojet 15,000 feet in the sky over South Carolina. The crew was scheduled to fly to the United Kingdom and continue on to North Africa. This was part of an ongoing training mission to track the accuracy of mock bomb drops. The bombs on board were very real. Tensions with the Soviet Union were at a height and the Cold War was becoming less cold by the day. For this reason, the aircraft taking part in this training mission, ominously dubbed Operation Snow Flurry, carried live nuclear bombs in case war broke out during the missions. The bomb being carried by Captain Koehler's B-47 that day was similar in size to the one lost in the Atlantic in February—a 7,600-pound Mark 6 nuclear bomb.

The first sign of a problem that day was when Captain Koehler noticed an indicator light telling him that a bomb harness locking pin did not engage. This wasn't the mechanism that held the bomb in place - it was an added safety measure. It was one of a few steps to secure it to the plane. When he noticed this indicator, the bombardier and navigator, Captain Bruce Kulka scrambled to the bomb bay area of the aircraft to check it out. As he reached around the bomb to lift himself up, he accidentally grabbed hold of the one thing he shouldn't have: the bomb's emergency release mechanism. This dropped the full weight of the ten foot long, 7,600-pound bomb, along with Captain Kulka, onto the bomb bay doors. The bombardier desperately reached his arm out to grab on to something. The bomb, however, weighed too much for the doors. He looked down through the open doors and watched in horror as the bomb started falling 15,000 feet to the land below.

The three children playing below at the Gregg house would have had no idea that the bomb was coming toward them. The Mark 6 nuclear bomb detonated 200 yards from the children. All three were injured, but none were killed. Luckily for those children, and for Mars Bluff, South Carolina, and for the southeastern part of the United States, the nuclear capsule was not on the bomb. The capsule, which contained the fissile nuclear core, was still on board the aircraft and hadn't been loaded into the bomb housing.

Even so, that bomb was carrying enough explosives to blow a crater into the ground that was 70 feet wide and 30 feet deep. In addition to injuring the three girls playing, it obliterated their playhouse, injured their mother, father and brother, and damaged seven nearby buildings.

After the incident and the victims' recovery, the Gregg family sued and was awarded $54,000 in damages. If you visit Mars Bluff, South Carolina, you can still see the crater today. It's overgrown with trees and brush, but the site is marked with a historical marker.

As for the bomb dropped outside Tybee Island in the Atlantic Ocean? Throughout the years, the military has mounted efforts to locate the bomb, even as recently as 2004. But to this day, it's one of six American nuclear weapons that have been lost and never found.

The Vulcan Salute: The Power of a Feminine God

Some of the best moments ever to appear on screen have been decisions that were made in the moment by the actors - things that weren't even in the script. Think of DeNiro's famous "You talkin' to me?" scene in *Taxi Driver*. That wasn't in the script. That was just DeNiro ad libbing. Or Humphrey Bogart's famous line "Here's lookin' at you, kid." Not in the script. Just Bogart repeating something he had said to Ingrid Bergman earlier that day off-camera.

So goes this story about Leonard Nimoy and the famous Vulcan Salute.

The salute was first used in the first episode of the second season of the original *Star Trek* series. It was called "Amok Time" and the plot was that Vulcans had a particular time that they had to mate with another Vulcan and Spock had to return to mate with a woman with whom he had sort of an arranged marriage.

Spock was the only non-human being on the Starship Enterprise—he was only half human—so providing a back story for this alien being provided some interesting depth and color to the series. He was one of the main characters, yet we didn't know much about his people. This episode was providing the first look into other Vulcans and as such, it was decided that they should have some sort of way of greeting each other.

This is where Leonard Nimoy remembered something from his Jewish upbringing. He recalled a time he went to the orthodox Jewish temple with his family in the north end of Boston and witnessed a group of five or six men facing the congregation and singing and shouting a Hebrew Benediction. The prayer was called the "Shekhina," which represents the feminine representation of God as she comes into the temple to bless the congregants. Along with the chanting and shouting, the men held their hands up, palms out and fingers together, except for the middle and ring fingers, which were separated into a "v." This split-fingered gesture—the Kohanim Jewish Blessing—stuck in Nimoy's mind as something powerful. It's a sign of the Hebrew letter "Shin" - the first part of words like "Shalom" and "Shaddai." For Nimoy, he saw this blessing occurring during a time in which congregants are encouraged to cover their eyes or look away to not be damaged by the power of the feminine divine being entering the temple. Nimoy looked anyway and felt like he was witnessing something secret and something powerful.

When Nimoy was looking for a choice to make for his character, he remembered this split-fingered blessing and decided to use that—with one hand instead of two like was used in the temple—as the way that Vulcans greeted each other. In the episode, he used the salute to greet the

Vulcan character T'Pau, played by Celia Lovsky, and his bride to be, T'Pring, played by Arlene Martel. It was an instant cultural phenomenon.

Star Trek viewers within just a few days would use the Vulcan salute to greet Nimoy in public. It became iconic. If you've seen the hand signal, you've probably also heard the accompanying greeting: "Live long and prosper." Not many people realize, however, that there is a correct response: "Peace and long life." Other times in the series, "Live long and prosper" was used as the response.

In the Vulcan language, it's "dif-tor heh smusma."

There are many possible attributions to "Live long and prosper." There's an ancient Egyptian blessing which says "may he live, be prosperous, be healthy." There's a phrase in Deuteronomy in the Bible that says "Live and prosper," and even Shakespeare's *Romeo and Juliet* has the line "Live and be prosperous," when Romeo says goodbye to his servant Balthasar. There are many phrases similar in literature throughout history, so it's tough to know exactly how they landed on this for the Vulcan greeting—but it too became iconic.

Leonard Nimoy died in 2015. That year, to honor him, astronaut Samantha Cristoferetti took a photo of herself doing the Vulcan salute…from space.

The goal was just to show a small glimpse of Vulcan culture and add background to one of the TV show's characters. But the result had a much larger impact. The result was a sort of cultural icon that became synonymous with the show itself. And with that, I wish you peace and long life.

The Confederados: The Confederate Flag Flies in Brazil

Something you hear a lot when it comes to patriotism or politics is "Love it or leave it"—this idea that if you have a complaint about this country or its government that you should just leave. This story is about a group of people who took that seriously.

In 1865 the American Civil War came to an end. Between the months of April and June, most of the Confederate soldiers surrendered. It had been four years of bloody battles and around 750,000 dead, about 2.5 percent of the total U.S. population.

Lincoln had a plan for reconstruction that was a threat to what many considered the southern way of living. Freed slaves would have joined the working class—they would have been given their own land—and amnesty would be given to those Confederate soldiers who took up arms against the United States. Lincoln wanted a swift reunification and so his plan was based on forgiveness. But as we know, Lincoln was assassinated soon after the end of the war. And while his successor Andrew Johnson wouldn't carry out Lincoln's vision for reconstruction, many Confederate soldiers worried about living in a country that didn't hold their values. Others had lost their land.

Starting just before the Civil War, America was experiencing westward expansion. The building of the intercontinental railroad and the Homestead Act had people flocking west. In fact, the argument as to whether these new territories would be slave states or free states was one of the significant factors to the start of the war. After the war, a lot of Confederate soldiers moved out of the south. They went west, seeking out fortune and a new life.

For some of the leaders of the Confederate Army, amnesty wasn't initially extended to them. Jefferson Davis spent two years in a Virginia prison. When he was released, he fled to Canada, then England. His Vice President, Alexander Stephens, was held in a Boston prison until October when President Johnson released him. He wouldn't flee the country at all and instead went on to be a U.S. Congressman and the Governor of Georgia.

Robert E. Lee fought against Black voting rights after the war and ended up poor and homeless before being made the head of Washington College.

General George Pickett fled to Canada for two years until he was pardoned.

But for some of the soldiers who still deeply held their Confederate pro-slavery values, they sought out to create new Confederate colonies outside of the United States. One plan was for a place called the "New Virginia Colony." The main settlement was planned in Carlota, halfway between Mexico City and Veracruz, but there were as many as four other colonies planned throughout Mexico. There were a few problems: Mexico wouldn't allow them to bring slaves, and eventually the Confederate-friendly emperor of Mexico was overrun with Mexican Republicans who didn't approve of the Confederate settlers.

Other Confederate colonies were attempted in Belize, Paraguay, and Cuba. But the most widespread and successful attempt at a new confederate colony occurred in the Brazilian state of São Paulo.

There's a small cemetery south of Santa Barbara D'Oeste in Brazil. It's called Cemtério dos Americanos. And there are several generations of American immigrants buried there, almost 500 interments in total. Every year in April, there's an unapologetic festival at the cemetery celebrating all things Confederate: the Festa Confederada. Members of the community meet to eat foods from the American South like fried chicken and French fries, listen to country music, dress up in replica Confederate uniforms and antebellum dresses. And they dance. The dance floor, a permanent outdoor surface, depicts a giant Confederate flag. It's a celebration of Brazil's interpretation of the Confederacy—stewarded by Brazilians who are the descendants of Confederate immigrants who moved there from America more than 150 years ago. I went to their Instagram page and it's absolutely bizarre. You'll find a combination of Confederate flags, American bikers, women in ornate Civil War era dress, men in costume, Trump flags, and quasi-American patriotism. Pictures of the festival include other icons of a conservative anti-government America, like the Gadsden "don't tread on me" flag. One Memorial Day post says "In honor of the fallen" with a pair of oak leaves, but inside the oak leaves is the Confederate flag. Why here? Why in the middle of Brazil?

In 1865, slavery was still legal in Brazil. In fact, it was the last of the western countries to outlaw slavery in 1888. Brazil relied on African enslaved people all the way back to the 16th century when the country developed a lucrative mining industry. Around 40 percent of the 11 million Africans that were forced into slavery in the Atlantic sale trade were brought to Brazil to work on sugar cane plantations. In addition to sugar cane, Dom Pedro the second, Brazil's Emperor, wanted to develop a lucrative cotton industry in Brazil. He offered southern farmers cheap land, tax breaks, and free travel to his country in order to cultivate this new industry. While some Confederate leaders discouraged southerners from emigrating to Brazil, thousands did anyway.

No one is sure exactly how many Confederates fled to São Paulo. Conservative estimates put the number at around 8,000 but port records of Rio de Janiero show that as many as 20,000 Americans entered Brazil after the war. These were people who no longer identified with an America that didn't value a slave-holding agricultural South. They were people who didn't want to feel conquered and saw the South without slavery as a south that would live in poverty. So they took Dom Pedro the second up on his offer and fled by the thousands. Many fled to Santa Barbara d'Oeste, a city northwest of Campinas. Others founded the city of Americana to the east. And it was there that these Americans put down roots. Some returned the U.S. once reconstruction failed and the Jim Crow era began. But most stayed.

So for now, their legacy continues. And just like how the "Lost Cause" narrative replaced the truth for some here in the states, the same is true for the proxy Confederacy that still exists 3,000 miles from where the Civil War ended. Today, the history and legacy of the confederados that left the U.S. is held by a group called the Fraternity of the American Descendants. Marcelo Dodson is a past president of the group, and in the 2017 aftermath of the white-nationalist rally in Charlottesville, VA, he made the argument that the Civil War was a battle not for slavery, but for small government, free commerce, and states' rights. This of course is a view of the conflict with which most historians disagree. In an era in which more and more Americans disagree with the flying of the

Confederate flag in the U.S., it still flies—proudly and strangely in one small part of Brazil.

Mind Your Business: Our First Minted Coin

Every American knows who Benjamin Franklin was: a man so important he's one of only two non-Presidents to be featured on U.S. paper currency. He was an inventor, a writer, a diplomat, a scientist, a statesman, and, most notably, one of the few men responsible for drafting America's Declaration of Independence in 1776. He was the only person to have signed all four major founding documents: The Declaration of Independence, The Treaty of Alliance with France, The Treaty of Paris, and the United States Constitution.

But there's something that Ben Franklin did that not as many people are familiar with. He was an artist and designer of American money.

About a decade after the founding of the new nation, a problem was arising. There were a lot of counterfeit and lightweight copper pennies in circulation. States were minting their own pennies and because of the inconsistency in weight and counterfeiting, businesses were losing money accepting these coins, which would occasionally be accepted as less than face value. This was hurting the economy of the thirteen original states. To fight the problem, the Continental Congress of the Confederation decided on a resolution in 1787. It was for the contract to mint a national copper cent.

About ten weeks after the resolution was signed, a design had been approved for the coin. The Reverse of the coin (a numismatic term for the back of the coin) would have an unbroken chain with thirteen links representing the colonies. In the center of that, the words "WE ARE ONE." The Obverse, or front, of the coin would feature a prominent sun dial with a sun shining down on it. On the right, the date 1787 (even though all these coins were struck in 1788) and on the left the word FUGIO. This is a Latin word meaning "I fly" and is apparently a reference to time flying by and the coin flying across the sky, represented by the sun and sun dial. But perhaps the most interesting part of the coin to me are the big letters on the bottom, under the sun dial. It's there that the coin features the intriguing words: "MIND YOUR BUSINESS."

Eric Newman was a Numismatist who wrote several books about the Fugio Cent, and he was able to show that the design of this copper coin was the handiwork of Benjamin Franklin. He was known for several of these mottos and designs like the thirteen-chain links. It's also very similar to a dollar coin that Franklin had designed in 1776 for the new nation, but which was never circulated.

But why the words "Mind your business"? It seems like a weird if not anachronistic phrase to have on a coin. When the coin was designed in 1787, this phrase didn't mean what it means today. Today when we use the phrase, we obviously mean "stop being nosy." But Benjamin Franklin meant "mind your business" literally. As in, "pay attention to your business," with "business" literally meaning business. Among all those things I listed about what Ben Franklin *was*, he was a businessman, with a strong worth ethic. These coins reflect that ethic.

The story of how these first coins were minted is rather interesting as well. The United States Mint wasn't established until 1792, so how did they mint this first national cent?

The Congress of the Confederation asked for bids on striking the coins, and several copper makers came forward wanting to make the coins. The contract went to a man named James Jarvis in Connecticut. Connecticut had opened the first state mint in 1785, and Jarvis owned a controlling interest in the company, called the Company for Coining Coppers. And in true fashion of politics in America, he won the contract by bribing the Head of the Treasury board, William Durer, with $10,000. Durer was the assistant to the Treasurer and was an old family friend of Jarvis, so he was awarded the contract and started the process of constructing the dies to make the coin.

To carve and build these dies, he looked to a man who was missing part of his ear and had a small C branded into his forehead. The reason for these disfigurements? This man, Abel Buell, was a known counterfeiter. He had been caught counterfeiting five-pound notes and his punishment was lopping off the top of one of his ears and branding him with a letter describing his crime. This was apparently a common type of punishment in those days.

He set up the dies and began striking the coins, along with the help of an enslaved man named Aaron, several children, a freed Black man and others. It was a group effort to get these coins made, and the problem became apparent quickly.

The coinage requested by the contract required 300 tons of copper. There weren't 300 tons of copper in the United States. He had put his father in law, Samuel Broome, in charge of mining additional copper, but it wasn't very successful. After Jarvis's mint produced 1200 pounds of coins, they ran out. This was a problem not only for the nation, not only for Jarvis, but for the Treasury. Jarvis had been given the first 30 tons of copper and he never paid the Federal Government back for it. Ultimately, he fled to Europe to look for more copper and to escape his troubles.

Eventually Abel Buell fled to England as well. He eventually returned and is credited for printing the first U.S. map, but he died penniless.

Samuel Broome, however, continued to mint coins at the Connecticut mint, but just made them lighter and thinner. In the end, he made about 400,000 Fugio Cents. This was 4 tons of copper instead of the 300 tons.

The Fugio Cents never did see a whole lot of circulation. There was a huge devaluation of copper and there just weren't enough coins to be in large use anyway. The population of the country at that time was just under four million, so there just weren't enough of these coins to be effective.

Today, collectors pay up to $10,000 for a Fugio Cent. Only 3,811 have been officially cataloged and graded. In 1926, a secret stash of these coins was found. They had been stored away in 1788. Those several thousand coins represent the largest chunk of the Fugio Coins that are now owned.

Who owns them? How do you get one? I think there's a saying about that from one of our founding fathers and from modern numismatists. Mind Your Business.

Polio Outbreak: The Illicit Lemonade Stand

About once a year, some local news station will run a story about how a little girl's lemonade stand got shut down because it didn't have the proper permits and such. And then there's always an ensuing argument about whether or not this is big-government regulation gone too far or if we should just let kids be kids and sell lemonade on the sidewalk.

When I first researched this story, it was happening as the COVID-19 vaccine was finally about to be distributed in America, and it was interesting to learn about the Polio vaccine and how we distributed it back in the mid-1950s. Obviously it's a different type of virus and a different type of vaccine, but people still talk about the hardships from Polio today. It saw outbreaks for a period of forty years before the vaccine. I grew up hearing stories about how my grandfather had to spend a period of a few months in an iron lung due to polio. And to put things in perspective, consider this. People still talk about how bad Polio was from the 1950s. In the 1952 outbreak, America saw 57,000 cases and just over 3,000 deaths. Compare that to the 111 million cases and 1.2 million American deaths from COVID. Makes you wonder how they'll talk about COVID-19 fifty years from now.

So, let's learn about this little girl that caused an outbreak of Polio in 1941. This happened outside of Chicago in Western Springs, Illinois. And it's true. It happened. There's a newspaper article from the *Kerrville Times* in 1941. The headline reads: "Girl's Lemonade Stand Gives Hot Tip on Paralysis." Before we learn about it, we should probably learn about Polio itself.

We have record of Polio, short for Poliomyelitis, all the way back in ancient Egypt. People suffering from unexplained paralysis and atrophied muscles are depicted in ancient drawings. But in 1916 and again in the early 1950s, Polio outbreaks ran rampant throughout the world. It peaked in 1952. Polio is caused by Poliovirus and is a viral disease that spreads through direct contact with people who have the infection. It's a disease that mostly affects the nervous system, causing paralysis. When you hear about "Iron Lungs," these were giant metal tubes that a patient would lie inside. It would simulate the muscle movement needed to draw and expel breath by changing the air pressure inside the tube. As the paralysis would keep patients from being able to move their diaphragm on their own, this kept them breathing.

Thankfully, we no longer see these contraptions. Partly because doctors and scientists have developed other ventilation machines, but mostly because we've nearly eradicated Polio thanks to vaccines.

I told you about this newspaper article I found from 1941. Here's a quote from that paper:

"Because a little girl kept a lemonade stand in suburban Western Springs and four of her playmates came down with infantile paralysis, scientists have struck the hottest trail of the deadly disease virus in the history of epidemiology. Because of the small size of the community, it was possible to examine everyone who came in contact with the little lemonade vendor. That she was the prime source was established early in the investigation. One hot afternoon in July, she did a lively business in front of her home. What did it matter if, as the day wore on, the glasses weren't rinsed after every using? Then she and four customers came down with the disease."

This case ended up being a great case study for epidemiologists of the time because the cases were very insulated to this one particular incident and the exposure was easy to trace. Contact tracing was easy in this case. Sadly, we don't have much more information on this particular story. Of course the children's names weren't included in the account and we also don't have any record of how the kids ended up. But we know that four cases of paralysis were caused from this one lemonade stand.

So maybe this is an extreme case, but it could be seen as an argument for setting up some sort of regulations for children looking to make a few extra bucks with their lemonade stand. Others might say that's ridiculous and we should just allow kids to learn about economy and capitalism through selling lemonade on the corner. After all, the free-market folks would say that if you want to keep doing business, don't paralyze yourself and friends, right? After all, people won't patronize the lemonade stand of the little girl who gave people Polio.

I think that when you look at lemonade stands these days, it's much more common for people to use disposable cups, so maybe this isn't something we need to worry about anymore. We do still see these stories about lemonade stands getting shut down every once in a while. I found an interesting one from 1997. A little boy in Indiana was shut down by health officials for not having a permit for his stand. He didn't have the required permits. So instead, he opened a sidewalk stand that sold items for which he didn't need permits. He sold squirt guns, balloons, magic tricks, and hats. And for every sale, the customer received a complimentary cup of lemonade.

When we look at the COVID-19 pandemic, we saw a lot of people step forward and donate their money and time to fighting the virus. And back in the 1950s, people did the same. They may have done it a nickel at a time, but they also did things on their own, separate from the March of Dimes organization to raise money to help fund the eradication of Polio. Eleanor Roosevelt wrote a column in her syndicated newspaper called *My Day*. In it, she talks about the efforts of everyday people to fight polio. And some of the efforts she cites are teens selling baked goods and….this is true….lemonade.

The Most Kissed Girl in the World

James Otis Elam was a physician and respiratory researcher in the U.S. who discovered the concept of "rescue-breathing" — that is, the idea that exhaling into a person's mouth gave them enough oxygen to help keep them alive. He had been working with iron lungs and, along with Dr. Peter Safar, helped to develop a new life-saving technique called Caridopulmonary Resuscitation, or CPR. This was in the late 1950s and soon the method of rescue breathing and CPR was being taught as a legitimate life-saving practice. Sidenote: it should be stated that television and movies have given people a false expectation as to the effectiveness of CPR. There was a study done by the *New England Journal of Medicine* that showed CPR in TV shows had a 75 percent success rate whereas in real life, the success rate is much lower in a person who is not breathing and has no circulation. But with that said, it's effective enough to still be used and taught, and in the absence of medical professionals, it's something that anyone can learn and could help some patients until medical assistance arrives.

But how can it be taught? When it was first developed, students practiced on each other. That's right. You had people blowing into the mouth and lungs of people who were breathing normally. After a while, we figured out that this is dangerous. Especially the chest compressions that are taught as part of CPR—it creates significant trauma. If you know anyone who has received CPR, you might know that it's common for the ribs or sternum to be bruised or even cracked in the process. This is where we meet the most kissed girl in the world: a fictional woman named "Resusci Anne."

Dr. Peter Safar knew there was a need for a way to practice CPR without using healthy people as subjects. He expressed this to a Norwegian Doctor, Bjorn Lind, who knew of a Norwegian toymaker, Aesmund Laerdal. He approached Laerdal about creating a life-like toy, a dummy that could be used to practice mouth-to-mouth breathing and chest compressions. Laerdal was on the forefront of creating toys with PVC faces—a doll called "Laerdal Anne," which was named "Toy of the Year" and became a best seller in Europe. This had led him to create realistic-looking dummies with wounds for military training. He was a natural fit to create the CPR dummy that Safar and Lind were talking about.

The result was a dummy that to this day we know as "Resusci Anne." It was unveiled at the 1960 International Symposium on Resuscitation in Norway and it was instantly so successful that the Laerdal Company was no longer a toymaker. Their new mission would be saving lives. Today, the American Heart Association credits Laerdal Products with training half a billion people in CPR and with having saved 2.5 million lives. The original Resusci Anne dolls were very simple in design, but today they make full-size mannequins that provide realistic biofeedback and sync data to smartphones as the training takes place.

When Laerdal was developing the Resusci Anne CPR dummy, they recognized that medical professionals were predominantly male at the time and might feel uncomfortable giving mouth-to-mouth resuscitation to a male dummy. They were looking for a female face to use as a model and it turned out there was already a quite famous one. Let's jump back in time all the way back to the late 1880s.

The story of L'Inconnue de la Seine has various roots, but the result of all of them are the same: a plaster casting of a young girl's face. The face has delicately closed eyes and a calm expression. Her mouth has a slight, almost knowing smile with the edges turned up. Her hair is short, parted down the middle.

Some claim that the cast was the death mask of a young girl who died of Tuberculosis in 1975. Some claim that it wasn't a death mask at all, but instead was the face of the daughter of a mask-maker in Germany who asked her to model for him.

But the predominant story is the legend of the young woman who was pulled out of the river Seine in the late 1880s. An unknown girl was found in the river near The Quai du Louvre, a walking area near the river Seine. She was anonymous. No one knew her identity, her social station, or her cause of death. Since she had no signs of foul play, suicide was suspected. The custom of the time was to put bodies on display at the Paris Mortuary for people to identify them. There were so many bodies pulled out of the Seine at that time that a special morgue with a public viewing area was built. That remained open from 1868 until 1909. And in 1889, the public viewing area of the morgue was a more popular tourist attraction than the zoo, the Louvre and the Eiffel Tower, which had just been built. But despite the crowds and despite days going by, this one particular girl went unclaimed and unidentified. They local population became intrigued by the girl, not only because she was a mystery, but because her facial features were so calm and beautiful. The mortuary had a local mask maker come and make a death mask of the girl —this was another practice that was a custom of the time when it came to notable figures. The face became known as L'Inconnue de la Seine—the woman of the Seine.

It was long before the mask of the mysterious woman started showing up for sale at shops along the river, and then throughout Paris, and before long, it was common to see the mask hanging in any high-class drawing room. Her face offered mystery and beauty, and Parisians would build their own stories around her. English Poet and Author Richard Le Gallienne wrote a novella in 1900 based on the face, called Worshipper of the Image, in which a poet falls in love with the mask. In 1910, a German author, Rainer Maria Rilke wrote the following passage in his novel: "The caster I visit every day has two masks hanging next to his door. The face of the young one who drowned, which someone copied in the morgue because it was beautiful, because it was still smiling, because its smile was so deceptive – as though it knew."

The mask lived on through these works, which still continue to this day, by the way: the mask is referenced in several films and albums of the last decade. So when we jump forward from 1900 to the late 1950s it makes sense that when Aesmund Laerdal was designing his CPR dummy and wanted to use a female face, he would choose this famous and intriguing mask as the face of his Resusci Anne doll.

If you look at those early CPR dummies from the 60s, you can definitely see the resemblance. And even today, when you look at Laerdal's Resusci Anne, you can see the face of L'Inconnue de la Seine. Using the death mask of a drowning victim to create an educational tool may seem morbid until you think about how famous and intriguing this image was. And the thought of a young girl without an identity going on to save millions is yet one more fantastic story that we have to tell about her.

Ted Slauson: The Man Who Beat *The Price is Right*

Retired weatherman Terry Kneiss had been called to "come on down" to be the next contestant on *The Price is Right* television game show. He got out of contestant's row by correctly guessing the price of a Big Green Egg smoker. When he made it to the final part of the show, the showcase, the first showcase included prizes like a karaoke machine, a pool table, and a 17-foot camper. Terry's opponent passed on the group of prizes, meaning it was up to him to guess the price without going over. A guess within $250 of the actual price would win him both showcases. The total value of the prizes was $23,743. Terry's guess? Exactly $23,743. It was the first time since 1973 that someone had guessed correctly to the dollar. But when the camera showed the show's host Drew Carey, he wasn't smiling.

I don't know about you, but for me, *The Price is Right* is indelibly linked to staying home sick from school. It will always invoke that sense of nostalgia - being home at 10am when you shouldn't be and feeling like you're getting away with something. The music, the colors, the stagecraft - it's all part of the image of a show that has changed very little since its first episode. The show rose to fame under its second host, Bob Barker, who hosted the show until 2007 when comedian Drew Carey took the reins. And for a show to have done so well through such a transition is saying something. It's a huge deal for a game show so iconic to pick a new host. A modern example would be the troubles that *Jeopardy* had trying to pick a new host after the death of long-time host, Alex Trebek. But *The Price is Right* continued to be popular and hardly changed a thing.

The show operates based on promoted brands and prizes that have won the valuable honor to have their products bid on by the contestants. The prizes that are often the most valuable are announced with a phrase that has transcended the show. "A new car!" And when a contestant loses, we hear the iconic "Sad Trombone," which has become a meme unto itself.

Even the show's theme song is iconic. But as the theme song played to close the show on December 16, 2008, Drew Carey and the producers were scrambling, trying to figure out what to do about Terry Kneiss's perfect bid to win the showcase. And they were looking into the audience at a man named Ted Slauson.

When you watch the broadcast of *The Price is Right* from Terry's Kneiss's perfect bid episode in 2008, you see the show go seamlessly straight from his bid to the announcer going through the next showcase into Drew Carey reading the actual prices. But in reality, the show taping had halted for a few minutes while executive producer Mike Richards and Kathy Greco, who had the official price lists, met with Carey to explain that something was up. He had bid the exact right amount, something that was seemingly impossible. They considered the idea that maybe he had been cheating. But they also had an idea of what was going on, and they were looking at a man in the front of the audience wearing a blue shirt. His name was Ted Slauson and they knew who he was.

Ted Slauson is a man who was a Superfan of *The Price is Right*. He was so famous to the cast and crew of the show, and to other show superfans, that people he didn't know would call him by name as he was lined up to enter the show. Slauson was such a fan of the show that he knew the prices of the items in the showcase. He remembered seeing those same prizes on previous shows. And he was loudly yelling and holding up fingers to convey those prices from his place in the audience to Terry Kneiss onstage.

There was another controversy that the show had just undergone. I mentioned *Jeopardy* earlier. The man who was set to be host of *Jeopardy* and then had his offer rescinded was Mike Richards. This was the same Mike Richards who in 2008 had just replaced Roger Dobkowitz as producer. Roger had been the show's producer for thirty-five years and was loved by fans of the show. But as Bob Barker retired, changes were being made. Between Mike Richards and new host Drew Carey, subtle things were changing on the show. And these superfans, just like any superfans, didn't like all the changes.

As Kathy Greco and Mike Richards heard Ted Slauson loudly yelling the prices to Terry onstage, they immediately connected those dots. To them, this was a fanatic who was angry that Roger had been replaced. Maybe he was even sent by Roger, they thought. Drew was angry. He was a new host of a popular show and now, if the show was corrupt, he was thinking it was the end of his reign as host. He recalled asking Kathy: "There's no way this is going to air, right?" And she replied, "I don't know how it could."

But there was a major problem with that. Terry Kneiss, and Ted Slauson for that matter, hadn't done anything illegal or wrong. The show encourages the audience to yell out their guesses. If Slauson was guilty of anything, it was watching the show too much.

It turns out the suspicions about Slauson being angry about the producer change weren't accurate. He just wanted to see Terry win. And we know this because Slauson was just doing what he had been doing since he first started showing up to tapings in 1989.

Theodore Slauson watched the show from the time he was a boy. And between 1989 and 1992, he attended more than twenty live tapings of the show. He recorded every show and kept a spreadsheet that recorded every prize and its value. Slauson made his living developing standardized testing and used those skills to build a computer program that allowed him to study his spreadsheet. When he would attend the show, he loudly shouted out the prices to the contestants. Several times, Bob Barker would interact with Ted during the show. He definitely knew who he was and when Ted got onto the show in 1992, Bob told him "Theodore you made it! He's been a loyal friend and true"

If you talk to Terry Kneiss about his win, he claims he didn't hear Slauson giving him the prices. He claims that he and his wife also kept spreadsheets of prices and memorized them. He claims that the 743 in his bid of $23,743 was from their anniversary and his wife's birth month. Terry and his wife were statisticians and loved numbers. He had worked in casinos busting card cheats.

It's totally plausible that he did it on his own. But according to Drew Carey, everyone knew that Slauson was yelling the prices. They even had to edit the show to remove Slauson several times.

As many of you know, I'm a professional magician. And there's a theory in magic called the "Too Perfect Theory." It's the idea that if something is fake and you're trying to make it look real, it can't be perfect. It would be like if you committed a crime and made up an alibi to the police, but then you started describing every person you saw and every car you passed in perfect detail. It would be too perfect. For this reason, you might see a mind reader or a magician mess up a small detail on purpose here or there. Well, the same goes for this. The only reason anyone knew that it wasn't a normal taping of the show was because Terry guessed the number on the nose. Had he guessed $23,500, he would had won and nobody would have thought any different.

The main problem was that *The Price is Right* was recycling the same prizes for the same prices for way too long. There wasn't enough variation. After the December 16, 2008 show, this all changed. They expanded the range of prizes to make it virtually impossible for anyone, no matter how good their memory, to be able to guess the prices. The example that Drew Carey gives is you could have the same car four days in a row, but with four different trim packages and the price could be anywhere from $20,000 to $25,000. So if you're an aspiring game-show contestant with a good memory and you plan on bringing *The Price is Right* down the way that Terry Kneiss and Ted Slauson did, you just might be hearing your own "sad trombone."

Adobe Flash and the Demise of a Chinese Railroad

If you weren't an internet user in the early 2000s, you really missed out on the best part of Flash. I'll try to tell this story without making it super boring for people who aren't into internet programming. I'm not, I'm just familiar with Flash because of all the internet media it created.

Around the time I was in college, there was huge internet phenomenon. One of the first internet-based regular cartoons. It was called *Homestar Runner*.

Homestar Runner was a comedy series made by Mike and Matt Chapman and it starred this main character, Strongbad. He was based on a character from an obscure wrestling computer game and he would basically just answer people's mail and it was always something funny. They were short form animated videos and some of the first viral content. They continue producing videos to this day, but they really saw their heyday in the early 2000s.

The Strongbad cartoons on *Homestar Runner* were flash-based animations. Flash is a file format and platform that was used to create simple animations. They were known for being able to use very small file sizes and load quickly in the early days of the internet when internet speeds were a fraction of what we have today. Most of them just played when a video was loaded, but some were made to be interactive, such as the popular "frog in a blender" Flash animation where you see a frog swimming in water in a blender and you have the option to press the button to turn the blender on. "Frog in a blender" has hundreds of millions of views since its release in 1999.

It was the popular choice for web-based games like online casinos.

One of my favorite Flash-based websites was called "you're the man now dog" which was just a site where people could upload their own full-page Flash animations that were always loud, bright, flashing, and put into a never-ending loop. That website still exists too, by the way. Their most popular page was just a recording from a radio show called "how to prank a telemarketer."

Even YouTube was powered by Flash until around 2017. Videos were converted to Flash because it was a way to compress information into something that loaded very quickly.

But it's much more than animation. It was a software platform that was used in desktop and mobile apps, games, and apparently some public utilities.

That brings us to the train system of Dalian in the Northern part of China. They built their train system to operate using Flash.

So when Adobe announced it was discontinuing Flash, there were a few places where that might have an effect— this train system was one of them.

Dalian, China is located on a peninsula just northwest of North Korea. It's not a city I've ever heard of before, but with a population of 6.6 million people, it's bigger than every American city except for New York. For reference, this one Chinese city has about the same number of people as the entire state of Indiana.

And the China Railway Shenyang Group in China is hugely important for getting people around. When it was constructed in 1903, the Dalian Railway Station was one of the most advanced and largest in China.

This railway was using Flash-based displays in its control rooms. The software used Flash to view train operation diagrams, formulate train sequencing schedules and arrange shunting plans. I didn't know what shunting was, so I googled that. Shunting is the process of sorting items of rolling stock into complete trains. In the U.S., we call it switching. So basically it's the way train cars are compiled into a train. Anyway, at 8 p.m. on January 12 of 2021, all these systems stopped working. Because Adobe disabled Flash.

Despite the name, the decision to disable it didn't happen in a flash. It might be the slowest obsolescence in software history. They announced in July of 2017 that they would be disabling Flash. Adobe acknowledged that it had served its purpose but wasn't needed anymore. More powerful open-source platforms like HTML-5 and CSS 3 had made it weak by comparison. Not only that, but a more efficient standard was also needed for the many platforms that web content needs to be displayed on: tablets, phones, desktops and…train control panels apparently. While they announced its demise in 2017, they waited quite a while to announce *when* that would be. Finally, in June of 2020, Adobe announced Flash's death date. It would no longer be supported after December 31st, 2020, and would completely stop working on January 12, 2021. This was because if you had kept your Flash software up to date, they had built a kill-switch into it. So, starting on January 12, if you tried to view anything in Flash, you'd see a message that said, "Adobe Flash Player is blocked."

That's why, at 8 p.m. that night on January 12, the trains stopped running. All the software to run them was inoperable. In the three and half years since the announcement of the end of Flash, no one bothered with updating their system software. So for 20 hours, all the way until 4 p.m. the following day, no trains ran on the Shenyang System in Dalian.

You may be wondering how they solved their problem. They could have hired a crack computer whiz to build a new system based on software that's still supported in that twenty hours. Sorry, no. They found a pirated "ghost version" of the Flash software to get the trains back on track. So there you have it…

Obsolescence problems… require obsolete solutions.

Dung Beetles: Crappy Celestial Travelers

I should offer a quick content warning. This story is going to talk about poop. I'll keep my language clean, but we're going to be talking about feces. We're going to be discussing crap, dung, excrement, fecal matter, feces, stool, waste, number two, defecation, turds, doodie, poo, dumps, dookie, droppings, butt dumplings, rusty nuggets, body boulders, sewer serpents, keister cakes, brownie bits, tushy tots, butt babies, smelly pebbles, POOP. We'll be discussing poop.

The Dung Beetle is an arthropod from family Scarabaeidae —that's right, there are TWO diphthongs in its family name. It's classified as an insect. They live in forests and grassland almost everywhere in the world except super cold climates. They live to be about three years old and they survive on a diet of poop. They're called the Dung Beetle because that's what they eat.

There are three main types of Dung Beetles. The difference is how they like their food. The main kind we think of is the beetle rolling the giant ball of dung. That's the kind we'll be talking about in this episode. But there are also Dung Beetles who tunnel through giant piles of poop and eat it that way. And then some of them just live inside poop. There's a saying: never eat where you poop. But for Dung Beetles, it's okay because it's not their poop.

Here's something crazy about Dung Beetles: In a way, they're the world's strongest animal. Relative to their weight, they can lift more than any other animal. How much more? Get this: When they're rolling a ball of dung, a Dung Beetle can pull 1,141 times its own bodyweight. So imagine a 200-pound man lifting 228,200 pounds. That's like one man lifting a blue whale, the largest mammal to have ever lived. For reference, the entire space shuttle weighs 160,000 lbs. So now imagine a 200-pound man on a runway pushing the space shuttle all by himself. And in this analogy, it's not even an empty space shuttle. In the payload bay of the shuttle is the anchor of a cruise ship. That's what we're talking about here. Dung Beetles are on average about the size of a gummy bear. Absolutely crazy. One of the things they use that immense body strength for is—for males anyway—fighting with other males. The male Dung Beetles lock horns and fight for female attention and for dung. Back to our example of comparing that to a human. That's two dudes fighting each other, each with the power to lift a BLUE WHALE by himself.

So *"why* do they roll the ball of dung?" you may be wondering. When an animal lays a fresh steaming pile, the Dung Beetles come in. The don't use their noses to smell poop like we do. They use their antennae. They have special poop-antennae on their head that's specialized for the scent of fresh animal droppings. They spend most of their time on the ground, but they can fly, sometimes up to several miles for a good pile of dookie. They eat the dung of herbivores, and herbivores suck at completely digesting their food. There tend to be a lot of nutrients leftover that are partially digested. Grass, liquid, and it's this nutrient-rich poop liquid that the Dung Beetles like. They eat it, and they lay eggs in it so their babies can have food. These beetles crawl into the pile, start rolling up some fresh dung, and then get it away. They want to get it away because they want to get it to a spot where they can save it for themselves and their eggs and so they're not fighting with other beetles for it. They roll it and the females lay eggs in it and they bury it—that keeps a safe food source for them later, and there are some added consequences like loosening up the soil, which nourishes the land and helps control fly populations.

Just like most insects, their movements are motivated by a couple things. Mating and eating. When it comes to the subject of this episode, we're talking about their movement as it involves them rolling the dung ball. A couple things to know: 1) The roll the ball in a straight line, and 2) they need to remember where the ball is that they've buried. This is where navigation comes in.

National Geographic journalist Christine Dell'Amore wrote a piece in 2013 with this title, "Dung Beetles Navigate Via the Milky Way, First Known in Animal Kingdom." In the piece, she cites to work of a biologist from Lund University in Sweden, Eric Warrant. Warrant co-authored a study that figured out this crazy fact. Scientists knew that the beetles rolled in a straight line, and it was important that they were rolling it away from the pile, but they didn't know how the beetles were doing it. One of the best guesses leading up to this study was that they were navigating at night using the position of the moon. But then they saw that the beetles were able to still do so on moonless nights. Eric Warrant said this caused scientists a lot of grief. So they conducted a study.

Here's what they found out: Dung Beetles, it turns out, can see the Milky Way, which from Earth creates sort of an oblong skinny oval. That oval points a particular direction, and that is what the Beetles use to navigate. Usually the human eye can't see the Milky Way, but Dung Beetles have this ability with super sensitive eyeballs. They use that faraway point much like sailors use the stars to navigate. The idea of celestial navigation is simple, really. Stars are really far away, so picking a point that doesn't move (or barely, imperatively moves), you can be sure you're following a straight line. For sailors, they have to know where certain stars appear in the night sky so they can orient themselves to the cardinal directions. For Dung Beetles, this doesn't matter; the important part is that they are moving in a straight line AWAY from the pile. And then using that straight line, they know their way back to the pile.

So YES. Now you know something crazy. Dung Beetles are the first insects discovered to use celestial navigation.

Overthrowing the Government: The Insurrection in Wilmington

This story is known by several different names. It's called "The Lost History of an American Coup d'État" in *The Atlantic*, while other articles refer to it as the Wilmington Insurrection, The Insurrection of 1898, the 1898 Race Riots or the Wilmington Massacre. While politics plays into this, it's immediately clear that this is a story about racial tension and white supremacy in America. And being so, it deals with a sensitive topic. I'll try to explain it the best I can, but some of this stuff is pretty uncomfortable.

To talk about the events leading up to what happened in Wilmington in 1898, I think it's important to paint a picture of where things were at politically. After the American Civil War, Republicans in the South favored and promoted a reconstruction that aligned with the view that Abraham Lincoln had: one where freed slaves were given land to farm and build a life for themselves. The Democratic Party at the time—remember this was before the parties sort of switched—was an all-white party fighting for small government and fighting against reconstruction policies that they felt threatened their power and land. The story of how the parties switched over the next 20 to 30 years is an interesting story, but the Democratic Party of 1898 looked more like the Republican Party that we know today.

In 1894, mostly white Populist Party members in North Carolina had joined together with mostly Black North Carolinians to create what was known as the Fusion Party. Five years later, members of this party had been voted to local offices, making for the first time a biracial government in Wilmington. Wilmington was a majority Black city, but had always been ruled by whites. They saw Republicans fighting for reconstruction as race traitors. In Wilmington, Black people had been elected to office and help positions of power in the city. One of those was the U.S. Customs Collector at the port. Following the election of Republican William McKinley, a Black man was put into that position, which had previously been held by a prominent white Democrat. *The Daily Record*, a Wilmington Newspaper was owned by Alexander Manly, a Black man. Economically, the people in Wilmington's Black population were moving out of service jobs and into higher paying jobs. This was ahead of its time, especially considering that governments around the country were making laws to raise barriers and promote racial segregation. In 1890, for example, Mississippi adopted a new state constitution that raised almost impassable barriers to allow black Americans the right to vote. These "Jim Crow" laws were being adopted all over the country. The 14th Amendment that allowed African Americans equal protection under the law was being circumvented and undermined by local and state governments.

Even though Wilmington's Black residents were seeing more power and money than in other areas in the country, there was still a huge disparity when compared with the white residents. The city was 60 percent Black, but they owned 8 percent of the property. The per-capita wealth for white people in Wilmington was $550 and less than $30 for Black people. Prominent white Wilmington residents wrote sentiments in the local paper that this proved white superiority over the city's Black residents. After all, they argued, they had seen thirty years of freedom and hadn't risen to the same level of wealth as the white man, an absolutely ridiculous white supremacist talking point.

One quote from *Washington Post* journalist Henry L. West says, "The Negro in North Carolina is thriftless, improvident, does not accumulate money and is not accounted as a desirable citizen." I know this stuff is hard to read, but I think it's important that we learn these things to understand. This was the overwhelming sentiment at the time by white Americans in the South. And the tensions continued to rise.

With this racial landscape in mind, it becomes easy to understand that when the Fusion party gained power in Wilmington with biracial members and some of their agenda which included debt relief and free coinage, the white Democrats were angry. They began a campaign in 1989 of White Supremacy and railed against what they called "Negro Rule." They specifically made this a major issue to try to regain power in the city.

What you can see brewing here is a perfect storm. And it all comes to a head that November.

This is where we start talking about a guy named Alfred Moore Waddell, a real piece of work. He was a four-time congressman who had lost his seat and began speaking around the country spreading a message of white people being oppressed. He riled people up everywhere he went, convincing them that the Black freed men were going to take their jobs and their power. He would stand outside voting locations to intimidate Black voters and distribute anti-Black propaganda. Waddell is going to become an important figure in this story.

The situation in Wilmington had become a boiling pot of racial tension, but it was a series of newspaper opinion articles that made it boil over. One of the threats that white southerners lobbied against Black men was the threat of the "black rapist." When white women would sleep with Black men, it was always painted as rape, no matter what. It was always painted as an attack that the white woman couldn't have wanted. And this was one of the most common causes that led to lynchings. After a prominent woman's suffragist made a speech complaining about the Black men as rapists and called them "ravening human beasts," Black newspaper owner and editor Alexander Manly wrote an op-ed to set the record straight on August 18, 1898.

In his article, he said that many white women were not being raped by white men, but instead willingly slept with them. As if that wasn't enough to incite anger in the local white population, he went on to say that if white women were really being raped, then, "we suggest that the whites guard their women more closely." He ended the article by calling out the hypocrisy of the white men who commonly slept with African American women.

Soon after this article, word had spread and militant white supremacists started gathering in Wilmington, including a group known as a the "red shirts," a paramilitary arm of the Democratic Party. Alfred Waddell traveled to Wilmington with the hopes that he could be seen as a Patriot and leader in this cause to solve the so-called problem for the North Carolina white population. They marched, rallied, and paraded around Wilmington through the fall of 1898 until the November election, when they won easily. And by "won easily," I mean they threatened to kill any Black voters they saw and rigged the election.

Even though they won the election, there were many Black officials and white Republicans still in power because they weren't up for reelection. But what this group of white supremacists couldn't achieve at the ballot box, they decided to achieve by force. The created a document they called "The White Declaration of Independence" and on November 9th had Alfred Waddell read the list of demands in front of a packed courthouse.

It listed eight bullet points. In them were complaints that the white men hadn't been given enough power in the city and that Black people should turn over businesses to whites, shouldn't congregate or speak to whites, that only whites should be employed in new jobs, and that Alexander Manly, who had written the newspaper article, should be removed from the city. The group gave Wilmington's Black residents twelve hours to respond.

What they didn't know was that Alexander Manly, the Black newspaper owner, was ahead of them. He had already shut down his press and left town after learning that the Redshirts were threatening to kill him. Nevertheless, the committee of white men needed a response. They asked to meet with a committee of thirty-two of Wilmington's prominent Black citizens, who pleaded that they didn't control Manly and didn't condone the editorial. But it didn't matter. They wrote a letter as a response to Waddell, but he never received it. The next morning, all hell broke loose.

500 white men raided the local armory, armed themselves with weapons, and then went to the building that housed *The Daily Record,* Manly's Newspaper. They torched the building. As the crowd of white men swelled to 2,000 people, they started marching through the city. Rumors

circulated that the Black men in Wilmington were arming themselves and had started fighting back. They hadn't. In fact, they hadn't done anything. The group of white men stormed through the Black neighborhoods, indiscriminately shooting into Black homes and attacking any Black citizen they could find. As they were being hunted, any Black person that could escaped into the swamps surrounding the city, many never to return again.

It wasn't just the citizens that were the target of the riotous mob. They wanted power. So they marched to City Council and forced all the Republicans and Black men to surrender their offices at gunpoint. This included the town's Republican Mayor. The mob instantly replaced him with Alfred Waddell, who was given a list of prominent black citizens in Wilmington. They were forced to leave the city.

By the end of the riot, lots of Wilmington's Black population had been killed. It's not known for sure how many, but estimates range from 60 to as many as 300. Two thousand others had fled the town and never returned, forced out of their homes and businesses. For the white Democratic Party, it was a success. They had successfully carried out a coup d'état to claim power by force. It was the only successful example of this happening in America.

I wish I could say that North Carolina used this as a lesson in what to avoid in the future. But they didn't. The insurrection was described in history books as a heroic effort to avoid disastrous reconstruction policies. The victims were portrayed in the books as the ones who incited the riot and were quickly put down. It wasn't until 2007 that the North Carolina Democratic Party acknowledged and renounced the actions of those party leaders. It's still not taught in school. All these years later, we see white supremacy rearing its head. Just three years ago, North Carolina installed a mile marker sign to commemorate the event. It reads:

"Armed white mob met at armory here, Nov. 10, 1898. Marched six blocks and burned office of Daily Record, black-owned newspaper. Violence left untold numbers of African Americans dead. Led to overthrow of city government & installation of coup leader as mayor. Was part of a statewide political campaign based on calls for white supremacy and the exploitation of racial prejudice."

Stupid Contagion: The Limping Ladies of London

There are several stories that I've heard over the years that are similar to the one you're about to read. Here's a particularly gross one: in France, King Louis the Fourteenth reigned from 1643 until his death in 1715. He was known as "The Sun King" or "Louis the Great." And the guy had butt problems. Specifically, an anal fistula. Listen: don't google that. Just understand, it's a butt problem. And at that point in history, physicians didn't perform surgeries where they cut into people. But barbers had blades they used to cut hair, so a barber named Charles Francois Felix created a special blade-like tool that he called "The Royal Probe" and used it to perform a surgery on the Sun King to cure him of his anal fistula. It was a huge success; Louis was fistula-free and the result was that his courtiers and subjects who wanted to appear king-like tried to get the surgery too—whether they had the ailment or not! Even people who didn't get the surgery wrapped their butts in swaddles to appear as if they'd gotten the surgery.

That's maybe the grossest example of a monarch becoming a trend-setter. Cleopatra had all the upper-class women in Rome wearing their hair in a bun at the back of their neck, and wearing eyeliner. If you know the rule about men's three-button suit coats? You know: *sometimes, always never,* meaning you never button the bottom button on a suit coat? That goes back to King Edward the seventh when he was Prince of Wales and he was too fat to button the bottom button. It started a trend that exists today.

So I guess it's not surprising that a trend started by a monarch had women walking irregularly.

Let's go back to the guy who couldn't button the button. England's King Edward the Seventh. His wife was Alexandra of Denmark, so she became Princess of Wales, then Queen of England. She was a beautiful woman, and was known to be very charming and joyful person. When her third child was born, she was stricken with rheumatic fever and almost died. After the birth, she had to use walking sticks to get around, and after a year, had begun to walk again without the crutches. She had a permanent limp for the rest of her life.

Alexandra of Denmark had already become a trend-setter as Princess of Wales. She was a huge fashion influencer and the women in England would copy everything she wore. She had a small scar on her neck from a childhood surgical procedure and she often wore choker collars and jewelry high on her neck to cover the scar. English women started wearing similar-style chokers. And just as they had been influenced and tried to mimic royalty before, they did so with her, even going so far as to imitate her permanent limp.

Here's a quote from an 1869 Edition of the *North British Mail* newspaper: "Taking my customary walk the other day, observant of men, women and things, I met three ladies. They were all three young, all three good-looking, and all three lame! At least, such was my impression, seeing as they all carried handsome sticks and limped; but, on looking back, as everyone else did, I could discover no reason why they should do so."

It was called the "Alexandra Limp" and it caught on like wildfire. A faked limp that was put on by women in the upper-class areas of London in order to appear more like Alexandra of Denmark. Women would walk with a pronounced limp and go so far as to use a cane that they didn't need. They didn't have any ailment. They faked it. In order to do so, they started wearing shoes of two different types, one high heel, one low.

The writer in the *North British Mail* continued, "A monstrosity has made itself visible among the female promenaders in Princes Street. It is as painful as it is idiotic and ludicrous."

But for shoemakers, they saw an opportunity. They began selling pairs of women's shoes with mismatched heels, so that walking in them would make the wearer hobble.

There is a happy ending to this story. Fads, by definition, fade away and get replaced with something else, and that's the story with the Alexandra Limp. Women of London could soon walk normal again. That is, until the next fad. As the Limp went out of style for ladies of London, a popular fashion journal reported the following: "The Alexandra Limp is to be discontinued forthwith. The skirt of the season, we are informed, is to cling closely round the feet, in consequence whereof ladies will be obliged to walk as if their feet....were tied together."

Evel Knievel: The Naming of a Legend

Evel Knievel was born Robert Craig Knievel in 1938. He was born in Butte, Montana, to Robert Sr. and Anne Marie Knievel. Raised by his second-generation German immigrant grandparents, he attended a daredevil show at the age of eight that he never forgot. The daredevil was a guy name Joie Chitwood who ran a death-defying automobile stunt show where he would do things like drive a car balanced on two wheels and jump from one ramp to another.

The bug for doing insane stunts was put into Knievel and as he grew up, he was known for doing crazy stunts on his motorbike. At the age of thirteen, he crashed a motorcycle into his neighbor's garage and started a fire. He was fired from his first job when he popped a wheelie in a front-loader and drove it into a power line, knocking out power to half the city. He was an adventure seeker at heart and was constantly pushing the adrenaline envelope.

This eventually evolved into a love for motocross. Knievel was really good at motocross, despite crashing a few times and breaking a few bones. But motocross wasn't enough to pay the bills, so he got a job as an insurance salesman. Not many people know this about him, but Evel Knievel was actually a really good insurance salesman. Like an award-winning insurance salesman. He sold 271 policies in one week! But then they figured out he sold them to inmates of an insane asylum. The insurance salesman thing didn't last that long.

He opened and closed his own motorcycle dealership and worked for another. Around this time, Knievel had a buddy who owned a car dealership in Moses Lake, Washington. It was 1965 and he had an idea that he'd stage a publicity stunt for his buddy to bring some notoriety to the dealership. He set it all up. He'd gather all the media, write the press releases, call the newspapers and let them know he was going to try jumping his Honda Scrambler motor bike over a pen with two mountain lions and a box holding a whole bunch of rattlesnakes. He took a long rolling start, left the ramp, and flew forty feet in the air, clearing the mountain lions and *almost* clearing the snakes. He hit the edge of the snake pit, crashed his bike, sprained his ankle, and a legend was born. The legend, of course, wasn't about the car dealership. It launched a world-famous fifteen-year career of being a one-of-a-kind daredevil.

I won't cover all of Evel's career. There's simply too much packed into those fifteen years to cover, but just about everyone knows the name Evel Knievel. His elaborate motorcycle stunts grew and grew in size, scope, and danger. He would jump over twenty-two cars lined up, or fourteen Greyhound buses. He performed a stunt in just about every one of the world's most famous stadiums and would make around $25,000 each time he did it. He became famous around the world and even had a popular

Evel Knievel children's toy patterned after him. He performed seventy-five jumps, the largest in a steam-powered rocket trying to jump Snake River Canyon. He didn't make it across the canyon, but he did travel 1730 feet and broke his nose. His jumps were legendary—and they weren't always successful. He broke thirty-five bones during his career, spending the equivalent of three years in the hospital. At one point, he tried to jump over the fountain at Caesar's in Las Vegas and crashed, putting him in a coma for a month. But it was the possibility of him failing that made people watch. He didn't crash on purpose of course, but if he landed every jump successfully, people would stop watching. The reason daredevil stunts are interesting is because of the risk. And Knievel lived a life full of risk. He was rough around the edges; not afraid to speak his mind.

And he had a lifelong hatred for the Hell's Angels Motorcycle Gang. Knievel was a motorcycle safety advocate and didn't like the "reckless" message that he felt the Hell's Angels promoted. Despite his crazy antics, he promoted bike safety to kids throughout his career and used his notoriety to speak at schools and clubs.

And because he didn't want to be confused with the Hell's Angels, he decided from the very beginning, all the way back in 1965 that he wouldn't wear black leather during his stunts. He designed and wore a bright white leather jacket with red and blue patriotic trim for that jump and kept the motif throughout his career.

I said a minute ago that Knievel was rough around the edges. Well one story of a brush-in with law is what led us to know him as Evel Knievel.

Let's briefly go back to a time when Evel Knievel was eighteen years old. At this point, he was still Bobby Knievel. He was a guy who, as I said earlier, was rough around the edges. He was a guy who didn't respect authority and did what he wanted. And in 1956, that included stealing a motorcycle, leading the Butte, Montana police on a chase, crashing the bike, and getting arrested.

Now for a second, I'm going to tell you about another guy. In Butte, Montana, there was a sort of notorious criminal; for right now, we'll just refer to him as William. He had done a stint in the State Pen and had escaped from the Butte City jail on three different occasions. He was a nasty guy and at this point in the story, he was the prime suspect in a murder investigation.

Well Bobby Knievel is in his cell in the Butte City Jail. And in the cell next to him is this notorious bad guy, William, whose last name was Knofel. He was known locally as "Awful Knofel." As the jailer was reading out loud the names of the folks he had in custody, he quipped to the men, "Look at that! We've got Awful Knofel and Evil Knieve.l" Knievel thought it was so memorable that he adopted the name. He spelled it E-V-E-L instead of E-V-I-L. He didn't want to be confused with the dark image of the Hell's Angels and thought spelling his name differently would help.

He was forever known as Evel Knievel until his death in 2007. But for the world, he was infamous—known for a being a little different, a little crazy, and for a lot of reckless driving. With that small stay in a jail, a legend was born. I know it sounds hard to believe, But: the Internet says it's true.

Human Sacrifice and Mexican Food

You know how you try to read an online recipe and you have to scroll through pages and pages of the history of the food and the writer's first influence of that dish and how it reminds of them of their first crush and how they met at the carnival and then they go on to describe all the things they saw that day and how inspired they were and eventually it gets to a story about how they fell in love and this was the first dish they made in their new home?

If you're not familiar, I'm going to read one of these; this is the first recipe that came up when I searched for Pozole. And I want to make clear I am in no way making fun of Mexican culture. I'm making fun of this white lady talking about a recipe for pages before listing the ingredients. Here it is:

"Years ago when I spent a summer studying Spanish in Cuernavaca, Mexico, my Mexican teacher told me that it was much easier to pronounce the language properly if you smiled as you spoke it. She was right! Good thing Mexican food is so delicioso, because just thinking about dishes like this pozole makes me smile. It's somewhat of a feast, pozole. I guess you could make smaller batches, but since you have to cook it for several hours, it just makes sense to make a large amount, and then have lots of friends over with whom to enjoy it. I made this for my parents, and they loved it. Mom told me she hadn't had pozole since she was a kid in Tucson. Lots of smiley faces around the table tonight."

So being that I'm looking for the story behind pozole, it's not the recipe I'm after, it's the history, so I actually had to read a few of these ridiculous intros to recipes. Let's talk about pozole.

Pozole is a traditional Mexican stew. Some people call it a soup, but I would refer to it as a stew with the basic ingredients of hominy and pork or beef with chiles, garlic, radishes, avocado, salsa, or limes, then topped with shredded lettuce or cabbage and chopped onions. It's a very popular dish with a long and rich history.

Hominy is just corn, but prepared in a special way. The field corn kernels are dried, then soaked in a solution with lye or slaked lime to break down the cell walls and soften the corn. After that, it's thoroughly cleaned and dried again. It looks sort of like a white, expanded, blown-up version of a kernel of corn.

So, hominy is the base grain of pozole, and it's cooked for hours in this stew of ingredients—chili peppers, or a puree of chili peppers and other ingredients to give it its unique spicy flavor. It's most commonly either red, green, or white, depending on the style and the region it's served in.

It's a dish that's common at special events, like New Year's Eve, Mexican Independence Day, birthdays, and other holidays. It's a warm dish perfect for a cold day. And it's got a really crazy backstory.

The time and the era we're going to talk about now is the Pre-Colombian Mesoamerican peoples known as the Aztecs. This was in the area we now know as the central and northern part of Mexico in the 14th, 15th and 16th centuries all the way up until the Spanish conquered Mexico and the Aztecs in 1521. They were believed to have started as a nomadic people, hunter and gatherers whose name came from the name of their home, Aztlan, said in their language, which was Nahuatl. Many Spanish words have their origin in Nahautl and were adopted after their invasion of this area. Words like "Chile," "avocado," "peyote," and "chocolate" all started as Nahuatl words from the Aztecs.

They had a festival every February and March called Atlacahualo in order to honor Tlaloc, the god of rain—in a harvest-based culture, praying to rain gods was important to them. Then once the food would be harvested, they would have a feast called Tlacaxipehualiztli. And there was a lot of symbolism with this feast.

Religious symbolism in foods is seen throughout history and throughout every major religion. For Catholics, there is of course the Eucharist where the wine represents the blood of Jesus and yes, I understand it could be argued that if one believes in transubstantiation that this isn't symbolic but rather literal, but I digress. Did you know the shape of pretzels is supposed to represent a child's arms folded in prayer? Baklava is supposed be made with thirty-three layers of dough, representing the thirty-three years of Jesus's life. The shape of dumplings has a Taoist beginning - it's supposed to represent money-related objects such as a Chinese measuring weight. And the Jewish Hannukah treat of Sufganiyot is a pastry filled with jelly and that jelly represents the miracle of oil, like when the oil lamp lit for eight days.

Here's where things get a little weird, so trigger warning if you are squeamish. Like other Mesoamerican religions—the Mayans come to mind—the Aztecs practiced human sacrifice. So during that feast of Tlacaxipehualiztli, they would offer to the gods ears of corn, and a human sacrifice. Forty days prior to the sacrifice, a person would be chosen, often a prisoner from an enemy party that had been captured. Pieces of human flesh were carved and consumed. The heart was offered to the gods. And the rest of the body would be put into a ceremonial pot of pozole.

When you read something like this, you have to be very careful because we know that gruesome stories like this one have been used throughout time to denigrate peoples. For example, an Islamic preacher on the Temple Mount in 2015 made the false and inflammatory statement that Jews cooked children's blood into their Passover Bread. There are sometimes cultural feuds and prejudices that create harmful lies about culture. So, as a white person, I wanted to be very careful about this story. But it is 100 percent true according to Mexico's National Institute of Anthropology and History. It's also referenced in a 16th-century book called *General History of the Things of New Spain* written by Fray Bernandino de Sahagun. It's worth noting that when the Spanish conquered the Aztecs, they outlawed the practice of cannibalism. In his book, Sahagun writes that they began using pork in the meal because of its similar taste to human flesh.

Now it's also important to say here that this wasn't how pozole was eaten all the time in Aztec culture—it was reserved for ceremonial times. When it wasn't a ceremony, the meat in pozole was typically provided by a rodent called the tepezcuintle, what we could now call a paca—it looks kind of like a miniature combination of a guinea pig, a deer, and a pig.

Next time you enjoy a nice ham steak, or a steaming bowl of pozole, you've got something to think about—and an interesting story to tell.

The Nebraska Miracle: The West End Baptist Church Explosion

During the Civil War, the government of the United States enacted the Homestead Act of 1862. Basically, it said that if you'd never taken up arms against the nation, you could go farm on 160 acres of undeveloped government land and if you worked the land for 5 years, it was yours. Thousands of hopeful Americans, including freed Black men, flocked west to begin a life in the plains. One of the first claims was that of Daniel Freeman, whose home in Beatrice, Nebraska, now acts as the Homestead National Monument of America, an historic site. One of these homesteaders was a man named Frederich Pahl, a German immigrant. Frederich settled in Beatrice, Nebraska, with his wife, and they had three children. One of those children had a little girl who, just two generations from the historic homesteading of Nebraska, is involved in our story.

Frederich's Granddaughter Marilyn Ruth Paul was eighteen years old and was the pianist at a local church, the West End Baptist Church. It was March 1st of 1950 and she decided to take a quick nap after dinner and before choir practice that night. She slept a little bit long and her mother had to wake her up, only ten minutes before choir practice was about to start. She was definitely going to be late.

That wouldn't have been such a big deal, except this was a pet peeve of the choir director, which just happened to be her mother, Martha. Martha was a stickler about punctuality. She stressed that choir practice began promptly at 7:25 p.m.—in fact, she demanded it from her small fifteen-member choir. Choir practice didn't begin at 7:30 p.m.—it began at 7:25 p.m. and you'd better be there.

That Wednesday evening was a cool one. The pastor of the church left at 4:30 p.m., but before he left, Pastor William Kempl turned on the heat to the building. But somewhere in the church's heating system, there was a gas leak and for the next three hours, the church filled with gas. At 7:27 p.m., a booming explosion could be heard throughout the entire town of Beatrice, Nebraska. It shattered the windows of nearby buildings. The town radio station lost its signal. The church was flattened. The roof fell in and the walls collapsed into a pile of rubble. It was an absolute tragedy. Martha Paul and her daughter Marilyn were spared. They hadn't yet made it to the church because Marilyn napped too long.

But this is where the story gets interesting. Despite choir practice being scheduled for 7:25 p.m.—two minutes before the explosion—nobody died. Nobody was in the church.

When the Titanic sank, a giant suite of three adjoining rooms, a sitting room, large closets, and a private balcony had been designed and intended for the American financial legend J.P. Morgan. But he was enjoying himself at a French resort and decided stay longer. So when disaster struck, he was not on board.

Mark Wahlberg was booked to fly on American Airlines Flight 11 from Boston to L.A. on September 11, 2001, but changed his plans at the last minute. That airplane tragically was flown into the World Trade Center. That same morning, Michael Jackson overslept and missed his meeting at the top of the twin towers.

When there are tragedies like these, it seems like we always hear about the people—or at least the celebrities—who narrowly escaped fate and avoided the tragedy. But the fact remains that there were countless others who weren't so lucky. I mean, sure, J.P. Morgan survived the Titanic, but more than fifteen hundred other people died. Marky Mark and Michael Jackson survived 9/11, but almost 3,000 other people died.

But in this story of the West End Baptist Church, 100 percent of the people strangely avoided what would have been an absolutely horrific fate. All fifteen choir members survived because they were all miraculously late to practice. For fifteen different reasons.

The pastor left at 4:30 p.m. that day, but his daughter Marilyn was in the choir. She was late because she spilled food on her dress and was quickly ironing another one.

Herbert Kipf randomly decided to stop on the way to the church to mail a letter.

Harvey Ahl was going to bring his two young sons to practice since his wife was out of town. He got caught up talking and lost track of time.

LaDonna Vandergrift got stuck on her geometry homework.

Joyce Black was cold, and had gotten comfortable in her warm bed, so she was late getting up.

The Estes sisters couldn't get their car to start.

Lucille Jones got caught up listening to a radio program and also caused her friend Dorothy to be late, whom she was supposed to pick up.

Joyce Black—she was the one that was comfortable in her warm bed—lived across the street from the church and actually opened her door to leave when the explosion happened.

She said she couldn't put it off any longer and when she opened the door, she saw the church disintegrate in front of her.

All these stories were documented in countless newspapers and magazines soon after it happened, including *Life Magazine*, just twenty-six days later.

The church was eventually rebuilt and frequently uses the story as proof of God's miracles.

If you know me at all, you know that I'm an intense skeptic. I did not believe this story was true. But I've found so many newspaper articles from the time that tell the story. Then there's the part of me that looks at this and it raises all kinds of questions about whether it was really an accident. When people bring up conspiracy theories about the government, I usually think there's no WAY that many people could have kept their mouths shut. And maybe that's the same with this story. Let's be cynics and say this was some sort of elaborate insurance fraud plot. Could fifteen people, most of them teenagers, really have kept the secret? They all would have had to have been in on it.

And then there was national coverage—national newspapers and magazines looking into it.

So then there's the next theory. If you're religious, maybe this story is something that strengthens your belief in miracles. After all, I have used the word miraculous to describe what happened here.

Then there's the chance that this was just a wonderfully crazy coincidence. Fifteen people from fifteen different places had fifteen different reasons for missing catastrophe. We'll never know how this happened. But the internet says it did.

A Titanic Hero at Dunkirk: Charles Lightoller

In America, we tend to focus on World War Two stories that occur after Pearl Harbor—that is, after America was provoked into becoming involved in the war. But one of the most amazing stories of heroism during the second World War happened during the Battle of Dunkirk between May 26th and June 4th of 1940.

The Allies were losing the war. Nazi Germany had invaded Poland the previous September and by early May, they had now entered Belgium, the Netherlands, and France. The British Expeditionary Force was sent to help defend France. But Germany's powerful Panzer Tank divisions had trapped the BEF, a small contingent of Belgian Troops, and three French field armies against the northern coast of France. There was no safe land route for escape and it was determined that the only course of action was a full evacuation from the nearest port city of Dunkirk, France, to safety in Dover, England.

To explain the events leading up to the evacuation of Dunkirk, I'd have to take more time than what would fit in a modest book like mine, because I'd have to explain the battle and the conditions that left the troops stranded, so we'll just skip past a fierce battle and jump forward to the point where the German tanks were stopped by canals outside of the port city and now it was up to a powerful German Luftwaffe air attack to drop bombs and complete strafing runs on the surrounded troops. They had all mostly filed out to the beaches, waiting without cover for ship transport to Dover, a passage that, at its shortest, was 39 nautical miles. There were somewhere around 400,000 troops waiting to evacuate Dunkirk. They were surrounded by twice that many German troops. British Prime Minister Winston Churchill said that with the available ships, he thought they would only be able to evacuate around 45,000 troops.

What occurred next has been referred to as the "Miracle at Dunkirk." The official codename was "Operation Dynamo." The word was spread that the troops needed help, and a giant flotilla of boats started arriving to aid in the evacuation—not just military ships, either! Anyone who could take on passengers started showing up and picking up the soldiers wading in knee deep water. One cruiser, 39 destroyers, 9 gunboats, 36 minesweeper boats, 13 torpedo boats, 8 hospital boats, 34 tugboats, 113 trawlers and more than 311 personally owned small watercraft came to the rescue. 693 boats in all. 223 of those boats were sunk by the Germans. Around 61,000 were killed or wounded. But miraculously, 338,226 allied troops were rescued and arrived safely on the other shore.

So what does this have to do with the Titanic?

There's not much I can say about the Titanic that hasn't been said by the many documentaries, not to mention the

James Cameron blockbuster movie in 1997. At least that's what I thought. But I had never heard the story about Charles Lightoller.

He was born in in Lancashire in 1874 and his naval career began as early as the age of 13 when he apprenticed on board a large sailing ship. The drama that would follow his career started during that early apprenticeship when they sailed into a horrible storm in the South Atlantic and had to make repairs in Rio de Janeiro despite the country raging with a smallpox epidemic while struggling through a revolution. Soon after that, a fire broke out on a ship where he was serving and he was promoted for his bravery in putting out the fire to save the ship.

He started working on board steam ships at the age of twenty-one and, during that time sailing around Africa, almost died from Malaria. He took some time away from sailing to try his hand at mining for gold and wrangling cattle, but the sea called him back when the White Star Line hired him as an officer.

That's how he came to be involved in the H.M.S. Titanic. On the fateful night of April 14, 1912, Lightoller was the Ship's Second Officer and had commanded the bridge watch late into the evening. Before retiring to bed in his cabin, he had told the ship's lookouts to watch out for small ice in the ocean ahead. But it wasn't until he felt the collision that he knew something was wrong.

This is where, according to some, Lightoller was a hero. According to others, he was a murderer. As the ship began to sink, his first job was to get the women and children into the light boats on the port side of the ship and lower them into the ocean. And that he did. He evacuated every woman and child into the ships on that side until there weren't any more. And that's why he faces criticism. Only allowing women and children on the boats meant that some of them had room to spare for the men aboard. His instructions were to only allow women and children, and Lightoller followed them strictly—so strictly, in fact, that when a man tried to board one of the boats, he jumped on board and threatened the man with his revolver. This scene was dramatized in James Cameron's 1997 film.

After the ship's lifeboats were all lowered, there were only a couple small collapsible rafts left and those were sent away as well with as many as could occupy them. Lightoller now found himself in the icy water as it crept up the Titanic's many staircases and hallways. He tried to swim to the ship's crow's nest, which he could see peeking above the surface, but remembered that a sinking ship created suction that would pull him under. He tried to swim away, but he couldn't. It was too late. The suction of the sinking ship pulled him underwater and pinned him against a grate. He tried to push away, but couldn't. He was sure it was the end.

A large boiler explosion deep in the ship underwater sent a rush of hot air upwards and had enough force to throw Lightoller away from the ship. He ended up finding himself underneath an overturned light raft. He would be the most senior member of the Titanic's crew to survive.

Long after the Titanic, long after Lightoller played an important part in the investigations into what went wrong, he found himself fighting for Britain in World War One. From his actions during the war, he was awarded on two separate occasions for gallantry—one being for sinking German U-Boat UB-110.

Charles Lightoller retired in March of 1919 and just ten years later returned to the sea on his own private yacht, the Sundowner. The Sundowner was a 58-foot motor yacht with a 72hp diesel engine and top speed of about 10 knots. It was a ship purchased for enjoyment and nothing more. Until a call went out in late May of 1940 about small ships being needed for a massive rescue effort from the shores of Dunkirk France.

On June 1st, Lightoller and his son Roger left the Port of Ramsgate and sailed to Dunkirk. Crossing the channel, they rescued the crew of a motor cruiser that was on fire. That was just the beginning of what they would face. Sailing past sunken ships and with the threat of the Luftwaffe overhead, the Sundowner wasn't able to board soldiers from the piers at Dunkirk because they were too high. Instead, Lightoller pulled up next to the HMS Worcester and began taking soldiers that were crammed on board. A total of 130 men squeezed on the Sundowner and she returned to England to bring them to safety.

Charles H. Lightoller had seen his share of high drama in his naval career. But none as heroic as being one of the hundreds of ships put into service of the War that day.

The Hartlepool Monkey Hangers

If you lived in Europe before the 19th century, and you witnessed an animal doing something wrong, it would be entirely possible to witness that animal go to trial and be punished the same as a human.

There are all kinds of cases of this going back to the 13th century when a pig was executed, and in the 14th century when a pig was hanged by the neck after killing a child. It had received full legal representation as if it were a person. Before its execution, it was dressed in a suit with pants and gloves and a human mask. In the 15th century, there's a story about a rooster being put on trial because it laid an egg. They said the egg was the spawn of Satan and contained a demon.

Most of these practices ended in the 1700s, but there was a case in 2004 when Katya the bear was imprisoned in Kazakhstan for 15 years after mauling two people. She was released in 2019.

But today's story is about a monkey in northern England. A monkey so famous, its still depicted and sang about today. The date of our story isn't certain, but its reported to have happened during the Napoleonic Wars, which puts it somewhere between 1803 and 1815.

In the early 2000s, the city of Hartlepool England voted to have an official elected Mayor, rather than a ceremonial one. Many residents of Hartlepool were angry. They didn't want an elected Mayor who had power for the first time in the city's history. So in 2002, when the election for Mayor took place, there was a protest candidate. His name was H'Angus the Monkey. He was the mascot for the local football club. We'll talk about why in a moment, but this monkey—this man dressed up in a monkey costume—first emerged as a candidate with 100-1 odds to win the Mayor's race against the Labour Party candidate, Leo Gillen. Soon, those odds became 4-1 and on May 6, 2002, H'Angus the Monkey won the election to be named Mayor of Hartlepool by something like 500 votes. He hadn't campaigned, at least not seriously. He ran on a platform of free bananas for school children. It was purely a protest vote for many citizens of Hartlepool. So that's how the man inside the costume, a guy by the name of Stuart Drummond, became mayor. In his official capacity as Mayor inside the Mayor's office, he didn't dress as H'Angus the Monkey. He was just Stuart Drummond. And people liked him so much, he was elected twice more.

So why was this mascot so popular? And why was the mascot named "H'Angus the Monkey?" It all goes back to a popular legend from the Napoleonic Wars.

The legend goes like this. Sometime between 1803 and 1815, a French ship sank off the coast of Hartlepool. Hartlepool is a coastal city on the Northeast side of the UK, just below Scotland on the East coast. It was one of the most important ports in England. The local fisherman had been observing a French commercial ship off the coast and a horrible storm blew in. The fishermen watched from the shore as the storm wrecked the French ship. The only one to wash up on shore alive was a tiny monkey, reportedly dressed in a decorative French Army uniform. It must have been the ship's mascot to keep the sailors entertained.

Now, this is where some versions of the popular legend say that the locals thought that the monkey was a French person—that they had never seen one, so that's what they thought the French looked like. It wouldn't answer their questions, so it must have been a French spy. This was during a time that everyone was on high alert waiting for a French invasion and here was a tiny French little spy. That's pretty hard to believe, but whether or not they thought the monkey was a French Spy or not, they decided that this only survivor of an apparent invading ship was to be tried, and if found guilty of being a spy, it would be hanged.

Like in the cases we talked about before, an animal is generally unsuitable to put up any sort of strong legal defense to argue their case, so the monkey was found guilty and sentenced to hanging.

So the townspeople of the Port of Hartlepool gathered near the beach where a gallows had been erected to watch the hanging of a French Napoleonic Monkey. They dropped the floor of the gallows and the monkey… survived. It didn't hang because it just climbed up the rope. They eventually—
I'm not sure how—*did* hang the monkey. And became famous for being "Monkey Hangers."

The story became so famous that sometimes residents of Hartlepool are referred to as "Monkey Hangers." The Hartlepool Football Club embraced the legend in 1999 when they named their mascot H'Angus the Monkey. Even the Hartlepool Rugby Club, whose official name is the Rovers, are known colloquially as the "Monkey Hangers."

So is any of this true? It's tough to say. We know that the legend really took off after a song that was written by Ned Corman in 1855.

In former times 'mid war and strife,

The French invasion threatened life,

And all was armed te the knife,

The Fishermen hung the Monkey, O!

The Fishermen with courage high,

Seized the Monkey for a spy.

Hang him says yen says another he'll die

And they did they hung the Monkey O!

They tried every means te make him speak,

They tortured the Monkey till loud he did squeek.

Says one that's French, says another it's Greek.

For the Fishermen then got drunkey, O!

There's really no evidence of the legend before this song. So some believe that it was the song - a work of fiction - that started the legend. But there's also some evidence to believe that the song just took an existing popular legend and wrote about it. The original lyrics of the song were "The Boddamers hung the monkey." Because this legend appears in the town Boddam, Aberdeenshire, which is a Scottish port up the coast from Hartlepool. There are at least two other Scottish towns with similar legends. So we really don't know if there's truth to the story. There's also a darker origin story.

Some people believe that there wasn't a monkey at all, but a small boy that washed up on shore. Boys ages 12-14 were employed during those times aboard ships. They were referred to as "powder monkeys" because their job was to carry gunpowder from the ship's holds to the cannons. So some people think that it was a young French boy who they found dressed in a uniform and unable to communicate with the Englishmen who found him.

Regardless of the truth, many townspeople, including Former Hartlepool Mayor Stuart Drummond—H'Angus the Monkey himself—believe it to be 100 percent true. So maybe it doesn't matter anymore whether or not it actually happened. What IS true is that the legend lives on, and that's how residents of this small town in England got one of the weirdest nicknames to ever exist. The Hartlepool Monkey Hangers. The Internet Says It's True.

Measuring Misfortune: The Pirate Who Stole America's Metric System

Today's story is about pirates.

But it's also about science, and bureaucracy, and just how close the United States came to joining the rest of the world in using meters and kilograms. This is a weird tale of swashbuckling sabotage—with the twist that it doesn't involve sword fights or treasure maps, but instead, a very specific copper cylinder.

Before we get into that story, I have to tell you about something I find absolutely fascinating.

If you drive parts of I-19 in Arizona or along I-394 near Minneapolis, you'll actually find highway signs marked in kilometers instead of miles. I-19 runs from Tucson to Nogales, right on the U.S.–Mexico border. When the road was constructed in the 1970s, there was a push for metrication in the U.S., and the Federal Highway Administration allowed metric signs as part of a broader metric test program. The thinking was that metric signage would help facilitate trade with Mexico, which uses the metric system. While the metric push fizzled out nationally, the signs stayed—so to this day, you'll see distances in kilometers along I-19.

In the early 1990s, a short section of I-394 in Minneapolis used dual-unit signage (both miles and kilometers) as part of an experimental project aimed at familiarizing the public with the metric system. That effort was also part of a brief national metrication push, but like I-19, it was never expanded. Most of the metric signage has since been removed, but some remnants linger. So in short, these are leftovers from the last time the U.S. seriously flirted with going metric in the 1970s and '80s. The signs are oddities now—but they're relics of a road not taken.

Despite the widespread use of the imperial system in everyday American life, the metric system quietly exists in more places than you might expect. Science, medicine, and the military all rely heavily on metric units—doctors measure medication in milligrams, scientists calculate distances in meters and kilometers, and military maps use metric grids. Bottled beverages are labeled in liters, and most car manufacturers list engine displacement in liters instead of cubic inches. Even track and field events measure races in meters. Yet despite these scattered adoptions, the U.S. remains resistant to fully embracing metrication. Road signs overwhelmingly show miles. Temperatures are Fahrenheit. People measure their height in feet and inches. It's as if the U.S. has one foot in the metric world—but refuses to take the next step.

Now we're going all the way back to the 1790s, when America was still figuring out how much things should weigh. In the early years of the United States, measurement was a disaster.

Different states used different units. Sometimes even towns used their own standards. There were British imperial units, leftover Dutch and Spanish measurements, and local adaptations. You might buy flour by the bushel in one place and by the stone in another. And good luck figuring out how long a "rod" was without arguing with your neighbor.

This wasn't just annoying—it made commerce harder. You couldn't trust the quantity you were buying or selling, and it stifled interstate trade. Even George Washington called for a standardized system of weights and measures in his very first address to Congress.

On January 8, 1790, he said in his First Annual Address to Congress, "Uniformity in the currency, weights and measures of the United States is an object of great importance, and will, I am persuaded, be duly attended to."

So when Thomas Jefferson became Secretary of State in 1790, he decided to fix it.

Now, Jefferson was a bit of a measurement nerd. He loved scientific reasoning and Enlightenment ideals. And he believed America needed a rational, consistent, universal system—something rooted in logic, not tradition.

At the same time, across the ocean, France was having its own revolution. And in the middle of all that chaos, French scientists were busy inventing a new system of measurement based entirely on the natural world.

They called it the metric system. Well, technically they called it, "Système métrique décimal." And this all happened while the U.S. was still dragging their feet debating a standardized system of measurement. Jefferson wrote: "The element of measure adopted by the National Assembly excludes, ipso facto, every nation on earth from a communion of measurement with them."

This new French system was elegant. A meter was one ten-millionth of the distance from the North Pole to the Equator along the meridian. A liter was the volume of a cube 10 centimeters on each side. And a kilogram? That was the mass of one liter of water at the freezing point. Everything was base-10. Simple. Logical. Standardized. Easy to teach to children. Jefferson loved it.

In fact, he wrote extensively to French scientists, expressing interest in bringing this revolutionary system to the United States. And the French, eager to spread their rational ideas across the globe, decided to help. They commissioned the creation of a set of official metric standards—one kilogram and one meter—to be sent to the U.S. as diplomatic and scientific gifts.

And to deliver these precious prototypes, they chose a man named Joseph Dombey.

Joseph Dombey was a respected botanist and scientist. He'd traveled South America collecting plant specimens, worked with the French Academy of Sciences, and supported the revolutionary government in France. But in 1794, he was tasked with something different: bringing the metric system to America.

He set sail for Philadelphia with an official kilogram—a copper cylinder, precisely calibrated to match the new French standard. This wasn't just a gift—it was a physical reference, something American scientists could use to create their own identical copies. It was, quite literally, the foundation of a future metric America. Jefferson was waiting. Dombey was ready.

And the United States was about to change... forever.

But then—something happened at sea.

His ship was intercepted.

Now, this wasn't the work of random criminals—it was British privateers.

At the time, France and Britain were basically in a constant state of war, and privateering was a common practice. Governments issued "letters of marque" to private citizens, giving them legal permission to raid enemy ships. So these guys were pirates, but with paperwork.

Dombey's ship was captured somewhere in the Atlantic. Possibly near the Caribbean. He was taken prisoner and brought to the island of Monserrat, which was a British held island in the Caribbean, and he died in captivity—never completing his mission. And so at that time in 1794, the metal kilogram weight never made it to the U.S. and was lost.

And that single event derailed the U.S.'s early flirtation with the metric system.

Back in Philadelphia, Jefferson never received the kilogram. The French revolution was making communication chaotic. And without a standardized reference in hand, the metric system remained just an idea.

Jefferson couldn't convince Congress to act without that physical object. And as administrations changed, so did priorities. The opportunity faded.

America stuck with the British imperial system, even after Britain itself began transitioning to metric in the 20th century.

Congress eventually legalized metric units in 1866, but adoption was never mandated. Today, the U.S. is one of only three countries in the world that hasn't fully embraced the metric system. The others? Liberia and Myanmar.

All because one man's voyage was cut short by pirates.

Here's a fun twist: that very same kilogram? It turned up later. Its exact path isn't certain, it was probably confiscated by the British—that's what happened to most of the stuff seized by these privateers back then.

Somehow it ended up finding its way to America around a century later. It was eventually transferred to the National Bureau of Standards, which is now the National Institute of Standards and Technology (NIST) in Gaithersburg, Maryland. NIST currently holds the artifact and confirms it as one of the earliest metric standards intended for the U.S.

But by the time it made it to the U.S., the imperial system had become deeply entrenched. Too many industries, too much infrastructure, and too many habits had formed around inches, feet, gallons, and pounds.

That single missed connection in 1794—caused by a pirate raid—may have been our best chance to make the switch.

So, what if Dombey had made it? What if Jefferson received the kilogram? Would we all be measuring our height in centimeters today? Would American ovens be set to 180 degrees Celsius? Would your speedometer have kilometers per hour on the outside ring instead of buried inside?

It's hard to say for certain—but historians agree that early adoption would've given metric a much better shot in the U.S. The country was still young, flexible and open to new systems. If it had been standardized from the start, Americans today might not even think about metric being foreign.

Instead, we have generations of students wondering why water freezes at 32 degrees, not zero.

All because one copper cylinder didn't make it to its destination. The Internet Says It's True.

Crowd Sourcing World War II: The Normandy Photo Contest

A major part of war is intelligence gathering. And this falls into a few different categories. One of them is signals intelligence. This is the stuff you think of when you think of military intelligence. It includes monitoring radio, internet and telephone traffic. Intercepting text messages, online chatter and things like that. But it also includes decrypting official military communications from other militaries and tracking vehicle movements and radar signatures.

But that's not all there is to the intelligence world. There's also reconnaissance and surveillance. This is usually the type of intelligence gathering that includes aerial photos from spy planes, drones and satellites. But it could just as easily include photographs from the ground. An offshoot of this is geographic and environmental intelligence, which is mapping out terrain and soil types, but also weather patterns, tides, and vegetation.

There's human intelligence—this is basically what we refer to as spies but also could include getting intel from civilians or captured enemy combatants.

And finally, there's open-source intelligence. This is using available public information in order to inform our military of what they need to know before going into an area. For instance, checking newspapers, public photographs and social media as well as monitoring the movement of civilians.

All these things are used together in order to learn about your adversaries, and we're seeing it in real time with a couple current conflicts. The ones I really want to focus on are the combination of human intelligence and open-source intelligence. Because social media has caused a confluence of these two things. People put personal stuff online and that information becomes public. Our current military members are trained to be aware of the things they put online for this very reason. Each branch has their own training protocol and they all revolve around protecting sensitive information like locations, names, military equipment, and movements.

In the current conflict between Russia and Ukraine, Open-Source Intelligence analysts and government agencies have used satellite images, social media photos, and videos to track Russian troop movements and equipment locations. The Ukrainian government and allied groups have leveraged geotagged social media photos to pinpoint and target Russian positions. This not only helps Ukraine learn about troop positions, but also the types of equipment in those locations. This was especially true during the 2014 invasion of Crimea, when intel was leaked to Ukraine because Russian soldiers had shared photos and videos without turning off their location services on their phones.

In the Syrian Civil War, governments used social media photos and videos to track the online activities of ISIS recruits and sympathizers. These materials often revealed locations and plans. There's also the case of photos and videos uploaded by activists and civilians being used to verify the use of chemical weapons in Syria.

Today's story is about the use of human and open-source intelligence during World War II, long before social media. And it was actually supplied by the public.

In World War II, the Allies were suffering heavy losses for the first couple years of the war, and it wasn't looking good. Things started turning in early 1943. The German forces had suffered horrible losses on the Eastern front and Mussolini's government collapsed in Italy. The Allied invasion of France, known during the planning as it's secret code name Operation Overlord, was starting to be planned early in 1943 and it really required a huge effort by the Allied intelligences agencies. These would have been Britain's MI6, and the American OSS, which was sort of a precursor to the CIA. There were other smaller agencies and groups involved, but these were the two main agencies responsible for gathering intelligence and planning the invasion, which we now know as D-Day or the Invasion of Normandy, which happened in June of 1944.

Normandy was chosen as the location because of its strategic location and weaker German defenses. And part of this intelligence was creating an entire web of deception to trick the Germans into thinking we were landing somewhere else. If you want to know more about that, research Operation Bodyguard, which is a CRAZY story and one too detailed to get into here. It could be its own episode, but it's been covered by so many other people— just look into it. But before this huge amphibious assault— which was the largest ever in history—could take place, the armies and navies needed to know as much as they could about the terrain of the landing site.

Think about it: if a bunch of Americans or British started showing up and surveying the ground in Germany-occupied France, it would send off all the red flags that maybe this would be the landing location. So how did they get all their intel?

They needed to know the layout of the land, the soil and sand density, the tide tables, and where ideal locations for German fortifications would be. This is where we come back to the different types of intelligence gathering. Aerial photography was used by the Royal Air Force and United States Army Air Forces. Covert agencies worked with French resistance fighters to gain intel on the ground like supply lines, German troop movements and weak points in their defenses. Allied submarines patrolled the coastline from a distance and divers were able to gather soil samples.

But a huge—and I mean HUGE—effort was made through a diabolical plot. They wanted photographs. The pictures they collected from tourist guidebooks and pre-war maps were great, but only showed so much. In order to piece together a complete picture of the beaches, MI6 and the Allied Naval forces turned to the BBC.

In March of 1942, this effort had already started - before the official planning of the Normandy invasion had even began. Director of British Naval Intelligence, Admiral John Godfrey, had gone on BBC and asked for people to send in their photographs and postcards of Europe that they had taken on vacation. Of particular importance to the Navy were pictures taken on Europe's beaches, from the Pyrenees in the West to Norway in the East. They didn't ask for photos from particular locations, but instead just asked for their beach photos and where they were taken, and the entire thing was framed as a photo contest. Hundreds of thousands of entries were immediately mailed in. They were photos of landscapes, photos of a toddler sitting on the beach, photos of a couple kissing next to a stream, and postcards they'd collected on their holiday vacations.

By 1944, more than ten million photographs had been collected and analyzed. They would look at the photo of the toddler and be able to see in the background how the beach sloped and dropped off into the ocean behind him. Or how the foliage hid the road behind the photo of the couple kissing. These photos were used extensively during the planning of Operation Overlord and map and 3D model makers used them to determine exactly where the Allied Forces would be able to focus and where paratroopers would need to land.

It was an ingenious combination of Open-Source and Human-Intelligence that absolutely helped guide the successful invasion of Normandy's beaches on D-Day. It was a deadly day, don't get me wrong. D-Day was deadly, with over 10,000 Allied casualties (a figure that includes deaths and injuries), including more than 4,000 deaths, as troops faced fierce German resistance, fortified defenses, and rough conditions on the beaches of Normandy. It was a success because meticulous planning, overwhelming Allied air and naval support, and the sheer determination of the soldiers overwhelmed German defenses, securing a vital foothold in Europe and marking the beginning of Nazi Germany's defeat. Those millions of photos sent in to the BBC marked a huge civilian effort in the landing. It was a 1940s version of Ukraine troops searching through geolocated Instagram photos. And it was all free and cost the Allies no dangerous spy missions.

World War II was won with a combined fifty million soldiers in the Allied Forces. But supporting those forces were the civilians of those nations. They helped by joining resistance movements in Europe. They manufactured war-fighting equipment at production rates that the world had never seen. They raised money and war bonds, and took part in rationing. And by supplying their old vacation photos, their direct contributions to the intelligence gathering was absolutely invaluable in helping the Allies win the war. The Internet Says It's True.

Pablo Escobar's Cocaine Hippos

When I first saw a headline that read "Pablo Escobar's Cocaine Hippos," I got excited for a story about cocaine-fueled hippos. That's not what this is. This is a story about hippos that have a nickname because, well, everything about the Pablo Escobar story has to do with cocaine. For this one, we've gotta travel to the Magdalena River Basin in the heart of Colombia. There's a spot about a three hours' drive from the city of Medellin known as Hacienda Nápoles. These days, there's a small water park and zoo, but if you look around, you'll see the foundations of demolished buildings. Those buildings in the small town of Puerto Triunfo, demolished almost thirty years ago, used to be the grand palace of famed Colombian cocaine kingpin Pablo Escobar.

At the height of his operation, Pablo Escobar had everything. His net worth was $30 billion, equivalent to around twice that in today's money. He was the world's richest man in 1989 and his cocaine cartel was earning him $420 million a week at its peak. He owned 141 houses, 142 airplanes, 20 helicopters, 32 yachts and, to this day, he's sort of seen as both a villain and a hero.

The reason that he leaves a complicated legacy is that, to many people, he ran a drug cartel that devastated several nations in their effort to combat drug crime and the crimes associated with it. He supplied 85 percent of the cocaine that the world was consuming. His reign killed over 4,000 civilians, 1,000 police officers, 200 judges and included unspeakable violence, including the purposeful bombing of Avianca Flight 203, which killed over 100 people. I want to make sure I'm not making light of the horrible effects of Escobar and Medellin Drug Cartel. The reason that he's seen as a hero in Colombia—specifically with poorer members of society—is that when you're that powerful in an impoverished area, you're the one supplying money, houses, and jobs to the community. For people who were in Medellin in the 80s and 90s, they remember a Pablo Escobar that provided the community with thousands of houses, a city sanitation system, parks and soccer fields, schools and cars and buses. Due to the fact that he had so much money, his riches truly did trickle down to the economy of Medellin.

That's why, in addition to a water park and zoo, the tourist attraction at Hacienda Nápoles includes a Pablo Escobar museum that showcases some of the vehicles, cars, airplanes that he owned as well as some of the burned ruins of his house. People revere him and wonder at the memory of his legacy, even though Escobar was a man that caused severe pain and anguish throughout Colombia, Mexico, and the United States.

A man like Escobar could have whatever he wanted. And at one point in the late 1970s, what he wanted were four hippos. Let's talk about hippos for a minute.

There's only one part of the world where the hippopotamus lives in its natural habitat: Sub-Saharan

Africa. It's up there with the elephant and rhinoceros as one of the top three largest land animals, weighing in at over 3,000 pounds fully grown. Despite their giant size, they can run up to 30 miles an hour and are one of the deadliest land animals. Back in their home region of Africa, hippos kill 500 people a year. They don't have too many predators in the animal kingdom and they're constantly facing threats from humans, including poachers and the effects of the war in the Congo. This has given the African hippopotamus a vulnerable status from the International Union for Conservation of Nature. And because they are so freaking rare, you can't just buy hippos because you want to see them roaming around your house. That is, unless your name is Pablo Escobar and you're the richest drug trafficker in history.

It started with just four hippos. He had a dream of having the biggest private zoo in the world, so he illegally smuggled three females and one male Hippopotamus from Africa to his ranch at Hacienda Nápoles. This initial bloat of hippos was allowed to graze on his Puerto Triunfo property. He showed them off to friends and was proud of the hippos.

I mentioned a little bit earlier about how influential and powerful Pablo Escobar was. It was because of his influence and political connections that when he was arrested for a five-year prison term in 1991, he was allowed to build his own self-built prison, La Catedral, which was basically just another home. Even then, he couldn't stand to be imprisoned and escaped from the home. Two years later, Pablo Escobar was found and killed in a shootout with the National Police of Colombia. At this point, the government of Colombia seized and/or destroyed a lot of Escobar's property. The planes, the cars, the houses—but when it came to the hippos, they simply didn't have any way of handling them. The hippos roamed free and couldn't be rounded up. They were left on his Hacienda Nápoles estate.

These days if you visit Hacienda Nápoles, you'll drive through a big white gate with an airplane on top of it. It's a replica of the airplane Escobar used to smuggle his first shipments of cocaine. There are water park slides, a small zoo, and a couple small museums and attractions. Gone are the private airport, the mansion, the many buildings, the racetrack, the brothel, the tennis courts but not the spirit of Pablo Escobar. You'll witness what's left of the giant dinosaur sculptures he had constructed for his son. His burned-out car collection is still there for all to see. And while most of his zoo animals were sent to other zoos in and out of Colombia, the hippos still roam free. One of them, named Vanessa, even answers to her name.

By 2007, the 4 original hippos had grown to a pod of 16. By 2014, locals were counting as many as 40. Now, it's suspected that the Magdalena River basin is home to more than 100 hippos, all roaming free in a land where they have no predators, and where the climate and food sources are perfect for them to thrive. The Magdalena River is slow-moving, which is ideal for them, and the region never experiences droughts, which is one of the factors that curb hippo populations in Africa. They seem to have evolved to mostly be more tame than their African counterparts, though there have been a few dangerous encounters. These hippos are also reaching sexual maturity at an earlier age than in their natural African habitat. A normal hippo starts giving birth around nine to eleven years old, but the offspring of Escobar's hippos are active as young as three.

It's not all sunshine and rainbows though. These are still incredibly dangerous animals. And they're spreading further and further away from the Hacienda Nápoles estate. Some have been found 155 miles from Puerto Triunfo. Fishermen in the Magdalena River are justifiably terrified of them. Ranchers and farmers have had run-ins with them as they eat valuable crops and have even trampled cows. In 2020, one hippo ran down and injured a farmer, but to this day, they have not killed any people.

The question of what to do with Colombia's hippos is a constant source of debate within the country. When authorities killed one of the hippos in 2009, the public became upset. Some see the small population of thriving hippos as a sort of conservation of a species that is vulnerable in Africa. Others see it as an extension of Escobar's legacy. But Colombian authorities are concerned with the population, which they say could pose a threat to the region's natural biodiversity. Their hope is to castrate the male hippos of the bloat. They argue that the giant animals could possibly carry disease and are seen as an invasive species. If unchecked, the hippo population in Colombia will grow to 400 in the next eight years. By 2035, that number will be 1,500. It will be at that point, experts say, that tragic interactions between Colombian citizens and Hippos will be unavoidable. In 2021, an American court determined that Colombian hippos could be given legal status as "people." But this obviously has zero bearing on what happens in Colombia.

As of right now, no definite plan has been agreed upon and no one is quite sure what to do with Colombia's cocaine hippos. So they remain, wandering the Magdalena River Basin and reminding everyone of the infamous drug kingpin who introduced them.

Nazis in America: The Madison Square Garden Rally

When a society experiences hardship, history shows us time and time again that political leaders deflect that hardship toward an enemy to blame. In 1929, the hardship was a global economic depression.

Like in the United States, the depression left millions of Germans unemployed and unsatisfied with the democratic system of the Weimar Republic that had stabilized the country after the first World War ten years earlier. The public blamed social democracy and big business. If a German was going to reject Social Democracy, they had a choice between Communism and National Socialism and while Communism's argument was a complex one, The

National Socialists had pointed their finger at a clear enemy: Jewish Financiers and Bolsheviks. Because of that and because Hitler was seen by many Germans at the time as powerful and charismatic, the Nazi Party rose in popularity. Between the years of 1924 and 1934, the Nazis went from receiving 3 percent of the vote to 33 percent. Even after their rise to power, a lot of Germans were still skeptical, but the party offered a populist appeal and promoted a nationalism that people liked. They called it Volksgemeinshaft: "The People's Community." And after a global economic depression, nationalism sounded like a good idea. Sadly, even many of those who disagreed with the hateful antisemitic views ignored them in favor of seeing a political party build a stronger Germany. By 1936, Germany saw full employment—of course, many of those jobs were because of the country building up the military strength to prepare for war.

The Nazi Party saw support in other countries as well. History tells us about their support in Italy and Japan, but we know of other instances of Nazi support around the globe. In Europe, these were sometimes nothing more than an alliance in fear of the Soviet Union. For instance, in Finland, the President made an agreement with Hitler for protection against the Soviet Union should they invade. Even Great Britain, who would eventually be absolutely devastated by German forces during the war, had made an Anglo-German Naval pact in the 1930s, something that was in violation of the treaty of Versailles. And while most British despised the Nazi Party, there was indeed a large swath of support—mostly in the north—through the British Union of Fascists, led by a member of Parliament, Oswald Mosely. They even changed their name to include National Socialists. They had 50,000 members. They were disbanded in 1940, but there were a handful of smaller groups that supported the Nazis within Britain. Some were funded by Berlin directly. Some were simply aligned with the Nazis antisemitic policies. Many in the country's high society admired Hitler and saw his politics as crucial to defeating communism. Most of these high society folks ended their support as soon as Hitler invaded Czechoslovakia. Even then, during the war, as many as seventy British men and women were convicted of attempting to aid the enemy and hundreds more were rounded up and interned by the British government.

Like in Great Britain, there was support for Nazism in America as well. Bradley W. Hart, author of *Hitler's American Friends: The Third Reich's Supporters in the United States,* argues that the support for Nazis in the U.S. was greater than most Americans remember today. There were a few different reasons for this. Remember the first weeks of Russia's invasion of Ukraine in 2022, when there were extreme right-wing talking heads who were celebrating Russia's strength and denigrating the Ukrainian government? It's still happening today. Well similarly, there was a far-right radio personality, Charles Coughlin, who would go on the air and promote Nazi fascist policies and apply them to American life. This guy was a Catholic priest out of Detroit and he would broadcast these huge antisemitic tirades to tens of millions of listeners.

In North Carolina, there was a guy William Dudley Pelley who started the Silver Legion—known as the Silver Shirts—who grew a group of 15,000 pro-Nazi, anti-Jewish members, mostly because he had convinced them that "Jews were possessed by demons." It was a Christian Nationalist group. This guy was particularly weird. He had developed a whole costume for his clan and even had ambitions of becoming an American dictator like Hitler.

There were even American Politicians in Washington distributing Nazi propaganda, like Congressman Hamilton Fish III, who was an isolationist and led a scheme to distribute Goebbels propaganda via U.S. Mail, and Senator Robert Rice Reynolds, who made pro-German statements in the Congressional record.

The German American Bund, also known as the German-American Federation, started as a group called "Friends of New Germany." They were Nazi sympathizers and were started by a German immigrant to the U.S. who was given the direction to start this group directly from the deputy Führer of the Nazis, Rudolf Hess. This wasn't a grassroots Nazi support campaign—it was a direct result of Nazi influence. Many of the members of the German American Bund were of German descent, but some were just antisemites. They had a headquarters in New York City, but had training camps in Wisconsin, New Jersey, and Pennsylvania. They publicly opposed and attacked Jewish-American groups, communism, F.D.R., trade unions, and American boycotts of German goods. They would display the American flag next to the Nazi swastika flag, perform the Hitler salute, and prop up George Washington as their icon, saying he was the first fascist. Of course Washington wasn't a fascist. This is the man that turned down serving a third term when he was asked. They appropriated his image to make Nazism seem more "American." And at one point, they claimed to have 200,000 members, though historians have disputed that fact.

One thing that's indisputable, however, is that this group was powerful enough to fill Madison Square Garden in a huge Nazi rally in 1939.

When I talked about support for Hitler and the Nazi Party in the United Kingdom, I mentioned that most of the support ended when Hitler invaded Czechoslovakia. That happened at the end of 1938. But this huge rally in New York City that we're going to talk about happened in February of 1939. It was before Germany invaded Poland, but after they had annexed Czechoslovakia.

It wasn't a small affair. For the previous several years, The German American Bund had run training camps and held Nazi parades in several states. In 1938, we know that they were becoming somewhat sensitive to the overwhelming American opinion of Nazis. Okay, they weren't sensitive to it. I guess we can say they "knew" how most Americans felt. We know this because they were careful to point out that by this time, they were not funded by any German relations, and they didn't allow actual German Nazis in their ranks. They also formally banned Nazi emblems to be used by the Bund. But I don't know if I believe any of this, because we have the giant rally in Madison Square Garden in 1939 as proof.

As many as 22,000 people attended the rally on February 20 of 1939.

Before the event, Mayor LaGuardia knew there was going to be a storm of counter-protesters, so he dispatched a force of 1,700 uniformed New York Police Officers around Madison Square Garden. Inside, 22,000 American Nazis and Nazi supporters gathered. They gave the Nazi Salute to the American Nazi color guard walking by in uniform. These were Americans who had drilled at the various camps like the one in New Jersey. German marches played over the speakers. The stage was adorned with a thirty-foot-tall image of George Washington, flanked by American Flags and Swastikas.

Fritz Julius Kuhn was a German Nazi activist, the current leader of the Bund, and was the featured guest speaker. He was a veteran of World War I, where he fought for Germany. He addressed the crowd in the uniform of a full German Storm Trooper.

As Kuhn said this, Isadore Greenbaum, a young Jewish

anti-Nazi protestor, stormed the stage attempting to reach the podium and was quickly tackled and beaten by the guards wearing red swastika armbands. They kicked and punched the man onstage and ripped his pants off. Police came in and intervened and the rally continued. At one point, the journalist and author Dorothy Thompson yelled the word "Bunk" in protest and was escorted out of the rally.

Outside Madison Square Garden, as many as 100,000 anti-Nazi protesters organized, waving American flags, tearing down Nazi flags and attempting to confront anyone who entered or exited the rally inside.

To see one of the overhead shots of this rally, it's shocking to think that there were this many Americans who supported the open and raw antisemitism. Whether they knew or didn't know, while that rally was being held in America, Adolf Hitler was finishing construction on his sixth concentration camp in Europe. Here were 22,000 Americans who supported these antisemitic views—and these were just the ones that attended the rally. Who knows how many tens of thousands silently supported the cause from around the country.

And I think one of the major causes of that was propaganda. It could be spread so easily around the world. Whether it was through film, radio, or newspapers, it was easy for Joseph Goebbels to plant messages internationally, especially knowing he had the support of several United States lawmakers. So these tens of thousands—maybe hundreds of thousands—of Americans had received Hitler's message and agreed with it. Hitler said, I'm paraphrasing, "Nature doesn't desire the blending of a higher race with a lower race."

I'm going to read you another quote. "This is why we have always fought. We are willing to mix with one another, but we do not want to become peoples of mixed-race." That quote wasn't from Hitler, or Goebbels, or from 1939. It was from 2022. And it was said by Hungary's Prime Minister, Viktor Orban, who was a guest speaker at CPAC, the Conservative Political Action Conference in Texas. He received a standing ovation from the crowd of conservatives there. Of course I'm not the first to draw this comparison. CPAC has been widely mocked for promoting anti-American and isolationist views that sound more like something from 1930s Germany. Americans heard a sitting U.S. Congresswoman call herself a "Christian Nationalist" onstage and heard speakers promote Trump's "America First" tagline—the same type of nationalist/isolationist sentiment of the German American Bund. In fact, a major Nazi-sympathizing group that came about in 1940 was called the "America First Committee." This was a group that showed up after the German American Bund sort of dissolved. So "America First" as a slogan has a dirty past that directly links to present-day politics.

And as we saw in the "Unite the Right" rally in Charlottesville in 2017, there are still plenty of Americans out there today spreading this same brand of hatred. At that event, and at the U.S. capitol attack in 2021, people were spotted carrying Nazi swastika flags. Some wore T-Shirts that said "Camp Auschwitz" and "6MWE"—an acronym for "Six Million Wasn't Enough." With his anti-immigrant, America-First rhetoric, President Trump riled up the new Alt-Right and fueled their antisemitism. White Christian Supremacy in the United States is still alive and well. And instead of newspapers and film strips, they're receiving their messaging from the internet and hyperpartisan news-entertainment television.

Sometimes people ask, "How could that have happened?" How could Hitler have risen to power with those types of views? The 1939 rally at Madison Square Garden is proof. It could happen then, and it could happen now. All it takes is an angry faction of the public looking for someone to blame for their hardships, some exciting-sounding slogans, a leader to help them along the way, and for good people to do nothing.

Stuart Little and the Hungarian Masterpiece

There's something about missing pieces of art that capture the imagination. Art theft—one of the most romantic types of heists out there, besides maybe robbing a bank—has been the subject of countless books and movies. The idea of stealing something that is on public display is daring and has this impact on people that other types of thievery don't. Our story today isn't necessarily about stolen art, but art that has gone missing. People love stories about lost treasures.

In 1990, two Police Officers entered the Isabella Stewart Gardner Art Museum in Boston. They told the museum security they were responding to a disturbance call. The men weren't police at all, but art thieves, who bound and gagged the security guards and proceeded to steal thirteen pieces of art worth a total of at least $500 million. One of them was Rembrandt's *Storm on the Sea of Galilee,* the artist's only seascape. To this date, all the works remain missing, including the famous Rembrandt piece.

One of Vincent Van Gogh's paintings is also currently missing. It's called *Poppy Flowers* and it's actually been stolen twice from the same museum. The first time it was stolen from the Mohamed Khalil Museum in Cairo, it was during a move between two wings of the museum. It was eventually recovered, but was stolen again in 2010. The piece and the thieves still remain at large.

But one painting that went missing wasn't stolen.

Róbert Berény painted *Sleeping Lady with Black Vase* in 1927 and 1928. It depicts the painter's wife Eta in a blue dress, sleeping. Berény was Hungarian but living in Berlin, and after World War I he had fled back to Budapest where he painted the piece. It was unveiled in the Ernst Museum in Hungary and was sold to a private buyer the same year, in 1928. That was when the painting was lost.

It's believed that the buyer was Jewish and fled Europe as a result of the events of World War II. That's how the painting ended up going missing for the next ninety years.

The painting in the meantime was missed in the Hungarian art world, and although the artist's works weren't valued like a missing Van Gogh or Rembrandt, it was referred to as Róbert Berény's missing masterpiece. Historians only had a black and white photograph of the piece of art and no leads as to what happened to the piece after the war. It's considered the most widely known piece of Hungarian art in history, but that's possibly due to the story of its unlikely rediscovery after being considered lost for so long.

In December of 2009, Gergely Barki, an expert on Hungarian art, was watching a film with his three-year-old daughter. They were watching *Stuart Little*, a 1999 Rob Minkoff film starring Michael J. Fox, Hugh Laurie, and

Geena Davis. Barki worked as an art researcher in Hungary's National Gallery in Budapest.

In the film, Mr. And Mrs. Little, played by Hugh Laurie and Geena Davis, are seen in their home with their son, played by Jonathan Lipnicki, and Stuart Little, a computer-animated mouse voiced by Michael J. Fox. And in their home, on a wall—plain as day—Barki noticed the painting. After all these years, he was convinced he was looking at a color version of *Sleeping Lady with Black Vase,* Berény's lost masterpiece.

The painting was in a prominent part of the house in the film, so it appeared a lot. Barki didn't have any method of recording the movie as he was watching it on television, so he kept watching, waiting for the next time it appeared on screen. By the end of the film, he was positive that this was the real thing. There would be no way for anyone to have duplicated this painting. At the time, it wasn't well known outside of Hungary and the only known image of the painting was black and white. Barki decided he was now on a mission to track it down.

He immediately started researching production companies in the U.S. and getting the names of crew members and set designers at Sony Pictures and Columbia. He had sent about fifty different emails when he finally discovered the set designer assistant who had the painting. And that's when we learned a little bit more about how it ended up in a Hollywood movie.

So the Hungarian art world knew that the painting had been sold to an unknown person in the leadup to World War II. The best guess is that a Jewish person fleeing Europe had bought the painting and fled to America. That's how the painting ended up in the United States and was finally rediscovered sixty-five years later. We only know the next part because the set designer's assistant—

whose name has never been reported—was able to provide a backstory. At an art auction in San Diego in the mid 90s, the St. Vincent de Paul auction house sold the painting to Michael Hempstead, an art collector, who made some money on the piece when he realized it was a Berény and sold it for $400. A while after that, it ended up in an antique store on Fair Oaks Avenue in Pasadena. That's where the set designer purchased the painting for $500.

It had been used for years by the set designer—and in more than *Stuart Little*. Apparently there are numerous soap opera episodes, like the show *Family Law*, in which the painting shows up in the background.

By the time the art historian Barki discovered the piece in *Stuart Little*, it was ten years after the making of the film and the piece was then hanging in the home of this set designer's assistant, who had bought it from the studio after *Stuart Little* wrapped. Barki flew to Los Angeles and met the assistant to confirm the authenticity of the painting. He rushed across the street to a hot dog vendor to borrow a screwdriver and started taking the frame apart. His suspicion was confirmed. The painting was indeed the long-lost *Sleeping Lady with Black Vase*.

Now this was all happening as prices of authentic Berénys were skyrocketing. The owner of the painting sold it to an art collector from Budapest for $137,000. It was sold again in 2014 to a private collector for $285,700.

The painting is considered the perfect embodiment of 1920s European art. And for decades, it was lost to the world. It's a crazy cinematic story with a turn that even M. Night Shyamalan couldn't have written. Which is why I was shocked when I looked up the writers of the film *Stuart Little*: the original book was by E.B. White, but the screenplay was written by Greg Brooker, and you won't believe this, M. Night Shyamalan. The Internet Says It's True.

The Vexing Vampires of Venice

It was the mid-2000s when the Archeological Superintendent of Veneto in Italy promoted a research project on mass graves. They were on an island just northeast of Venice called Lazaretto Nuovo.

A few years ago, Jack White had an album and a song named "Lazaretto" and I remember googling it then. It's a word for an annexed area for isolating undesirables. In the ages of plagues, it was necessary for people to be quarantined to these islands, but they also used them for criminals and those deemed to be insane.

Lazaretto Nuovo was the second lazaretto in Venice; it literally means "new lazaretto" as opposed to Lazaretto Vecchio, meaning "old Lazaretto," an older and much smaller island that housed plague victims in the 1400s. Lazaretto Nuovo was a larger island, around twenty-two acres of land. It was established in 1468 when the Venetian Senate decided there needed to be more space to quarantine those afflicted by plague and the old Lazaretto wasn't big enough. It remained as a health quarantine until the 1700s when it started being used as a military fortification to protect the Venice Lagoon. It stopped serving any military function in the 1970s, but now the island is opened for archaeological and education tours.

It was one of those archeological studies in 2005 that our story starts to take shape. An archeological dig had discovered a mass grave from the plague. Hundreds of skeletons were discovered, but one in particular raised the eyebrows of researchers.

They had found a skeleton with a brick firmly placed into its gaping open jaw. There were no other bricks nearby. It wasn't a coincidence or accident. It was evident to the scientists that this brick had been deliberately placed there, so they set to out to find out why.

They were first looking at why those graves were there to begin with. The first black plague tore through Europe in 1348 and Venice was hit incredibly hard. They responded with these two Lazarettos, the old one in 1423 and the new one in 1468. The new Lazaretto also acted as a quarantine station for people coming to Venice from the sea. They could be checked for symptoms of the plague there before being allowed to come into the city. There were two additional plagues that hit Venice, one in 1576 and one in 1630. Most of the people who were sent to the island with plague never left. That helps to understand the mass grave, but not the body with the brick in its mouth.

By measuring the bones, they could tell that the person was a woman who most likely died in her sixties. The researchers started looking around at burial practices around the world from the era, and that's where we find out about "The Shroud Eaters."

In German folklore, the Nachzehrers, or "Shroud Eaters," were a very particular type of vampire. They're a little different than the normal vampire we hear about. They don't become a vampire from being bitten or scratched by one, and they don't spread their vampirism to other people. But it's related to communicable disease. The first person to die from a plague is said to be a shroud eater. They were called that because they would begin by eating their own burial shroud. Then the shroud eater would feed on their own bodies. Finally, their loved ones and family members would then become weak or die as the shroud eater was feeding on their life force from the grave. I found a couple other sources that said shroud eaters were created when a death occurred from suicide or by accident.

The brick in the mouth was a practice that was put in place to prevent the person from eating their shroud. In the case of the body recovered in Venice, it's believed that the body was not initially buried this way, but rather was exhumed and reburied with the brick. The likely explanation for this is that when the body was uncovered, it was seen that the burial shroud had a hole around the mouth area, and was assumed to have started to eat the burial shroud, and thus deemed to be one of these vampires. Another thing that would have clued them toward vampire is that parts of the body were thought to have continued to grow, like fingernails. The brick in the mouth would of course prevent the body from eating more of the shroud and would protect other people from losing their life force.

Of course all of this sounds pretty crazy, but there's a logical explanation for much of it.

So what's the truth about this story? Well we know that the body with the brick in the mouth was definitely uncovered. And most accounts point to the brick not being there by accident, though some theories do state that it could have happened when dirt was being moved around on the island. This is an island that's been purposed and repurposed so many times, lots of buildings were built and demolished through the years.

Most seem to think that the vampire story is the likely explanation for the brick. Of course there's no evidence that anything like a vampire exists, but the folklore and the ancient beliefs are very true. There's an ancient book, "De Masticatione Mortuorum in Tumulis" from 1728. That title translates to "On the Chewing of the Dead in their Tombs." It's quite literally a scientifically worded dissertation by Michael Ranft of Germany about this phenomenon of shroud eaters.

We know that science evolves and improves with time. And before we knew how bodies decompose, it would make sense that when a body was dug up, the mouth would be the place that would show signs of decomposition, which would then affect the burial shroud in that area. The brain is the first organ to decompose, and if insects and critters—
I'm sorry this is gross—were to have access to the body, that would be a pretty easy place for them to enter. Critters and insects also help to understand the idea of a shroud eater feeding on its own body. I already discussed about how they thought the nails continued to grow, yet another case of people not understanding the science. And then there's the idea of the vexed family and loved ones. Remember, we're talking about the age of the plague. If you had the plague and lived near people, there's a good chance that they would become sick too. And there were some really backwards ways of thinking about health back then. In the age of the plague, people were told not to bathe. This is before people knew about germs and bacteria. So it would make sense that they would see family members of the sick also getting sick. They would see these corpses with their long nails, hair, and exposed teeth, and just assume that these were signs

of a shroud eater.

So this ritual of blocking their mouth with something like large rock or brick was born. According to Matteo Borrini, an anthropologist from the University of Florence, "To kill the vampire you had to remove the shroud from its mouth, which was its food like the milk of a child, and put something uneatable in there. It's possible that other corpses have been found with bricks in their mouths, but this was the first time the ritual has been recognized."

So while The Internet Says It's True, remember that there's no such thing as a shroud eater, just stupid humans who didn't know any better and those of us here to tell the stories 400 years later.

The Dublin Whiskey Fire: Why Thirteen People Died

I want to state here at the top of this story, I spelled Whiskey with an "e" in the title. I know that it's a topic of debate whether or not there should be an "e" in Whiskey. You may notice some bottles have it, some don't. For some distilleries, it's a matter of tradition, but the most common distinction here is geographical. America and Ireland tend to use Whiskey with an "E-Y" at the end, but when you get into Scotland, Japan, or Canada, they go without the E: just "S-K-Y" at the end. Since we're in Ireland for this story, we use the E. But before we get into that story, it reminded me of a more recent piece of news.

For the Jim Beam distillery, Fourth of July Weekend in 2019 wasn't one to celebrate. On the evening of July 3rd, a lightning strike hit one of their Frankfort, Kentucky warehouses and started an uncontrollable blaze. Between wood and flammable alcohol, the fire spread quickly. Fire units from four different nearby counties responded and the fire was so hot that the plastic lights on the firetrucks melted.

They made the decision to let the fire burn itself out. They contained it, but they wanted the distilled spirits to burn down because one of the major results of this fire was contaminated runoff. As the barrels burned, they leaked ethanol into Glenn Creek, which then led to the Kentucky River and the larger Ohio River. Firefighters wanted to minimize the amount of bourbon entering the river. Even so, environmental experts found a large fish kill-off in the sixty-two miles of river where the bourbon runoff traveled. Jim Beam paid $600,000 in fines for the damage to the environment.

As far as the whiskey goes, the warehouse was a total loss. 45,000 barrels were destroyed—that's approximately 6 million bottles of bourbon. "Take one down, pass it around, five million, nine hundred-thousand, nine-hundred ninety-nine bottles of bourbon on the wall!" Now, to put that into context, it was about 1 percent of Jim Beam's total bourbon being stored. They have 126 warehouses in Kentucky with 3.3 million barrels, so the fire didn't affect supply at all. And Jim Beam ages their barrels for four years—these barrels hadn't yet broken the one-year mark, so it wasn't a huge loss in that regard.

It seems like other than a small financial loss, the biggest impact was to the fish in the ecosystem. But in Dublin, Ireland, a distillery fire that raged in the Liberties district in 1875 took thirteen lives. And none of them were due to the fire itself.

There's a long history of distillery fires in Kentucky. One of the worst ones was the Heaven Hill Fire in 1996. It was said to have destroyed 2 percent of the world's total amount of whiskey overnight. But no one died as a result. The fire we're going to talk about now ended up with the death of thirteen Irishmen. Let's go back to 1875.

The inner-city area known as the Liberties is the oldest part of Dublin, Ireland. It's so old it can trace its origins all the way back to the Vikings. On Ardee Street in the Liberties neighborhood stood Laurence Malone's Pub and Bonded Storehouse. A bonded storehouse was a place where barrels of whiskey from various distilleries were stored, and a Whiskey Bonder would make private-label blends and small-batch bottles from those barrels. Malone's storehouse held 5,000 barrels of whiskey—half-a-million liters. He was the largest and most successful Whiskey Bonder in Dublin.

Around 4:35 p.m. on June 18, 1875, someone from Malone's checked on the storehouse and all was well. But sometime between then and 8:30 p.m., a fire started. No one knows exactly how it began, but again: high-test alcohol plus wood equals quick-spreading fire. By 9:30 p.m., the fire was raging so hot that barrels were exploding, throwing flaming alcohol into the air and out the windows of the storehouse. It was a combination of immature spirits, whiskey, brandy and wine. It was basically like gasoline flowing out the doors and windows of the building, burning with a blue flame as it ran.

The fire brigade was a tiny group of twenty-three men, led by Fire Captain Robert Ingram. He had worked as a fireman in both New York and London and was the very first Superintendent of the relatively new fire brigade. They had only organized thirteen years prior, and most Dublin citizens didn't support the idea of a centralized fire brigade for the city. Some Dubliners didn't like the idea of poor citizens who didn't pay into the system getting the benefit of a fire service for free.

Even though the fire brigade was a group of twenty-three, only fifteen could be rounded up to fight the blaze at Malone's. It wasn't enough. The police showed up and immediately called for 150 more police officers and 200 military men. By this time, two buildings were burning—both Malone's storehouse and the adjoining Reid's Punch House Pub—shooting flames high into the air, thirty feet above the roof, as burning whiskey continued spilling into the streets, glowing blue with flame. The loss was somewhere around $6 million of whiskey in today's money.

The river of burning whiskey was rushing down the street six inches deep. It destroyed entire houses as it flowed down Cork Street, Ardee Street, Chamber and Mill Streets. The firemen couldn't fight it with water—that would just help spread the burning whiskey, which would float on top of the water. They started tearing apart the street and trying to dam the flow with gravel and rocks. It didn't work. Finally, Captain Ingram ordered the men to bring wagons of horse manure, something they had in plentiful supply. They mixed horse manure with supplies from the nearby tannery and ashes to finally stop the flow of burning whiskey. They stopped it just in time to save the convent as the fire spread toward Coombe. The scene in the Liberties was chaos. Animals were panicking, crying, and running everywhere in the streets. The citizens of Dublin had crowded around at the spectacle of a blue glowing river of alcohol in the night.

By the end of the entire debacle, thirteen people died. But strangely, NONE of them died from fire. None died from smoke inhalation. Every single death was attributed to alcohol poisoning. A total of twenty-four hospitalizations and thirteen dead—all from drinking too much.

As the river was flowing through the neighborhood, people were grabbing bowls and drinking it. Men took off their hats and filled them up to get a sip. Some even were reported to remove their boots to fill them up with free whiskey! And much of that whiskey was immature, unaged pure alcohol. Much stronger than what they were used to drinking.

Peter Paul McSwiney, the Lord Mayor, thanked the fire brigade and police for evacuating the buildings so quickly, but lamented the loss of life due to alcohol poisoning. He said that the deaths of those who drank the fire whiskey would have happened in "any city where there was a tendency to indulge immoderately in drink." He said, "In the present case, the unfortunate victims apparently could not restrain themselves, as I understand, from the burning fluid."

There is a happy ending, though. This fire was the catalyst to add certain fire-protection measures to storehouses. And it helped Captain Ingram finally convince the public of the importance of a large, centralized fire brigade. They had proven their value in saving not only countless lives, but a large part of the city. Had it not been for their efforts, it definitely would have been worse.

The newspapers were afraid of the story making Irishmen look like uncontrollable drunks and played it down. Whiskey manufacturers didn't talk about it because they didn't want people to think that drinking their whiskey was deadly. So, while it plays into the derogatory stereotype of the Irish, it definitely happened. The Internet Says It's True.

Poisoned: 344 Meals and a Miracle

To tell this story, we have to talk about something very small, very light, and often ignored unless you're about to need it desperately: the barf bag.

If you've flown in an airplane, you probably know about the waxy white envelope in the seat-back pocket. Most planes still have them, some don't. But there was a time—particularly from the 1960s through the 1990s—when every seat on every commercial airline first started carrying motion-sickness bags. It was like an air travel rite of passage to see them, and for many, to use them.

The modern barf bag was patented in the 1940s by a guy named Gilmore "Tex" Tilton. Before that, sick passengers were handed cardboard containers or, bizarrely, small canvas bags that had to be cleaned and reused. The paper version was cheap, disposable, and surprisingly collectible. Some airlines printed jokes or slogans on theirs. Delta once printed the question "Feel Better?" on theirs. There's even an online museum dedicated to barf bag design.

But even in the worst turbulence, they were rarely used en masse. Air sickness is usually isolated—one person here, another a few rows back. The story we're telling today isn't about motion sickness. It's about what happens when 344 people eat the same thing, and it turns out that thing should never have been on the plane in the first place.

Let's set the scene. It's February 3, 1975. Japan Airlines Flight 404 is preparing to depart from Anchorage, Alaska, bound for Copenhagen. It's a Boeing 747-246B, and this leg is part of a longer journey that originated in Tokyo and was headed for Paris. On board were 344 passengers and 20 crew. Almost all those passengers were part of a corporate group: Coca-Cola Japan had arranged an international trip for hundreds of their executives, salespeople, and family members. It was a working vacation—a reward for high-performing employees.

So this was not your average passenger list. These were business travelers, company people. And Japan Airlines wanted to make a good impression. In the 1970s, JAL was known for its elite service, immaculate uniforms, and meals that were better than average for the time. And with this being a high-profile group, they rolled out the best they had to offer.

Shortly after takeoff, the flight attendants began serving a hot breakfast. The main dish was a ham and cheese omelet, served with rolls, butter, and dessert. The trays were clean. The food looked great. The passengers ate and settled in for the long transatlantic flight.

Then it started.

First, one or two people asked for motion sickness bags. Then five. Then ten. Then entire rows of people. One witness later said it was like watching dominoes fall—one after another, passengers began vomiting, shaking, clutching their stomachs.

The plane was halfway to Europe when the scale of the outbreak became clear. Flight attendants were overwhelmed. Lavatories were full. Some passengers had collapsed in the aisles. Others were passed out in their seats. Diarrhea, vomiting, nausea—all at once. There was no panic, just a kind of stunned horror.

Out of 344 passengers, 197 became violently ill.

And this wasn't regular food poisoning, where you might feel queasy and get over it after a few hours. This was the kind where your body goes into full evacuation mode. Dozens of people were dehydrated before landing. Some were drifting in and out of consciousness.

The only reason this didn't become an air disaster is because the flight crew ate different meals. Airline policy often has pilots eat different dishes from passengers, as a safety precaution. And that policy likely saved every soul on board. Had the pilots been incapacitated by the same illness, it's possible the aircraft wouldn't have made it to Denmark. That's the miracle.

When the plane landed in Copenhagen, it was met by emergency crews, ambulances, and medical personnel. But the airport wasn't prepared for this many sick people at once. The language barrier only made it worse. Most of the passengers spoke Japanese. The medical staff spoke Danish. So officials did something creative: they called in Japanese-speaking restaurant staff from local sushi and noodle shops to serve as emergency translators.

One by one, passengers were triaged. 144 were hospitalized, and 30 were considered in critical condition. Some had to be carried off the aircraft. Others were taken straight to emergency rooms with fluids being administered on the tarmac.

And still, nobody knew exactly what had caused it.

When almost 200 people got violently ill on board the Japan Airlines flight, the airline immediately began an investigation. So did the U.S. Centers for Disease Control. Japan Airlines grounded certain routes. And in Alaska, health inspectors turned their attention to a company called International Inflight Catering—a subsidiary of Japan Airlines that was responsible for preparing the food at Anchorage International Airport.

This was the kitchen that had made the breakfast omelets. And when investigators looked into their practices, they were horrified. There were no proper health screenings for staff, no required glove use, and no protocols for reporting illness. Food was not stored according to modern cold-chain standards. And then they discovered the source.

One of the kitchen workers, a man who had been tasked with slicing the ham used in the omelets, had shown up to work with infected open sores on his fingers. He had bandaged them. But he hadn't told his supervisor, and no one had asked. That alone might've been enough to cause contamination. But it was what happened next that made it deadly.

After slicing the ham, it was left out for hours at a temperature where bacteria thrive. Specifically, *Staphylococcus aureus*, a common bacteria found on human skin and in wounds. Once introduced to the ham, it began to multiply rapidly.

Now, here's the science part: staph bacteria produce enterotoxins, and those toxins are heat-stable—meaning they're not destroyed by cooking or reheating. So even though the omelets were heated again in the galley ovens on the plane, the toxins remained fully active.

It wasn't bacteria making people sick. It was the poison the bacteria had already released.

The CDC confirmed this in their final report. It was one of the clearest documented cases of mass foodborne illness linked to a specific bacterial toxin. The mistake wasn't just one person's failure—it was a systemic breakdown. A worker came in sick. The kitchen let him prep food. That food wasn't cooled properly. And then it was loaded onto a plane where nobody could escape it.

But the story doesn't end there.

Shortly after the investigation began, Kenji Kuwabara, the head of International Inflight Catering in Anchorage, took his own life.

He left a note accepting full responsibility for what had happened.

It's not clear whether he was pressured, or whether the guilt was simply too much. But in Japanese corporate culture—particularly in the 1970s—honor and shame were serious business. To be publicly associated with a massive failure was a cultural weight few could bear. His death shook the airline world.

In response, Japan Airlines completely overhauled its food safety protocols. Medical checks became mandatory for kitchen workers. Glove use was enforced. Cold storage requirements were raised. The entire in-flight catering industry took notice. Airlines around the world updated their standards.

And despite the staggering number of sick passengers, no one died. That may be the biggest miracle of all. Nearly 200 people consumed a toxic meal, 144 of them ended up in the hospital—and everyone lived.

It remains the worst food poisoning incident in commercial aviation history. And today, when you lift the foil lid off a steaming airplane meal, you're seeing the legacy of what happened on Flight 404. There are temperature logs, health screenings, entire safety checklists. All because, one day in 1975, someone didn't report a few bandaged fingers—and the consequences flew across an ocean. The Internet Says It's True.

Inglorious Bruin: Wojtek the Soldier Bear

In the chaos and carnage of World War II, heroes emerged from the most unexpected places—not just from the ranks of soldiers but also from the animal kingdom. Dogs, pigeons, horses, and even bears were enlisted to serve in the world's greatest conflict, carrying messages, transporting supplies, and boosting the morale of weary troops. These brave creatures performed astonishing acts of courage, sometimes in the face of gunfire, and their loyalty was unwavering. From the fearless war dog who charged enemy lines to the homing pigeons that saved lives with their speed, animals proved to be more than companions—they were indispensable warriors.

In the dense jungles of Burma, elephants proved invaluable to both British and Japanese forces during World War II. Their immense strength and size allowed them to carry heavy artillery, construct bridges, and transport supplies through terrain impassable for trucks or tanks. Working tirelessly alongside the soldiers, these gentle giants played a crucial role in the brutal Burma campaign, where human lives depended on their unwavering service.

Mules were the unsung heroes of the Italian Campaign, often carrying artillery, food, and medical supplies across the treacherous Apennine Mountains. The British Army in particular relied heavily on mules, as they could traverse areas where vehicles would get stuck or destroyed. Though their role was less glamorous than that of combat troops, the survival of entire divisions depended on these hardy animals, which braved enemy fire and grueling conditions.

But there are also stories of individual animals. Take the case of "Unsinkable Sam" the cat. Originally a ship's cat on the German battleship Bismarck, Sam survived its sinking in May 1941 and was rescued by British sailors. After the Bismarck, Sam survived the sinking of two more ships—the HMS Cossack and HMS Ark Royal—each time being found alive and rescued. Following these incredible escapes, Sam retired to a peaceful life in the UK, becoming a symbol of survival and resilience during World War II. But he wasn't the only cat. Simon, the ship's cat aboard the British Royal Navy ship HMS Amethyst, became a hero during the Chinese Civil War's Yangtze Incident in 1949. After surviving injuries from a shell blast that killed several of his crewmates, Simon continued his duty, killing rats and protecting the ship's food supply. For his bravery and morale-boosting presence, Simon was awarded the Dickin Medal—the animal equivalent of the Victoria Cross—the only cat to receive such an honor during or after the war.

Even birds fought in the war. In 1943, G.I. Joe, a homing pigeon with the U.S. Army Pigeon Service, flew twenty miles in twenty minutes to deliver a message that saved a thousand British soldiers in Italy from being bombed by their own planes. The message was sent just in time to halt an airstrike that had already been ordered. G.I. Joe's lightning-fast flight earned him the prestigious Dickin Medal, proving that even the smallest creatures could turn the tide of battle.

As far as dogs, there were many dogs that helped with boosting morale. Chips, a German Shepherd-Collie-Siberian Husky mix, was part of the U.S. Army's 3rd Infantry Division. In 1943, during the invasion of Sicily, he singlehandedly charged a hidden enemy machine-gun nest, forcing its crew to surrender despite being wounded in the fray. For this, he was awarded the Silver Star and Purple Heart. Now this was sadly later revoked as animals were no longer eligible, but Chip's bravery remains a testament to the critical role dogs played in saving countless lives.

Smoky was a tiny Yorkshire Terrier. Little Smoky was found by American soldiers in the jungles of New Guinea in 1944, became a morale booster and a military asset. Though only 4 pounds, she crawled through seventy feet of piping to help lay a crucial communication wire, saving the troops days of dangerous work. Smoky also visited wounded soldiers, comforting them in ways only a devoted animal could, becoming one of the most famous therapy dogs of the war.

We've talked about elephants, cats, dogs, mules, even birds! But today's story revolves around an incredibly unlikely animal. A bear.

The story of the 2nd Polish Corps is interesting by itself, even without learning about today's story about a bear. The Polish Army was basically created inside Soviet territory when thousands and thousands of Polish prisoners were finally released from Soviet gulags in 1941. Between then and 1943, this new Army was formed and fought for the Allies.

In 1942, as these thousands of new troops were traveling to Tehran, Iran, some of these Polish soldiers encountered a young Iranian boy who had discovered a bear cub. He said the bear's mother had been shot by hunters and he had rescued the cub. A polish civilian refugee who was traveling with the troops convinced them to purchase the cub from the boy, and for a while after that the young refugee, Irena Bokiewicz, took care of the cub and raised it in a refugee camp there in Iran.

After a few years, this bear somehow found its way to being the official mascot of the 2nd Transport Company, which later became the 22nd Artillery Supply Company. The bear was given the named Wojtek, which is a play on the Slavic word "Wojciech," which means "happy warrior."

After being fed fruit, honey, syrup, and marmalade, the bear was fed beer, which was his favorite. This obviously gave a kick to the soldiers, who also took to feeding Wojtek milk from an emptied-out vodka bottle. He also took to cigarettes, but it turned out he was more interested in eating them than smoking. In the morning, they'd give the bear coffee and at night, the soldiers would take turns cuddling up to Wojtek to stay warm. Yes. They cuddled with the bear. He was that friendly.

He was so friendly, in fact, that the soldiers would even play-wrestle with the bear. Wojtek the Bear stayed with the 22nd Artillery Supply Company as they left Iran, traveled through Syria, and ended up in Egypt, then later fought alongside the British Army in the Italian Campaign. The only problem with this was that to get to Italy, the British Transport ship proved to be a problem. Mascots and animals in general were forbidden from riding on the ship.

To address this, the Polish Army officially drafted Wojtek. He was now a Private in the Polish Army. They assigned Henryk Zacharewicz and Lew Worzowski as his handlers. And it was just about as official as you could be. He had a serial number and rank, just like the other Polish soldiers.

In Italy, Germany fought the Allies at Montecasino from January 17 all the way until May 18, 1944. And on May 17 and 18th, at the end of the battle, the 2nd Polish Corps was the group that helped to launch the final bombardment on the German position. When Allied flags were raised over the ruins, it was the Polish flag that stood next to the British flag.

In this battle, Wojtek the Soldier Bear became famous. At this point, keep in mind, he was still very much a cub, but he was quickly growing. He weighed somewhere around 200 pounds when they got him, but by the battle of Montecasino, he was around 485 pounds. He had watched the Polish soldiers and was pretty good at mimicking their actions. One of these actions that proved valuable during the battle was carrying crates of ammo. The bear had seen men carrying these ammo crates, which weighed over a hundred pounds. They were filled with twenty-five-pound artillery shells and, after observing the men carrying the crates, the bear would do the same. They'd point the bear in the right direction and Wojtek would carry the ammo crates to soldiers in need and never dropped a single crate. It would take multiple men to carry these things, but for Wojtek, it was no problem. British soldiers even confirmed the reports of a bear walking on two feet, calmly carrying ammo to soldiers during the battle. The Allies went on to win in Montecasino, despite losing more than twice the amount of men as the Germans. Because of his heroism during the battle, Wojtek was promoted from Private to Corporal!

After Montecasino, the 22nd Artillery Company was sent to Scotland and the bear went with them. But when they were demobilized in November of 1947, no one knew what to do with this bear. In Scotland, he had become a very popular member of the military. Civilians were infatuated with the bear and would come to visit often. Poland wanted the bear to be returned after the war, but Edinburgh fought to keep him there. And that's how Wojtek's retirement was carried out at the Edinburgh Zoo.

He lived in the Zoo the rest of his life and would even seem to respond when Polish tourists would speak to him in Polish. He was frequently featured on UK television, which made him even more popular. When former army mates of his would come to the zoo to visit, they'd toss him cigarettes to eat, which he still loved. In 1963, Wojtek the Bear finally passed away. He weighed 1,100 pounds and had lived to the age of twenty-one.

There are multiple statues and commemorations to Wojtek. The most popular stands in Edinburgh's West Prince's Street Garden where the bear is depicted carrying an artillery shell on two legs. But he's been memorialized in London, Poland and at the site of the Battle of Montecasino in Italy. The Internet Says It's True.

The Woman Who Fell from the Sky and Lived

On The Internet Says It's True podcast, I've covered hundreds of stories. They all fall under the category of stories that sound made up but aren't. If someone were to ask me which one is the hardest to believe, it's the story you're about to read. It's one of my favorite stories from the show, it's 100 percent true, and I'm happy to include it here in this book.

In 1968, German biologists Maria and Hans-Wilhelm Koepcke bought an abandoned cabin in a lowland rainforest in Peru. It was at the western foothill of the El Sira mountain range, and their purpose in buying the cabin was to establish a new research station to study the local flora and fauna. They had worked for the Museum of Natural History in Lima and had decided to embark on what was only meant to be a five-year mission at the research station, which they named Panguana. It was there that Maria and Hans-Wilhelm's fourteen-year-old daughter Juliene got an unusual education.

Instead of being in school in the bustling city of Lima, she was homeschooled in this Amazon rainforest research station. She would go out with her parents on their many trips into the wild. She learned things that a fourteen-year-old girl normally doesn't get to learn, like how to identify various types of insects, plants, and animals in the rainforest and how to survive among them. Even though this education was great for her, the school back in Lima eventually said she had to return. And so she went back to the city to finish high school.

When Juliene was seventeen, her mother had the idea to fly her back to Panguana to visit her father for Christmas. Maria returned to Lima to pick up her daughter, and the two of them would fly together. The plan was to fly from Lima to the small Iquitos airport on the 19th or 20th of December, but young Juliene was about to graduate high school. She wanted to attend her graduation ceremony and a dance and leave after that. So the two were forced to fly out on Christmas Eve, December 24th, 1971. The only airline that they could book was LANSA, which stood for Lineas Aéreas Nacionales Sociedad Anonima, a struggling Peruvian airline with a poor reputation. Hans-Wilhelm protested the decision to fly with LANSA, but it was all that was available.

At noon on December 24th, LANSA Flight 508, a Lockheed L188A Electra Turboprop carrying 86 passengers took off from Lima's Jorge Chavez International Airport. The final destination of the flight was Iquitos, Peru, with a scheduled stop happening at Pucullpa. But the airplane would never arrive.

The first half of the flight was relatively smooth, but as the flight with eighty-six passengers and six crew members flew over the Puerto Inca province, it encountered severe turbulence and heavy thunderstorms at 21,000 feet.

The plane shuddered, dipped, dropped, and bounced in the horrible storm. Items were thrown around the cabin and the passengers began to scream. Suddenly, passengers witnessed the flash from a bolt of lightning…

The lightning struck the right wing of the L188A and ignited the fuel tank, blowing a hole in the aircraft. When Maria exclaimed "That's it. Now it's all over," it would be the last words that Juliene would hear her mother say.

The plane fell from an altitude of 9,843 feet. As the plane broke apart, Juliene's seat stayed connected in a row of three, which may have helped to slow it down during its descent. It fell through tall trees, further slowing her down. When she came to a stop in the mud, still strapped to her seat, she had suffered a broken collarbone, and gashes to her left leg and right arm. Her right eye was completely swollen shut. But somehow, despite falling nearly two miles from the sky, she was alive. For the next day and a half, she laid there, fading in and out of consciousness until she gained enough strength to start moving around and begin looking for her mother, who had been seated right next to her. She couldn't find her.

Not being able to find her mother, and suffering from wounds on her body, she made the decision to start trying to find help. She had one sandal left from the crash and would throw it ahead of herself to scare off any dangerous animals that might be in front of her. She stumbled upon a small creek and began following the water. It led to a bigger creek, and eventually to a river. She remembered something her dad had taught her in her days at Panguana: following a river downstream will always lead to civilization. So downstream she headed.

She lived by drinking rainwater off leaves and eating a bag of candy she had found in the plane's wreckage. Her wounds began to become infected and infested with bugs and larva. She continued on, even after she ate the last piece of candy from the bag. Her watch had stopped working. At one point, she came across an empty boat on the river, but no one was around it. She passed the boat to find a path to a small hut. That's where she found temporary shelter and a gas can. Despite the stinging pain, she poured the gas on her wounds to disinfect them — or at the very least, to clean them of infestation. Juliene had no idea of how many days it had been. She used that small hut for shelter for the next day and a half.

As the sun started to set the following evening, she heard voices approaching the cabin. It was three Peruvian fishermen who discovered her laying in the hut. They were amazed. This white girl in the middle of the rainforest appeared from nowhere. They brought her to the nearest village. The nearest village had a pilot who flew the seventeen-year-old to Pucullpa where she was taken to a hospital and reunited with her father. Julianne had been walking through the rain forest of Peru by herself for eleven days.

She was the only survivor out of ninety-two people on board LANSA flight 508. Her mother's body was found two weeks later.

There were many investigations and inquiries into why the plane crashed. Examining the wreckage showed that the plane was mostly made up of spare parts. LANSA had a poor safety record to begin with. And it's thought that the pilots felt pressure to push through the hazardous weather conditions because of the holiday. LANSA was stripped of their operating authority. They never flew another flight after the crash.

Experts aren't entirely sure how Juliene survived the almost ten-thousand-foot fall to earth. As I said earlier, one of their theories is that her row of seats stayed together and may have acted as sort of a parachute to slow her rate of descent. They also believe that falling onto a tall tree allowed her impact to be lessened by breaking through so many branches on the way down.

Juliene's story has been made into several books and movies, most notably the film *Wings of Flight* by director Werner Hertzog, who was interested in the story because he was originally scheduled to be flying on LANSA flight 508 that day.

As for Juliene, she honors the life of her mother through a long and successful career as a biologist. She's currently the director of a thriving research station that's now grown into a small camp responsible for publishing more than 180 biology research papers. She's the director of Panguana—
the very place her parents founded and the place that taught her how to survive!

The Battle of Los Angeles: Real Bullets and Imaginary Targets

In the height of the cold war in October of 1962, security cameras at the Duluth Air Defense Center of the Air Force picked up an intruder climbing a fence. It was midnight and no one should have been in that area. The guard on duty shot at the figure and activated the alarm. Bases in the entire region were put on high alert that a Soviet attack may be underway. There was an error with the alerting system and instead of the appropriate alarm for this type of event, a loud klaxon warning blared at every base. This was the sound that told them to scramble the fighter jets carrying nuclear warheads. The fighter pilots ran to their posts and started their jet engines. But an officer appeared, racing his truck down the runway at the jets. He was flashing his lights and laying on the horn, keeping the jets from taking off. He had reviewed the security footage and investigated the area. The fence of the base DID have an intruder. It was a large black bear.

There have been several close calls and false alarms like this throughout history, where the military sprang to action later to find out that there was no enemy attack. This story is about one of these defensive actions that took place in a huge way during World War II.

It happened on February 25th, 1942, in the city of Los Angeles. Just two days before, President Roosevelt had held his fireside chat with the nation about the progress of the war. In his address, he reassured the American people, but was also blunt with them about the scope and seriousness of the war. Pearl Harbor had been attacked just two months prior. And while Americans gathered around their radios listening to their President, something else was happening in the Pacific Ocean off the coast of Santa Barbara, California. A Japanese Imperial Submarine, I-17, surfaced and began shooting 5.5" rounds into the Ellwood Oil Facility. Pearl Harbor had shocked the nation, but now the Japanese had begun to attack the mainland United States. For twenty minutes, the submarine fired at the coast. Hardly anything was hit. No one was injured, and the damages totaled around $500. But the blow that was struck was a psychological one. The Japanese had seven submarines in the waters off the coast of California, and now the nation would know about it. Fear struck America.

Cities on the west coast issued black-out orders to their citizens, mandating that all lights be extinguished at night to prevent a Japanese air attack. This was taken seriously by most, but not by all. In Seattle, for example, when a few businesses didn't adhere to the blackout order, a mob of two thousand citizens showed up to bust out their lights. People in California were scared for what they feared would be a land invasion by the Japanese. The state sent five hundred United States Army troops to protect the film industry in Hollywood and nearby factories.

The United States counterattack began at around three in the morning on February 25th. But there was no enemy. They were firing at ghosts.
It was 2:15 in the morning on February 25th when radar detected something in the air twenty-five miles off the coast of Los Angeles. Air-raid sirens were triggered and a mandatory blackout was ordered from LA all the way south to the Mexican border. Panic set in when radar contact with the object was lost.

The coastal defenses were already on high alert. For the entire day previous, the Office of Naval Intelligence had issued a warning that an attack was expected. Throughout the night, every flare, blinking light, and sparkle was reported to the coastal defense. So when thousands of air-raid sirens were now blaring, everyone thought, this was it. They were sure mainland USA was under attack.

Search lights scoured the sky looking for what had been seen on the radar. At 3:16 a.m., the shelling began. The 37th Coast Artillery Brigade started shooting their 50-caliber machine guns into the night sky. This was followed by 12.8-pound anti-aircraft shells. Defensive stations in Inglewood, Santa Monica, and all throughout the Los Angeles area were firing into the sky. One report noted that the "air over Los Angeles erupted like a volcano."

Finally, an hour later, the all-clear signal was given and the shelling stopped. The American forces had fired 1,440 rounds of ammunition, but had hit nothing. No bombs were dropped. No planes were hit. None were even spotted. The entire thing was a false alarm.

That doesn't mean the barrage, which came to be known as "The Battle of Los Angeles," didn't have tragic consequences. Five civilians died in the attack. None of them died from the gunfire. Three were killed in panicked car accidents on blacked out streets, and two died of heart attacks. Property damage from the falling shell fragments was significant—perhaps worse than the damaged caused by the Japanese submarine the previous week.

There were many reports after the fact that attempted to justify the attack. Some said that there were enemy submarines with the capability to launch airplanes. We didn't know it for sure at the time, but this was a technology that Japan possessed and would use later in the war to attempt an attack on Brookings, Oregon. Some said it was a Japanese attack blimp. Others thought that Japan had secured secret air bases in the middle of a California Desert or perhaps in Mexico. Those who are inclined to believe in UFOs claimed that a huge flying saucer appeared in the sky that night. This was fueled by a famous photograph of the incident showing search lights illuminating a patch of sky. When it was retouched for the papers, the convergence of light appears to look like a floating blob being fired upon.

Paranoia was at an all-time high, and sadly, these fears were permanently cast into American history by the internment of more than 110,000 Japanese American citizens in camps that occurred shortly after the Battle of Los Angeles. It's understandable to imagine the fear that citizens were feeling at the time. But history is the judge of whether or not their ensuing actions were appropriate. And in the case of the Japanese internment camps, I think just about everyone agrees that it was a huge overstep and, to put it simply, wrong.

After the war, Japan came out and said unequivocally that they did not launch an air attack on Los Angeles in February of 1942. And we know that because we now know the truth of what happened that night.

In 1983 the Office of Air Force History released the official report of what occurred to set off the radar. It was never a Japanese airplane. The simple story is this: it was a weather balloon. The Internet Says the Government Says It's True.

Edgar Allan Poe and the Cabin Boy, Richard Parker

In *Life of Pi*, a 2001 Novel by Yann Martel, a young boy is shipwrecked and stranded at sea with a host of wild animals, one of them being a Bengal Tiger named Richard Parker. The use of the name Richard Parker was deliberate. Martel wanted to pay homage to the crazy literary coincidence that we'll be discussing. This is the story of the very unfortunate case of a man named Richard Parker and his fate at sea. To tell that story, we go back to July 5, 1884.

Captain Tom Dudley was commanding the yacht Mignonette with a crew of four. It was a fifty-two-foot inshore boat, and when it was built sixteen years earlier, it wasn't made for long ocean voyages. Nonetheless, Captain Dudley had selected his crew to sail it 15,000 miles from Southhampton in southern England to Sydney, Australia. An Australian had purchased the boat and selected this particular captain to deliver it to him in Australia. The crew was made up of Dudley, Edwin Stephens, Edmund Brooks, and Richard Parker.

Parker was the youngest of the bunch at only seventeen years old. As the ship's Cabin Boy, he was an orphan and inexperienced at sea. On the night of July 5th, the Mignonette was in the middle of the ocean, around 1,600 miles off the coast of Cape Town, South Africa. The seas were calm, so the crew was enjoying a good night's sleep. During their sleep, a rogue wave washed onto the boat, ripping away one of the ship's bulwarks and badly flooding the Mignonette. Within five minutes, the ship sank. In that time, the four-man crew had enough opportunity to scramble onto their small, poorly constructed lifeboat. They only had time to grab a couple navigational instruments and two cans of turnips.

On the first night, they fought off a shark with their oars. They waited a couple days to break into the first can of turnips and split it evenly among the men, which lasted them another two days. Then Captain Turner caught a sea turtle, and the meat from the turtle helped to keep them alive for a few more days. After one week at sea, the men had run out of any drinkable water and hadn't collected any rainwater. They were forced to drink their own urine. And despite knowing how it would affect them, Parker and Stephens couldn't resist the urge to start drinking sea water. Both men became ill.

Delirious and suffering from extreme hunger, the men started having a conversation about killing and eating one of the crew on the 16th of July. But after another week, the conversation became more serious. During that time, young Richard Parker had fallen into a coma. Captain Dudley suggested that they sacrifice Parker so the rest of them could live. The men argued amongst themselves about the idea. There was an old unspoken rule called the "Custom of the Sea" that was about keeping crewmen alive at all costs. Dudley felt that this custom of the sea protected his plan, morally and legally, of sacrificing Parker.

The men decided that it was important to not only have flesh to eat but also blood to drink in order to stay alive. So allowing Parker to die naturally wouldn't do, apparently. They decided they needed to murder the boy. Dudley said a prayer on the morning of July 25th, and with Stephens helping to hold the boy's feet, Dudley pushed his pen knife into Richard Parker's jugular vein, killing him. For the next few days, the three men stayed alive by cannibalism. Even though Edmund Brooks disagreed with the killing of Parker, he too took part. This next description that was later provided by Captain Dudley is pretty gruesome. "I can assure you I shall never forget the sight of my two unfortunate companions over that ghastly meal. We all was like mad wolfs who should get the most and for men—
fathers of children—to commit such a deed, we could not have our right reason."

Four days later, the men were rescued by a German sailboat and returned to England. And we may have never known about this case. I mean, it's a tiny boat with no passengers or cargo of note. There weren't famous sailors on this vessel. And it's not the only instance of cannibalism at sea, either. The story of the whaling ship Essex is a very famous example. There are two main reasons that the killing and eating of Richard Parker is remembered. One of those reasons is that it resulted in a very famous court case.

Dudley thought the men would be protected by the Custom of the Sea, but they were arrested for murder.

Brooks acted as a witness against the men, but Stephens and Dudley were found guilty of murder and sentenced to death. That sentence was later reduced to six months imprisonment, but it was a landmark case that established a precedent that you can't kill someone in order to keep yourself alive. It destroyed this concept of the Custom of the Sea.

The other reason this story is remembered is because of an uncanny coincidence. The story coincides with a story told in Edgar Allan Poe's only full-length novel. And that novel was written forty-six years before the sinking of the Mignonette. And before any of the crew members were ever born.

"...suddenly, a loud and long scream or yell, as if from the throats of a thousand demons, seemed to pervade the whole atmosphere around and above the boat. Never while I live shall I forget the intense agony of terror I experienced at that moment. My hair stood erect on my head-I felt the blood congealing in my veins-my heart ceased utterly to beat, and without having once raised my eyes to learn the source of my alarm, I tumbled headlong and insensible upon the body of my fallen companion."

That was a passage from the 1838 novel *The Narrative of Arthur Gordon Pym of Nantucket.* It was the only novel that Edgar Allan Poe ever wrote. Famous for his gruesome short stories, this book was a departure from his normal format, but not from the gruesome depictions that most people think of when they think of Edgar Allan Poe. This was yet another work in the pulp-fiction genre that Poe invented and it told a story of a stowaway on a whaling vessel, a shipwreck, mutiny, and eventually cannibalism.

The novel was met with mixed reviews. One reviewer, Lewis Gaylord Clark, said it was "too liberally stuffed with horrid circumstances of blood and battle." But then again,

Clark was always feuding with Poe. Others criticized the book for its inaccurate depictions of nautical life and navigation. Even Poe himself referred to it as "very silly book." But authors from Jules Verne to Herman Melville said that Poe's novel influenced their writing.

But nonetheless, we know about this book because of this eerie coincidence. In *The Narrative of Arthur Gordon Pym of Nantucket,* Poe tells a tale of a shipwreck and four sailors who are adrift in a sailboat. After catching and eating a sea turtle, they again become hungry and decide to kill and eat one of their party. They drew straws and the unlucky person among them was eaten and killed. He was the cabin boy and his name…was Richard Parker.

Again, this was forty-six years before the real Cabin Boy Richard Parker would be killed and eaten after being shipwrecked. There are some other strange coincidences with this name Richard Parker. For instance, in 1879, there was an English Sailor named Richard Parker who was tried for organizing a mutiny on board the HMS Sandwich and was very publicly hanged for it. In 1864, a man named Richard Parker was the last person to be executed in Nottingham. He had killed his parents.

Now when Yann Martel wrote *Life of Pi*, he had heard these stories about the various Richard Parkers and how this name kept popping up throughout history, and he thought that in dealing with themes of fate, he needed to use the name in the book. Although he also mentioned another case of "Custom of the Sea" cannibalism of a third man named Richard Parker on board the Francis Spaight in 1835, I did some research and can't come up with anyone with that name on board. They did cannibalize a fifteen-year-old cabin boy named O'Brien on that ship, however.

In any case, it's just a crazy coincidence. There's little to no chance that anyone on board the Mignonette had ever read Poe's novel. And none of the men on board had ever been born when it came out. Sometimes the universe just aligns in uncanny ways. Even still. If you're listening and your last name is Parker, just to be safe, maybe don't name your son Richard.

Real-Life Jaws: The 1916 New Jersey Shark Attacks

In May 2023, fifteen-year-old Maggie Drozdowski was surfing in Stone Harbor, New Jersey, when she felt a sharp pain on her left foot. She had been bitten by a shark.

She managed to free herself and return to shore, receiving prompt medical attention for her injuries and was able to get away with nothing but some stitches on her foot. It was the first recorded case of a shark attack in New Jersey in a decade. Experts attribute the increase in shark sightings along the Jersey Shore to warming ocean waters, which attract sharks closer to the coast in search of food. Despite the heightened awareness, shark attacks in New Jersey remain rare, with only fifteen confirmed unprovoked incidents since 1962. Authorities continue to monitor shark activity and advise beachgoers to stay vigilant while enjoying coastal waters. But in recent years, there's been an uptick in unprovoked shark attacks. In 2023, there were sixty-nine worldwide shark attacks, with more than half of those coming from the United States. Experts think that warming ocean waters are partly to blame, but they also cite human activity and the migration of food sources moving closer to shore.

There was a time when scientists didn't believe that sharks proved any risk to humans. Prominent scientists of the time, such as ichthyologist (that's a fancy word for a person who studies fish) Henry Weed Fowler and curator Henry Skinner of the Academy of Natural Sciences in Philadelphia, both asserted that a shark's jaws were not powerful enough to sever a human leg in a single bite. Frederic Lucas, Director of the American Museum of Natural History, even questioned whether a shark as large as thirty feet could snap a human bone, stating that "it is beyond the power even of the largest Carcharodon to sever the leg of an adult man." Carcharadon is the family of sharks that includes the Great White Shark.

Shark attacks were thought to be so improbable that in 1891, millionaire Hermann Oelrichs offered a $500 reward for any authenticated case of a shark attacking a human in temperate waters—a reward that went unclaimed for years.

This belief wasn't challenged until 1916, when our story takes place. Sure, there had been shark attacks in the U.S. before, but they were extremely rare. There was an attack in New Jersey in 1882 and another in 1905. Neither were deadly. There was an attack in 1850 in California and another in Florida in 1912. Also not deadly. In fact the only notable death from a shark attack had happened back in 1852. In that instance, a fisherman named James Gorman had been swimming near Long Beach Island in New Jersey when he was bitten by a shark and succumbed to his injuries.

In 1916, it had been sixty-four years since that attack and nobody was worried about sharks. That's why it was so scary when the first attack of 1916 happened. And it happened only six miles from where Gorman had been killed. It was the first in what would be a rash of attacks that would reshape the way the public thinks about sharks.

The concept of shark attacks has launched a huge industry. Books, movies, documentaries, and annual television programming events like "Shark Week" are all based on the idea that sharks are deadly predators of humans.

But the chance of being bitten by a shark is incredibly low, even with those attacks being on the rise in recent years. The odds of being bitten by a shark while swimming in the ocean are something like 1 in 11.5 million. You have a greater chance of being struck by lightning, being in a car accident, or being bitten by a dog. In fact, you have a greater chance of being bitten by a swan, a wombat, a honey badger, an octopus, or a giant clam than being bitten by a shark. That's statistically true. And if we're talking statistics, if you're going to die in the ocean, it's much more likely to be from drowning than from anything else. Where shark attacks are 1 in 11.5 million, ocean drownings are 1 in 2 million.

So shark attacks are rare. But before 1916, scientists didn't think sharks posed any risk to humans at all. Some even thought they weren't strong enough to bite through human limbs. This all changed on the first of July, 1916.

Charles Epting Vansant was visiting Beach Haven, New Jersey from Philadelphia. He wanted to take a quick swim with his dog before dinner, so he ran out into the waters of the quiet beach community. That's when he was bitten on both legs by a shark. Immediately, lifeguards Alexander Ott and Sheridan Taylor pulled him out of the water and later reported that the shark followed them to shore the whole way. They attempted to save Vansant, but couldn't.

The story made headlines in all the newspapers the next day. The story in the *New Jersey Herald* read, "Charles Vansant, 25, was attacked by a large shark Saturday, July 1, while swimming in chest-deep water. He and his family were vacationing at the luxurious Engleside Hotel. Mr. Vansant, known by all as a man of exceptional charm and great promise, was swimming with a dog when the attack occurred. The beach was filled with fashionable ladies and gentlemen enjoying the early evening breezes, when panicked shouts suddenly echoed through the air. A large black fin could be seen swimming toward Mr. Vansant. Onlookers screamed warnings. But it was too late."

The event was tragic, but not enough on its own to create widespread panic. That is, until five days later when another event occurred an hour north in Spring Lake, New Jersey.

This time, a local bellhop from the Essex and Sussex hotel was taking a break by swimming in the ocean. Charles Bruder was about 130 yards from shore when a shark bit him, severing both of his legs instantly. Again, there were lifeguards on duty and they hurried to get a boat out to reach Bruder, but the lifeguards couldn't save him. Now the public was starting to panic. One attack is a tragedy, but they saw two attacks as a pattern. Locals blamed the attack on local fishermen who used this area to discard unwanted fish scraps, inviting sharks.

Despite these two attacks, beaches on the Jersey Shore remained open. Even boat captains who were working in the area were reporting sightings of increased shark activity, but were ignored by authorities.

Thomas Cottrell was one of these captains and he reported an eight-foot shark in Matawan Creek, which is further north, a sleepy midwestern-feeling beach community. He was ignored.

Six days after the death of Charles Bruder, on July 12, it happened again. This time in Matawan Creek, the very spot where the boat captain had reported a large shark. An eleven-year-old boy, Lester Stillwell was swimming with friends and they thought they saw an old log or board floating in the water. But when they saw a dorsal fin, they knew it was a shark. Before they could react, they heard Lester scream and disappear under the water. The boys searched the water for Lester and local businessman Watson Fisher dove in to help. He thought he located Lester, but was bitten on the thigh by the shark. This caused him to lose Lester and, sadly, his life. He bled to death at the hospital. Lester's body wasn't recovered for two more days.

The sharks had now claimed four victims: Charles Vansant, the vacationer; Charles Bruder, the bellhop; Lester Stillwell, the child; and Watson Fisher, the man who tried to rescue Stillwell.

But there would be one more attack. At Matawan Creek, just thirty minutes after a shark had killed Lester Stillwell and mortally wounded Watson Fisher, Joseph Dunn was swimming in the ocean. He was a fourteen-year-old boy who was swimming near the same area as Lester and his friends, an area known as Wyckoff Dock. He felt the shark bite his leg and knew exactly what it was. He said he could actually feel his leg going down the shark's throat. When he tried pulling his leg out, the shark held on, stripping the skin off of his left leg. In the newspaper, Joseph was quoted as saying "Don't tell mother." Of course we have these quotes because thankfully, Joseph Dunn made it to Saint Peter's University Hospital in time to save both his leg and his life.

The community knew they had messed up by ignoring the sea captain the previous Sunday. But they were taking it seriously now. I'm reading the following from *Evening News* from Perth Amboy, New Jersey:

"Believing that they have caught a glimpse of the shadow of the big man-eating shark which caused the death of a boy, Inflicted fatal injuries to a man and Injured another boy here yesterday, searchers here for the body of the boy victim are completing plans to dynamite the big fish. They confidently believe that the shark is in about the same spot where it made its death dealing attack yesterday afternoon. The discovery was made about 11 o'clock this morning when the tide became very low, It is believed that the shark is still in a hole in the bottom of Matawan Creek."

And that's what they tried to do. They dropped dynamite into the waters throughout the next several days, to no avail. On July 14, a taxidermist and former Barnum and Bailey Lion Tamer, Michael Schleisser, caught a shark just a few miles from Matawan Creek. It was seven and a half feet long and nearly sank the boat while he was catching it. He beat it to death with an oar and was able to drag it to shore. It was a Great White Shark and when he opened the belly of the beast, he found what were believed to be human remains.

This was the last of the New Jersey Shark attacks of 1916. The fact that Joseph Dunn had lived and seeing a photo of the man eater hanging dead from the docks was enough to help calm the nervous visitors to New Jersey's beaches. For now, the threat was over.

There were some weird fringe theories from the public. Some people who still didn't believe sharks could do this thought that the attacks came from sea turtles. Let me repeat that. There were people who thought sharks couldn't have done this, but sea turtles could have. Another wild theory some people put forth was the idea that sharks had grown fond of the taste of flesh in the waters of the Atlantic, where the war was happening thousands of miles away, and had followed German U-Boats to the waters of America, where they continued looking for more human flesh to consume in the water. This is a pretty interesting snapshot of the fears and insecurities of Americans during the First World War.

But this largely reshaped how people thought about sharks. Most people knew the sharks were responsible. There were nationwide shark hunts. People questioned whether one shark was responsible or multiple man-eaters. The scientific community was forced to reevaluate their understanding of shark behavior and acknowledge that sharks could indeed pose a danger to humans. Ichthyologist Hugh McCormick Smith acknowledged the dangerous nature of certain shark species. He wrote in the *Newark Star-Eagle* that some sharks were "harmless as doves and others the incarnation of ferocity." He specifically highlighted the Great White Shark. This shift in scientific perspective marked a significant turning point in the understanding of shark behavior and their potential danger to humans.

Another thing came from this. A fascination with shark attacks that has spawned movies, films, books, and television ever since. This includes the most famous piece of work surrounding shark attacks: the 1975 Steven Spielberg thriller *Jaws*. The screenplay came from Peter Benchley and Carl Gottlieb and Benchley credited the 1916 New Jersey shark attacks as a major inspiration for the film in multiple interviews. People have pointed out similarities between the stories, and even if *Jaws* was simply based on lore surrounding the idea of shark attacks, that lore was largely created or at least inspired by a period of fourteen days in July of 1916 when the world was shocked by a rash of deadly shark attacks. The Internet Says It's True.

Bat Bombs: A Crazy Military Idea That ALMOST Happened

In the history of militaries around the world, there have been some ideas that seem crazy when we look at them through a modern lens. One of them that comes to mind is the U.S. Camel Corps, which was developed in the late 19th century. There have been other strange ideas that never actually saw combat.

One of these crazy ideas was an aircraft carrier made entirely out of ice! An unsinkable aircraft carrier made of a combination of wood pulp and ice was planned by the British and a prototype was actually built in Canada. It was incredibly expensive to build and very impractical, so the project was never implemented. The U.S. Army once tried to build a hover jeep. It was a jeep that could fly like a helicopter over landmines. It was impossible to control and crazy expensive.

During the Cold War, the CIA implanted listening devices into a cat to spy on the Soviets. The first test run failed when the cat was released… and promptly hit by a car. The project was then scrapped.

There are dozens of examples of these crazy-sounding ideas that have never seen the light of day. One of them occurred during World War II. Around 1942, the American military wanted a way to guide their bombs once they were dropped from a plane. So a famous behaviorist, B.F. Skinner, trained a bunch of pigeons to ride on the inside of the nose cone of a bomb and peck at a small target that would turn the bomb's direction. Of course, later in the war, radio-guided bombs were invented and used, so Project Pigeon was scrapped.

Around the same time that scientists were working with training pigeons, another winged creature was being looked at to see if they could help the war effort.

It started from an unlikely source. A civilian dentist, Lytle S. Adams, was friends with Eleanor Roosevelt. And it's a good thing he was, because otherwise his crazy idea would have probably never been heard or taken seriously.

Adams was a Pennsylvanian who had been vacationing at Carlsbad Caverns in New Mexico. While in the caverns, he was struck with an idea. While Adams was a dentist by trade, he spent a lot of time thinking up inventions. In the 1920s and 30s he tried to develop an airmail system to get mail to and from rural and low-income areas. But this new idea was all about what he found in that cave. He looked around and saw hundreds of hibernating Mexican Free-Tailed Bats, otherwise known as Brazilian Free-Tailed Bats, on the walls and ceilings of the cave. He was incensed about the recent bombing of Pearl Harbor and was thinking of ways the U.S. could make their revenge.

Seeing the bats, Adams thought if there was a way to put incendiary devices on these animals, they could be sent into Japan to roost on the walls and ceilings of buildings there and remotely cause chaos and destruction to Japanese cities. Again, this idea would have been considered crazy if any old person brought it to the White House. But Lytle had the ear of the First Lady. He had influence in Washington that he had gained during his airmail project in the previous decades and he was determined to use this influence to get his bat idea off the ground.

In addition to the First Lady, Adams's idea got another supporter. Donald Griffin was a researcher who had pioneered studies on the echolocation abilities of bats. And Donald Griffin happened to work for the National Defense Research Committee, which was a group tasked with coordinating, supervising, and conducting scientific research to improve and invent new methods of warfare. So when Griffin heard Adam's bat bomb idea, he endorsed it to the President of the United States. Lytle S. Adams had written an abstract of his idea, espousing the bat as the lowest of the low creatures. He argued that "reasons for its creation have remained unexplained" and "bats were created by God to await this hour to play their part in the scheme of free human existence, and to frustrate any attempt of those who dare desecrate our way of life." With the First Lady and Donald Griffin as advocates for Adams, Roosevelt took the idea seriously. He must have known what the public might say, because F.D.R.'s exact words were, "This man is not a nut. It sounds like a perfectly wild idea but is worth looking into."

Not only was the idea looked into, it was quickly put into development.

Franklin Roosevelt, with urging from his wife Eleanor and National Defense Research Committee member Donald Griffin, set the Bat Bomb program into motion by recommending it to the Army Air Force. Lytle S. Adams, the man who devised the idea in the first place, headed up the project even though he had no zoological or military experience. He put together a team of people to help bring the idea to fruition. That team included a former hotel manager, a former gangster turned TV actor, and a mammalogist, Jack von Bloeker. Some of these people actually enlisted in the Army to join the project and Adams was given the authority to make them Non-Commissioned Officers.

The goal was to find a way to attach incendiary devices to bats, who would be released into Japanese cities and burn down the buildings. Many of the Japanese buildings were made of paper and wood and were highly flammable. Initially, they wanted to use white phosphorous as the incendiary material, but when Louis Fieser was added to the project, he convinced them to use his new invention. It was a substance that mixed a fuel with a sort of gel—he had named it napalm. So it was determined the bats would carry napalm. The napalm would be put into a small cellulose payload carrier and attached to the front of the bat's chest with glue.

As for the bats themselves, it was determined that the Mexican free-tailed bat would be the best type to use, the same ones that Adams had seen in Carlsbad Caverns. They started collecting bats from the caves of New Mexico and Texas, a total of between six and seven thousand. They had ventured into these caves with giant nets and used smoke to get them to leave their roosting places on the cave walls and ceilings.

It was essential that the bats would be forced into hibernation to be transported and loaded up with the napalm, so they put the bats into ice cube trays in refrigerated vehicles, which artificially triggered their hibernation response and made them easy to handle.

The napalm payload they put on each bat was about the size of a walnut, about half-an-ounce of material. But how would they deploy the bats? They couldn't just drop them loose from a high-flying B-29.

What the team came up with was a sort of bomb-looking carrier for the bats. It was about five feet long and looked like a bomb. But inside the carrier would be 1,040 bats. The bomb would be dropped from a plane and at an altitude of around 4,000 feet off the ground, the carrier would deploy a parachute to slow its descent. When it got close to the ground, a door on the carrier would open, allowing the bats to fly out. As part of the release mechanism, a thirty-minute fuse would be ignited. This would give the bats enough time to naturally find places to roost inside the buildings before the napalm would ignite.

Once the bats were collected and the carrier containers were built, it was time to test. With eight thousand bats collected and prepared, and millions more that could potentially be harvested from caves, they started some test runs at Carlsbad Army Airfield Auxiliary Air Base in New Mexico. At first, they had a problem figuring out the right temperature to force the bats to hibernate because when the carrier would drop to a thousand feet and open, the bats would fall out, having never woken up. Or if they did wake up, they would fly off and end up far off-target.

Another issue was with the bats' mating rituals. If a female bat became pregnant, the male bats refused to eat. Because of this, the program had to be run when the bats weren't in mating season, which limited them to five months out of the year.

By May of 1943, the program was in full testing phase when a huge setback happened. During a test on May 15, armed bats were accidentally released at a time they shouldn't have been. They flew underneath a fuel tank to roost and blew up part of the test range at Carlsbad.

At this point, the Army was ready to give up on the project. They handed it off to the Navy, who expressed interest and continued the testing under a new name, "Project X-Ray." By December, they were over it. They passed it off to the Marines and moved the bats and the equipment to the Marine Air Base in El Centro, California. From this airport, they were tested at a fake Japanese Village that had been built in the deserts of Utah. After that testing, one officer remarked, "A reasonable number of destructive fires can be started in spite of the extremely small size of the units. The main advantage of the units would seem to be their placement within the enemy structures without the knowledge of the householder or fire watchers, thus allowing the fire to establish itself before being discovered. Expressed in another way, the regular bombs would give probably 167 to 400 fires per bomb load where X-Ray would give 3,625 to 4,748 fires."

The project was approved and it was decided that Project X-Ray would be carried out in war, ready to go by mid-1945. The total cost spent on the project at that point was $2 million—equivalent to $35 million in modern dollars. All the while, the United States was conducting devastating firebombing campaigns in Japan. They dropped 1,700 tons of incendiaries on Tokyo in March of 1945 and after that, did the same in more than sixty Japanese cities, killing hundreds of thousands of Japanese civilians and displacing millions.

The Bat Bomb Project X-Ray would have done the same with fewer bombs and fewer flights needed. But as the project was moving so slowly—we're talking three years of development so far since it was thought up by Lytle S. Adams—it was soon surpassed by another technology.

By that August, the atomic bombs were dropped on Hiroshima and Nagasaki. Less than two weeks later, Japan surrendered and Project X-Ray was scrapped entirely.

The people involved in Project X-Ray said that they never really considered the ethical problem of killing thousands and potentially millions of bats for the project. Not only were they preoccupied with avenging Pearl Harbor, they didn't see the bats as valuable. But viewed through today's lens, the idea is absolutely crazy. And I'm betting you didn't know how close it came to actually happening. It seems fake, but the Internet Says It's True.

Real or Fake? Palisade, Nevada's "Wild" West

If you've ever taken the train ride to the Grand Canyon on the Grand Canyon Railway, it starts in Williams, Arizona, and before you get on, you get treated to a Wild West show with a fake shootout and whatnot. Then on the train ride back, the bandits come and pretend to rob the train. It's a fun little recreation of the old Wild West.

But those types of things really did happen back in the days of the Wild West. As mining towns started popping up in the primitive American West, men mixed with liquor, money, and the disappointment of not finding the success they sought. Thieving, fighting, guns, and a lack of law enforcement led to some of the stories that would populate an entire genre of literature back east. You've heard of Tombstone, Deadwood, Dodge City, Cody, and Sante Fe, but one town that's lost to history was the rough and tumble mining town of Palisade, Nevada.

The name Palisade doesn't exactly evoke an image of the Wild West—not by today's standards. It sounds like the name given to a nice quiet community filled with good people. And when early train travelers visited the town, that's exactly what they saw.

Let's go back. When the Wild West started growing with boom towns and the gold rush, eager tourists back east left home seeking adventure. Not everyone who ventured West was looking for precious metals. Many of them had heard about how "wild" the West was. They had read about these things in dime novels and newspaper columns. Once word got out about the gun fights, the saloons, the fighting with local tribes of Native Americans, people wanted to see it for themselves. With the expansion of the railroads westward, they had the opportunity to travel there themselves without actually having to pick up and move.

One such railroad was the Central Pacific. The Central Pacific didn't exist for a long time because it was quickly absorbed into larger railroads. But when it did, it spanned from Sacramento, California, eastward to Promontory, Utah, where it met up with the Union Pacific. One of the stops was the mining town of Palisade, Nevada.

At the time, Palisade was a hub for several nearby mining camps like Mineral Hill and Hamilton Eureka. Because it was a hub, it grew to have stores, a post office, and a population peak of 600 residents. When tourists looking for Wild West adventure stopped, they had a lovely time but often wrote that they felt "let down" because they didn't see what they expected. They expected the gun battles, the fights, the Native Americans, the dirty, rough "Ole West" they had read about. That was until 1876.

When the passenger train stopped for lunch at noon and people got off, they saw Frank West and Alvin Kittleby involved in a heated exchange near the Palisade train station. West was leaning against the fence of a corral and was approached by Kittleby, who yelled, "There ya are, ya lowdown polecat! I've been waitin' for ya. I'm gonna kill ya for what ya done to my poor little sister!" The bystanders then witnessed Frank West draw a revolver and shoot Alvin Kittleby in the chest. The tourists watched, screamed, and ran for cover back in the safety of the train. Citizens of Palisade scurried to disarm West and carried Kittleby's lifeless body away.

Soon, the train was once again departing. And as the train chugged into the distance, the townspeople of Palisade laughed and cheered. The entire thing was a show—all of it fake.

You may be familiar with *Westworld*. It's a popular dystopian science fiction franchise first written and directed by Michael Crichton in 1973, but made popular recently with an HBO series by the same name. Basically, it's about a Wild West town that tourists can enter where they can feel like they've gone back in time. They witness shootouts and fights and interact with the town as if it's real, but all the residents of the town are robots. It was created to let people experience the adventure and danger of an Old West town.

The tourists traveling on the Central Pacific Railway from San Francisco, Sacramento, or Chicago were looking for the same thing. They didn't know what they'd experience when they got to cities like Palisade, NV, but they had read about it in fantastical dime novels and stories.

So when that train load of passengers saw Frank West murder Alvin Kittleby in cold blood in the streets near the train station, they were seeing their fantasies realized. They never knew that the whole thing was a set up. It was all fake.

So why did the citizens of Palisade agree to go along with this plan? I mean, a lot of people were required to make this plan work. Well, this was a tourist stop and it's possible that people in Palisade had heard tourists complain that it wasn't the Wild West they'd imagined. It was in their best interest to give people what they wanted, so that they would go back home and tell stories. Another theory is that they were just bored. But whatever the reason was, it didn't stop with West and Kittleby.

They started staging events to take place every time a train stopped. There would be fights in the streets, frequent shootouts, brawls breaking out all over. People would walk through the main street of the town and witness a bank robbery or a duel between two angry men. Many times, there would be elaborate backstories and citizens of Palisade would intervene. At one point, when the train pulled into the station, a man was staged to appear to be hanging from a noose at the station. When someone would "die," they'd be dragged into Johnson's Saloon—something that seemed to go unnoticed by the tourists—especially considering that these victims would be revived and come outside to watch the next event. Shooters would use blanks in their guns and victims would use cattle's blood from the slaughterhouse to make it look more realistic.

As this went on, local Native Americans from the Shoshone Tribe even got in on the action, staging war parties and huge elaborate battles with the men of Palisade. They'd stage massacres and even pretend to stab and scalp victims. For small sums of money, they'd agree to be tied up and laid on the train platform, accompanied by proud lawmen.

They had essentially created one of the first theme parks in existence, except the tourists didn't know it was all fake. Each time, they left thinking they had witnessed the real Wild West—but not before they screamed and ran back to the safety of their train cars, sometimes even jumping underneath the train to hide. They didn't know the truth: Palisade was so safe that it's been said it went years without even having a sheriff.

By all accounts, these fake shows went on for just over three years, from 1876 to 1880. In those years, Palisade had gained the reputation and nickname of "The most violent place west of Chicago." Journalists who traveled in on the trains would go back home and write about the violence and record what they had seen to stoke the wild imaginations of their readers. The violence was just a mirage, much like the town of Palisade, Nevada, today. If you visit the area that used to be Palisade, it's mostly all gone. There are just a few structures and foundations left. When mining dried up, it became a ghost town.

There's no doubt that the accounts of those few years in Palisade helped to inspire countless works of fiction about the Wild West—and all those bystanders who saw it firsthand were none the wiser. Palisade, Nevada was the Wild West that never was. The Internet Says It's True.

The Amazing Pearl Harbor Prediction of Billy Mitchell

If you ever fly through the Milwaukee airport, it's a tiny little airport, but there are two things there that are really great. One of them is the Renaissance Bookstore, which is a used bookstore that's a lot of fun to go through. The other is an entire museum dedicated to hometown hero Billy Mitchell. Let's learn a little about this amazing aviator.

Billy Mitchell is often considered the "Father of the United States Air Force." That's because he was the first one to argue that it would be possible to create bombers that could fly over and attack battleships from the air. Mitchell was born in 1879 in Nice, France, while his American parents were on vacation. His father was a wealthy Wisconsin senator who had served in the Civil War. His grandfather had established a railroad and bank in Milwaukee, so he was born into wealth. Mitchell went to Racine College and Columbian University (that was the original name of George Washington University) but dropped out to fight in the Spanish American War. He fought for General MacArthur—this was Arthur MacArthur, the father of the famous General Douglas MacArthur in the Philippines during the Philippine-American War in 1899—and eventually joined the U.S. Army Signal Corps, which was the group that handled the Army's communications and information systems.

In 1901, he was in Alaska helping to lay telegraph lines through the wilderness, and he experienced Otto Lilienthal's experiments with gliders. In 1908, he had watched Orville Wright fly his 1908 Flyer in Virginia. Wright had spent the week flying his aircraft daily and showing it off to the military at Fort Myer. These were his first experiences with aviation and he became particularly interested in the use of aircraft to fight wars. When he was eventually promoted to serve on the General Staff of the Signal Corps, he was the natural choice to head up the new Aviation Section of the Army Signal Corps. He had been the one talking nonstop about how future wars would be fought using aircraft. This was around 1913 and by 1916, at the age of thirty-eight, he took private flying lessons and became an aviator himself, just before the United States entered into World War One.

Until the First World War, the United States military had only used aircraft for reconnaissance, mostly through the use of balloons, but then later with the 1909 Wright A Flyer. In France, Mitchell studied the production of aircraft for the use in military. He met with Royal Air Force Commander Sir Hugh Trenchard, who was also calling on the use of offensive military aircraft at the time.

In 1918, Billy Mitchell had been promoted to Brigadier General, and in the battle of St. Mihiel, Mitchell conducted aerial attack campaigns that wreaked havoc on German forces. He spent the war and the next few years arguing that the Air Force should be its own dependent armed service separate from the Army and should be used to bomb enemy naval forces. In 1921, he started lobbying to the military that he could use a Martin MB2 bomber to sink battleships. So he arranged for a demonstration, moored an out-of-commission captured German battleship in place, gathered a bunch of big wigs like the Secretary of War and the Secretary of the Navy, and showed them once and for all that he could bomb the ship, which he did successfully. And while the test showed how effective aerial bombing could be, the military, particularly the Navy, did not like Mitchell's heavyhanded tactics and criticisms of the armed forces.

There is a lot to cover in Billy Mitchell's military career, so much that we can't cover it all here. The important part of this story happened in 1923, just after his bombing demonstration. Mitchell traveled to the Far East on an inspection tour. And it was that tour where he really saw the destructive threat of air superiority. In his report submitted to his commanding officers after his trip, he warned that Japan was dead set on expansionism and would one day attack the United States.

When Billy Mitchell returned from the Pacific in 1924, he submitted a 328-page manuscript. It ended up getting hidden by the military and eventually lost in the files of the War Department for decades, but when it was rediscovered, people who read it were amazed at what they saw.

The report detailed what Mitchell thought would happen in the future. Keep in mind, this was 1924—seventeen years before the attack on Pearl Harbor. He said Japan would attack Hawaii as part of their expansionist plans, and they would focus that attack on Oahu. These are his exact words as written in the report:

"There is no adequate defense against air attack except an air force. This can be supplemented by auxiliaries on the ground, such as cannon, machine guns, and balloon barrages, but without air power these arrangements act only to give a false sense of security, such as the ostrich must feel when he hides his head in the sand...."

He continued, "Attack will be launched as follows: Bombardment Attack to be made on Ford's Island (Oahu, Hawaii) at 7:30 A.M....Attack to be made on Clark Field (Philippine Islands) at 10:40 a.m."

The details in the report were staggering. He went into great specificity on what forces Japan would have, the time it would take to reach their target, the defense of the Hawaiian Islands, and more.

The military didn't take it well. They saw it as more criticism and insubordination. That was just one of the reasons he was court-martialed in 1925, an act that General Douglas MacArthur described as "one of the most distasteful orders I ever received." The blimp "Shenandoah" had crashed in 1925, killing fourteen people, and additionally three different sea planes had crashed, killing their pilots. After these events, Mitchell had written a statement blaming senior military leaders. They obviously saw this as mutiny and President Coolidge himself ordered the court martial. They ended up finding him guilty and suspended him from active duty while reducing his pay by half for five years. He resigned the following year and spent the rest of his life preaching about air power. In 1936, he died from heart disease at the young age of fifty-six. This was five years before the unthinkable would happen in Hawaii. It was, of course, unthinkable to everyone who wasn't named Billy Mitchell.

Remember, his prediction said Pearl Harbor would be attacked at 7:30 a.m. and the Philippines would be attacked at 10:40 a.m. On December 7, 1941, Pearl

Harbor was attacked by air by the Japanese starting at 7:48am. They also attacked Clark Field in the Philippines. His prediction on that attack was only off by about an hour.

Of course, Mitchell never lived to see his prediction come true. He never lived to see the Air Force become its own entity. He never lived to see the American military's air superiority. He was right about all these things and died before they ever happened. He's been given his due respect since then. He's the only person to have a military aircraft named after him. He's widely regarded as the father of the American Air Force. The Internet Says It's True.

Bamber Bridge: American Racial Tension in the UK

Prior to the 1950s, the United States Military was entirely racially segregated. Black Americans were not allowed to serve in the same unit as white Americans. When the U.S. drafted people for World War One, the numbers show that Black Americans were drafted more often than white Americans, particularly in the south. They made up 10 percent of the U.S. population, but were drafted at a rate of 13 percent.

By the time the Second World War came around, it was starting to become known that Black soldiers weren't receiving the same treatment as white soldiers and this impacted their ability to serve. Black soldiers had fought in every previous American conflict, yet they were facing exclusion and discrimination at every turn. They were disproportionately given service jobs and support roles rather than front-line combat or command staff. Some efforts were made to address this, like the nondiscrimination language in the Selective Service Act of 1940, but the Army's treatment of Black soldiers continued to be less than ideal. The push for desegregation didn't begin until 1948. Roosevelt had set the quota for Black soldiers at 9 percent, but the Army never reached that percentage during World War II. Other nations sometimes initiated this discrimination and exclusion of Black American soldiers. As a result, most Black soldiers were never sent overseas during the conflict. Many who volunteered for combat roles had to give up their rank and take a pay cut.

This week's story revolves around a Black regiment in World War II that did serve overseas: the 1511th Quartermaster Truck Regiment. It was part of the Eighth Air Force and their job was to deliver supplies to Eighth Air Force bases in the region. During World War II, they were headquartered in a place called Bamber Bridge. This is a small town in Lancashire, South of Preston in England and to find it in a map, you go Northeast from Liverpool and Northwest from Manchester. The 1511th was made up of all Black soldiers. As far as the officers, all but one were white and all the military police on the base were white. And one of the things that the Army tended to do in the days of segregation was dump less competent officers on these Black regiments. So if an officer was causing trouble or unwanted by the white regiments, they would assign them to groups like the 1511th Quartermaster Truck Regiment. And that's how they got people in their command staff like Captain Julius F. Hirst and Lieutenant Gerald C. Windsor.

Jim Crow was alive and well, even on American bases in England. There was an order by the United States Military to segregate the pubs in England. They didn't want Black service members drinking in the same places as white service members. And while this had been the standing order, something happened back home in 1943 that exacerbated the issue. Tensions were already high within the 1511th due to horrible discriminatory conditions. The

Black soldiers were receiving barely edible food and were ordered at times to sleep in their trucks. They were already unhappy with their mostly white command staff, so when race riots erupted back home, everyone took notice.

In Detroit, Michigan, race riots in June had led to $2 million in property damage, 6,000 troops responding, 433 injuries, and 34 tragic deaths. Racial tensions were at a high point and, in addition to an influx of immigration amid a housing crisis, much of the angst that led to the riots had to do with social unrest due to the the fact that Detroit had converted its auto-making capabilities to help the war effort. A false rumor about a mob of white people who had murdered a Black baby started the riots and the violence spread from there.

In response to these race riots, the military commanders felt emboldened in their decision to segregate not only Army units, but even the social actions of service members like visiting English pubs. In many places, the Army put in place a rule where white soldiers could visit pubs on certain days of the week, Black soldiers on others.

They demanded that the English provide at least one separate bar for people of color. But the English locals didn't like the idea. Racial tensions in the UK at the time weren't as severe as in the United States. The English saw Black Americans as Americans—deserving of the same treatment as any U.S. Soldier. And so the people of Bamber Bridge respected and supported the Black troops of the 1511th and as a protest to the segregation order, all three of the town's pubs put up signs reading "Black Troops Only." You can imagine how this was received by the almost all-white command staff and MPs.

It was only three days after the Detroit Race Riots when the incident took place. After the Detroit riots, the command staff for the 1511th was on edge thinking about racial tensions. It was normal for the soldiers of the unit to frequent the local pubs and on June 24th, a group of them were enjoying themselves with some British locals, including ladies from the Auxiliary Territorial Service, and they were all having drinks at a pub called Ye Olde Hob Inn. At this point, there are a few differing accounts of exactly what happened, but it's clear that there wasn't initially any sort of issue. One account stated that the Black soldiers were drinking later than what the law allowed. Nonetheless, two MPs were called by Command to report to the pub to deal with a problem. It seems like the only problem was that the soldiers were committing a few very minute offenses. They had standing orders to arrest soldiers who were out of camp without the proper pass or who were not in the proper uniform.

When the military police entered the pub, they saw Private Eugene Nunn from the 1511th. He was in uniform, but dressed in a field jacket rather than the Class A uniform the regulations said he should be wearing. They asked him to step outside. A few of the local British military members tried to intervene explaining that he wasn't bothering anyone or hurting anybody. The only Black officer of the 1511th, Staff Sergeant William Byrd, calmed the situation down and convinced the MPs to let it slide. As the MPs got back to their jeep and were about to drive away, all hell broke loose. Someone threw a beer bottle at their car. What happened next is now known as the Battle of Bamber Bridge.

The situation at Bamber Bridge on June 24, 1943, was all but defused when someone threw a beer bottle at the truck of the military police. The two MPs were on their way back to the base, convinced by Staff Sergeant William Byrd to leave the soldiers alone.

The MPs, Corporal Roy A. Windsor and Private First Class Ralph F. Ridgeway, picked up two more reinforcements and reported to Captain Hirst and Lieutenant Gerald Windsor and were ordered to find and arrest the soldiers at the pub. By this point, the soldiers were walking back to the Mounsey Road base and when they got to Station Road, the four Military Police riding in their Jeep with a machine gun mounted to the top, caught up to the soldiers and a fight broke out.

The soldiers knew there was about to be trouble. In fact, some of them had walked up and down the street telling locals to stay inside because there was about to be a fight. Others went back to base and raided the armory.

This entire skirmish—not between the Axis and Allies, but between Black and white U.S. troops—was about to explode. And it was all caused by a command staff who was looking for any excuse to punish Black soldiers. The fighting that night wasn't caused by one man being in the wrong uniform. It was likely just the straw that broke the camel's back after months and months of building racial tension, and of course made worse by reports of riots back at home.

History doesn't know who fired first, the white MPs with a Jeep-mounted machine gun or Black soldiers who had armed themselves with guns taken from the base's armory. But within the next several hours, the main thoroughfare of the town of Bamber Bridge was filled with gunfire. At least four hundred shots rang out on Station Street, lasting until the next morning.

Private William Crossland from Pittsylvania County, Virginia, had been shot in the back and killed. An officer, one member of the military police, and three of the GIs had also been shot and injured. Two other soldiers had been badly beaten. By 4 a.m., the fighting was over as the

MPs were ordered to cease firing. The Battle of Bamber Bridge had ended, but the matter wasn't over.

Immediately after the fight, a military court martial was held against 32 of the Black soldiers. They were accused of mutiny and related crimes. By August, four of the soldiers who were involved were sentenced to several years of hard labor and dishonorably discharged. One of those sentences was overturned on review. But a second trial was held the next month and on September 28, more of the soldiers of the 1511th were convicted. Their sentences for mutiny ranged from three months to fifteen years. Now there was again a review of these sentences and all of them were reduced. Most of these soldiers were free and returned to duty by the following summer. None of the MPs or Command Staff saw any sort of punishment. Not even the one who killed Private Crossland. According to the Courts Martial, all the blame was placed on the Black soldiers.

But the Commander of the Eighth Air Force, General Ira C. Eaker, saw things differently. He thought the Officers bared most of the responsibility. He had heard the reports of how the white leaders had mistreated the soldiers of their unit, including providing poor eating and sleeping conditions and even went so far as to frequently use racial slurs. The result of his assessment was a decision—in combination with President Harry Truman's Executive Order 9981 of 1948 to integrate the U.S. Army—to combine the trucking units of the Eighth Air Force into a single unit. Officers that were found to be inexperienced, inept, or overtly racist were kicked out. MPs also became racially integrated.

I had trouble finding any contemporaneous newspaper articles detailing the Battle of Bamber Bridge. And what I discovered was that the entire ordeal was censored to protect the American Army from embarrassment and further race riots throughout the armed services. And while there were a couple other similar racial battles within the Army, Bamber Bridge was the worst.

Today, only one of the barracks on Mounsey Street remains. But in the late 1980s, a maintenance worker Clinton Smith was cleaning the exterior of the Nat West Bank in Bamber Bridge. He found some bullet holes in the woodwork of the building and began to ask around how they got there. Back then, there were still people alive to tell the story. This reinvigorated the discussion and publicity around the Battle of Bamber Bridge and the fascination with a military battle in England during World War II that didn't involve the enemy.

The Battle of Bamber Bridge was a precursor to the American Civil Rights Movement. It was used as an example of why racial integration in the military was necessary in the following years. The contrast between the way American southerners treated Black Americans versus how they were treated by the English was a stark depiction of how Jim Crow was affecting American race relations. It's an ugly part of American history, but important to tell the story. Like Tulsa, Oklahoma; Clinton, Mississippi; Wilmington, North Carolina; Colfax, Louisiana; and dozens of others, it's a story that was covered up and hidden because it was embarrassing to admit the difficult history this country has with Civil Rights and race relations. But the Internet Says It's True.

Dumbest Civil Unrest Ever: The Straw Hat Riots

You may have heard about the tradition that forbids the wearing of white after a Labor Day. It's a social taboo to do so and it's one of those traditions from the past that has long been removed from its origin. It's an antiquated social rule that nobody adheres to anymore, but the reason for it is status.

Before we could brag about our vacations on Instagram and Facebook, the clothes we wore let those around us know what sort of vacations we could afford, if we could afford them at all. People who were of means and wealth could afford to vacation, traveling away to warmer climates where it was customary to wear white linen clothing. Then, when they returned back home, those members of the upper echelons of social and economic class felt the need to separate themselves from poorer members of society. In a place like New York City where there was little or no geographical separation between the classes, the way they would separate themselves was by wearing these white clothes. After all, a working-class person wouldn't be able to wear white because it would get dirty. So light colors were commonly worn by richer people, dark colors by poorer people. Labor Day was seen as the end of the summer, so if you wore white after Labor Day, it was signaling to society that you had the money to take fall and winter vacations. It's an antiquated social rule rooted in classism.

There's a similar tradition in other countries, involving fingernails. Men in Greece, Italy, Portugal, and Turkey have a tradition of wearing one of the nails of their pinky finger much longer than their other nails. The reason they do this is the understanding that if you worked a manual labor job, you wouldn't be able to wear that fingernail long without it being broken or worn down. It's another tradition rooted in showing your social and economic status.

And that's what brings us to Straw Hats. For men in the late 19th and early 20th centuries, a hat was an important part of clothing, particularly in public. Men wore the homburg-style hat with their semi-casual clothing, which was a popular felt-style hat with a short brim. Any time you were wearing a jacket or blazer, you would be wearing a homburg hat. But for summer months, that would often be replaced with a hat called a boater. Now these days, you've probably seen a boater hat associated with political rallies or barbershop quartets. It's a straw hat with a flat top, a short, flat brim, and a ribbon around the base. This type of hat was the equivalent in formality to the homburg, but worn in the summer to signify the change in seasons. A less formal version was the Panama hat, which is a larger brim version that Teddy Roosevelt had made popular when he was photographed wearing one while observing the construction of the Panama Canal. These straw hats were only accepted as summer headwear. It's similar to wearing white clothes in that way. Different regions would switch to straw hats on different days, but there would usually be a regionally-declared "Straw Hat Day" when men would switch from their felt hats to straw —usually around May 15. It was sort of a celebration that summer had arrived. Everyone loved to switch to their straw hats.

Likewise, when September 15th arrived, that meant Summer was over and it was time to switch back to felt hats. And if you didn't...there was hell to pay.

Think about the last time you celebrated St. Patrick's Day. You might have eaten some traditionally Irish food like corned beef and cabbage, drank a green beer, and you may have gotten pinched if you forgot to wear green that day. It's a weird tradition for sure, but where did it come from? Well according to the New York Irish Center, wearing green symbolizes Irish Republicanism, the group that campaigned for Ireland to become independent in the late 18th century. And the reason we get pinched is because of the folklore that green makes you invisible to leprechauns, and naughty leprechauns apparently like to pinch people. So if you don't wear green and someone pinches you, they are cosplaying as a leprechaun. That or they're grossly appropriating leprechaun culture. Either way, here's a social clothing rule that is openly enforced and understood with a sort of transgression against the culprit. And that's what happened if a man wore a straw hat after Felt Hat Day.

The date to switch back to felt hats was originally September 1st, but had eventually been pushed back a few weeks. In some areas, it was September 13, in some areas it was September 20th. But as we talked about earlier, men were supposed to switch from their summer boater hats to warmer felt hats when the seasons got colder, and regardless of the actual weather, this date was September 15th in New York. If a man was seen wearing his straw hat after that date, then his buddies would taunt him and, for some close friends, it was even acceptable to knock the hat off his head and stomp on it, ruining it. This was common practice between stockbrokers on Wall Street. They were friends, and it was friendly ribbing.

At some point, this started moving from being a practice between friends to being a prank that mischievous teenagers would do to complete strangers. If they saw a man wearing a straw hat past the acceptable date, they'd knock it off his head and smash it before running away. This became so prevalent that newspapers would run warnings to men leading up to September 15th to be sure to switch hats. Of course, many of these warnings were put in the paper by the local Hat Salesman, next to an ad for their finest felt homburgs.

In 1922, September 15 was only two days away and a group of kids decided that they couldn't wait for Felt Hat Day. They were going hat-smashing in Mulberry Bend. Mulberry Bend was a rough area of New York. It's now the area known as Chinatown, but in that time, it was a part of the city filled with young street gangs like the Dead Rabbits and the Bowery Boys. It was known throughout New York as one of the worst neighborhoods. Upper-class people didn't go there. It was seen as the place where poor immigrants lived with crime, filth, and depravity.

On September 13th, a group of teens ran up and down Mulberry Bend, knocking and smashing straw hats off factory workers who were wearing them. After all, they wanted to smash hats, and in two days, there'd be a lot less hats to smash. When they smashed the hats of a group of dock workers, the dock workers fought back, turning into a huge brawl that is said to have even stopped traffic on the Manhattan Bridge. Police stopped the fight, arrested some people and everyone else went home. But the next night, the same thing happened. This time it was worse.

This time the group of hat-smashers had grown to over a thousand. Some of them were armed with baseball bats. Some of those baseball bats had nails driven through them protruding from the barrels. The thugs went up and down lower Manhattan, knocking off straw hats, smashing them, and beating up anyone who fought back. Multiple men were hospitalized. Huge groups of teens smashed hats on Amsterdam Avenue and more on 109th. The police once again did very little, but they eventually stopped the rioting. Only a few of the boys were jailed—and the longest sentence served was three days.

The *New York Tribune* printed a story about the Straw Hat Riots a few days later. The article says "Boys who were guided by the calendar rather than the weather, and most of all by their own trouble-making proclivities, indulged in a straw hat smashing orgy throughout the city last night. A dozen or more were arrested and seven were spanked ignominiously by their parents in the East 104th police station by order of the lieutenant at the desk."

Hat smashing continued every year until the fashion of wearing the boater hats died out. Some years, hat-smashing incidents were worse than others, but 1922 in New York was the largest scale incident—except for the time in 1924, when a man was actually murdered for wearing a straw hat past the acceptable date.

So there you go. The Straw Hat Riots. A ridiculously stupid reason to riot.

Eternal Neighbors: Nick Beef and Lee Harvey Oswald

It was an unseasonably warm day in November when Ray Carney showed up at Rose Hill Cemetery in Fort Worth. His floral company had been hired to deliver flowers to the gravesite of Lee Harvey Oswald exactly four years and one day after he was charged with killing the President of the United States, John F. Kennedy. On that Thursday, he delivered the flowers and a card from an anonymous sender that simply read "You will never be forgotten." But when he found Oswald's plot, the headstone was missing.

The headstone had been engraved with Oswald's full name, birth date, death date, and a floral border with a large cross in the middle. But now it was missing, so Carney reported this to the cemetery superintendent Earl Johnson, who placed a small temporary marker in its place. In the meantime, newspapers came to report on the theft of the notable marker. While they were there, another bunch of flowers was delivered with a card that read: "As these flowers hold sweet scent, this grave does hold me innocent. I am. No other voices speak that louder grow. No longer weak. Who if legal means do fail, will some names, true killers tell." It was signed "C.D.E., Jr," but again no one has ever identified the identity of the sender. 3 years later, Marguerite Oswald, Lee's mother, replaced the headstone with a much more discrete version, simply reading, "Oswald" in the hopes that it maybe wouldn't attract as much attention. She was the one that purchased the plot for her son and planted a large weeping willow tree next to it.

Lee Harvey Oswald is the man who is blamed for the assassination of President John F. Kennedy. Of course, since the assassination on November 22nd, 1963 and continuing today, there are all sorts of theories on whether or not Oswald fired the fatal shot, or if there was a conspiracy involving possible other assassins. This chapter isn't about that. It's about Oswald's grave in Fort Worth.

Lee Harvey Oswald was born in New Orleans. His father died shortly before he was born and when Lee was five, his mother moved the family to Fort Worth, Texas. His mother moved the family around a lot, requiring Lee to attend multiple different schools around the area. His difficult childhood landed him in juvenile detention by the age of twelve, and this continued into adulthood. He had tried living with his half-brother in New York, but that didn't work out because Lee tried to stab his brother. They moved around a ton—Texas, New York, New Orleans—and eventually his brother co-signed for him to join the Marine Corps at the age of seventeen.

The reports on Oswald's military service are kind of confusing. On one hand, he scored very high on his shooting test, sort of teetering on the levels of sharpshooter and marksman. But on the other hand, he shot himself in the arm at one point, fought with the sergeant about it, and was court martialed, demoted, and imprisoned. While some of his fellow Marines described him as a "very competent crew chief," he continued to face punishment for insubordination and was referred to as "Oswaldkovich" by some fellow service members because of his affinity for the Soviet Union and its causes. He taught himself Russian while serving and eventually left the Marines on a hardship discharge because he told the Marine Corps that he needed to take care of his ailing mother.

So, there's a lot of weird stuff that happened after this. And I'm trying to pull myself back from talking about all of it, because again—this chapter isn't about that. But a few bullet points.

- In 1959 Oswald defected to Russia
- Tried to kill himself in a Russian bathtub
- He unofficially renounced his U.S. citizenship
- Fell in love with a woman from Belarus and proposed to her, but was rejected
- In 1961, he starts to rethink his defection, marries a Russian woman and they apply to return to the U.S. which they do in 1962.
- This whole time, the CIA has been keeping a file on Oswald.

So then we get to 1963. He actually attempted an assassination in April of 1963. This was a new piece of information for me—I had never heard about this and it all came out from the Warren Commission, which was the group that investigated the JFK assassination. Oswald sent away for this Carcano Rifle through the mail and used it to try to shoot U.S. Major General Edwin Walker, who was an anti-communist and a segregationist. None of this was tied to Oswald until after his death.

It was that same rifle that was found in the sixth floor of the Texas Schoolbook Depository building after the JFK Assassination. But in between April and November, Oswald had moved back to New Orleans where he was notably handing out flyers for the Fair Play for Cuba Committee. This was a pro-Castro, anti-U.S. government, activist group that supported socialist causes, and was outspoken against the failed Bay of Pigs Invasion. Now some have claimed that he was only part of this group as a spy to infiltrate the organization. There's no evidence of that, but who knows what we'll learn in the future as more and more files are released. Between New Orleans and the Kennedy Assassination, he traveled to Mexico City with apparent plans to then go to Cuba, and eventually back to the Soviet Union. He was denied a visa and ended up returning to Dallas in October.

The official published Warren Commission conclusion was that Lee Harvey Oswald and only Lee Harvey Oswald was the person responsible for that fateful day on November 22, 1963. And this is where my story is going to do something that I bet every other story about Lee Harvey Oswald doesn't do. I'm skipping past the thing he's known best for. We're not talking about the JFK assassination. So, let's skip forward to November 24, two days after the shooting.

Lee Harvey Oswald was being escorted through the Dallas Police Headquarters to the county jail. It was just before noon and the basement was filled with press, so the whole thing was caught on camera. There was even a crowd outside the police station.

Jack Ruby, a Dallas nightclub owner, stepped forward out of the crowd of reporters in the basement and pressed forward a small .38 Colt Cobra revolver toward Oswald and fired a shot into his abdomen. It injured several organs and major arteries. He was taken to the Parkland Memorial Hospital—the same hospital where the President had died. At 1:07p.m., almost exactly two days after Kennedy, Oswald died. His last recorded words were "I want to see the American Civil Liberties Union."

Lee Harvey Oswald was buried at Rose Hill Cemetery in Fort Worth. Before finding a burial space there, multiple other cemeteries had refused to accept his burial. The public obviously hated Oswald—so much so that he had no friends to be his pallbearers. The local press carried his casket.

Most of the public blamed Oswald alone for killing the President. In those early days, there wasn't the massive speculation and doubt that exists today. The Warren Commission didn't release their report until two years later, which caused more doubt about the official story when people read what came to be known as the "magic bullet theory." So it was interesting that there would be the occasional flowers and messages of support laid at Oswald's grave.

Like most graves of famous—or infamous—people, it was frequently visited whether people supported him or not. And after that gravestone near the northwest corner of the cemetery was stolen four years later, Oswald's elderly mother replaced it with one she thought would garner less attention. It read "Oswald." But from here on out, we're changing stories. This isn't about Oswald's gravestone. It's about a strange and mysterious gravestone that appeared immediately to the right of it thirty years later.

In 1997, visitors to the Lee Harvey Oswald burial site saw a strange name next to it. The grave marker said nothing more than the name "Nick Beef." Nick Beef? Who the hell is Nick Beef? For the next sixteen years, no one knew. But we know now.

For years, people wondered who this person was. History buffs or curious locals would visit the grave and wonder if Nick Beef was part of the story or perhaps a distant relative. This *Houston Chronicle* newspaper article from 2005 brings up the mystery with the headline, "Mysterious headstone beside Lee Harvey Oswald grave puzzles Kennedy History buffs." The article displayed a photo of the gravesite and mentions something that only made things more interesting: the grave was empty. The manager of the cemetery, Deby Alexander, said nobody is on file for that plot, and a burial has not been done there. One theory that people spread was that the cemetery would refuse to give directions to Oswald's grave, so a couple local reporters bought the plot next to it, so people could ask for the name "Nick Beef" in order to find the Oswald burial plot. But that was just a rumor.

One of America's most debated and controversial events now had another element of mystery. But in 2013, sixteen years after the stone was placed, Nick Beef came forward.

It was coming up on the 50th anniversary of the Kennedy Assassination and the man who owns the Nick Beef grave marker decided it had been long enough and it was time to tell the truth. The truth is: Nick Beef isn't anyone. It's a pseudonym made up by Patric Abedin—a man who considers himself a comedian and performance artist, which is funny because he doesn't perform and he's never done stand-up comedy. He told his story to NBC News.

He said when he was a child, his parents had brought him to see the President when John F. Kennedy visited Texas in 1963. He was there on November 21st, cheering in the crowd at the airport to greet John and Jackie Kennedy when they landed at Carswell Air Force Base before continuing on to Dallas the next day. He recalled sitting on the shoulders of a nearby Military Police Officer so he could get a glimpse at the President and First Lady as they went by. The next day at school, he told his classmates about how he got to see the President in person. And that day, it was announced over the school loudspeaker that President Kennedy had been shot. Like many people, Abedin remembers exactly where he was when he heard the news. But for him, it was a little bit more personal.

As he grew older in Texas he and his mother would drive to Carswell Base and, as part of their ritual, they would stop at the Rose Hill Cemetery on their way home and visit the grave of Oswald. His mother said to him, "Never forget that you got to see Kennedy the night before he died." And when he was eighteen, there was a newspaper article talking about how the grave beside Oswald's stood empty because nobody wanted to be buried next to one of history's most famous assassins. Without so much as a thought, he drove to the cemetery and put down $17.50 and a promise of a further $10 payment for the next sixteen months. That was 1975—and the plot that he purchased stayed empty for the next 22 years. In that time, he had moved to New York and dabbled in comedy, at first as a player in an improv troupe and later as an occasional humor writer, using his pseudonym of Nick Beef.

Why "Nick Beef?" It was an inside joke between Patric and his friend from years earlier. They had gone into a restaurant and his buddy had jokingly referred to himself as "Hash Brown," so Patric played along and said, "I'll be Nick Beef." It became a running joke between them and a sort of alter-ego for Abedin.

In 1996, Abedin's mother died and he returned to Texas to help conduct her funeral. During that trip, he visited his plot on a pilgrimage to visit Oswald's grave like he and his mother had done so many times in the past. And this time, he decided he would place his own marker there. He bought a stone that almost perfectly matched the size of Oswald's. And when they asked him what he wanted on it, he told them "Nick Beef."

For a lot of people, putting your name, even a fake name, next to a notorious killer would seem morbid. But for Abedin, it was a way to remember that day and the special bond he had with his family and his mother. Maybe he knew that the general public would find that morbid, so maybe that's why he chose to put his fake name there. He doesn't plan on being interred there. He wants to be cremated. The plot isn't for a body — it's for his memory. It was his way of commemorating a formative memory in his life. And that's pretty morbid. But Patric Abedin, who is still alive and living in New York — a non-performing performance artist — readily admits he's sort of a morbid guy.

The Internet Says It's True.

22 Caliber Surgery: George's Horrible, Awful OCD Cure

There's a famous story of a man named Phineas Gage. Gage was a foreman for the Rutland and Burlington Railroad in Vermont. His job was to oversee the construction of new railroad tracks and manage the crew who was responsible for both clearing the land and laying down the track. He was described as a capable, responsible, and hardworking man, but also one who had excellent social skills and a kind demeanor. That's how he rose to the position of Foreman by the time he reached his mid-twenties.

The year was 1848 and the railroad crew was clearing land near Cavendish, Vermont. Part of the job was blasting rock out of the way to clear the lane for the railroad. This involved drilling a hole in rock, loading it up with explosive powder, then filling the rest of the hole with sand and tamping it down with a tamping iron—a 43-inch iron rod about an inch and a quarter in diameter. On September 13th, Phineas Gage went to use the iron tamper and didn't realize he had made a fatal mistake. He forgot to pour the sand into the hole. So instead of tamping down inert sand, he was shoving the iron rod directly into the exposed black powder. The first thrust of the tamping iron caused a spark in the powder and huge explosion.

The ensuing explosion propelled the tamping iron out of the hole and directly back toward Gage. It entered his face through his left cheekbone behind his left eye and exited out the top of his skull, landing several feet away. Remarkably, he never lost consciousness. He was talking with those around him, despite having a hole through his head. But the reason we know about this horrible accident is because of what happened after the mishap. It made him into a landmark figure in the fields of neuroscience and psychology.

After the accident, Gage was able to recover physically. His speech remained intact, as did his comprehension and memory. The problem was that he turned into a total jerk. Gone was the pleasant demeanor, the social skills, the work ethic, and the responsible Phineas Gage everyone knew. He was reported to be unable to stick to plans, prone to outbursts of anger, and indifferent to the feelings of others. He became unreliable in work settings and had difficulty maintaining relationships. Descriptions of him included being profane, irreverent, and impatient, all of which were stark contrasts to his previous temperament.

The rod had damaged Gage's left frontal lobe. The shift in his behavior highlighted the role of the frontal lobes in regulating personality, decision-making, and social behavior. This is what made his case a foundational study in neuroscience. The prefrontal cortex is critical for executive functions such as decision-making, impulse control, emotional regulation, and social behavior. The damage to this region is believed to be responsible for the profound changes in Gage's personality and behavior following the accident.

Similar stories have happened throughout history. One of the more interesting cases was in the case of the man who became the infamous Texas Tower Shooter at the University of Texas in 1966. Charles Whitman was later found to have a brain tumor near his amygdala, a part of the brain involved in emotional regulation and aggression. This discovery led some experts to speculate that the tumor might have influenced his violent behavior, causing him to lose control of his emotions and impulse regulation.

Today's story is a similar situation. It happened on November 11, 1983. It's a dark story, but one with a happy ending.

Most of the following information comes from one source. It was reported in 1988 in a bunch of newspapers, the February 23 edition of the *Los Angeles Times, The Washington Post*—just about every major newspaper ran this story, but I did some digging and was able to track down the story's origin. They all quoted the psychiatrist Dr. Leslie Solyum. I found his body of published papers and I actually found the academic paper that he wrote about the subject. Rhis comes direct from the 1987 *British Journal of Psychiatry*, issue 151. It tells the story of one of Solyum's personal patients. The patient's identity was kept anonymous, but he refers to the man as "George."

At an early age, George started experiencing symptoms of severe obsessive compulsive disorder. He had come out as gay to his parents and while his dad was accepting, his mom didn't handle the news well. The OCD started after telling his parents and continued through the age of fifteen without interfering too much with his life. At that point, it amounted to excessive hand washing, constantly checking things, and being obsessed with dirt and contamination. The older he got, the worse it became until he was admitted to the hospital for it. The treatments he was given didn't work—they tried exposure therapy, response prevention, and supportive psychotherapy. His grades in school suffered and a heavy cocktail of psychoactive drugs didn't work for him, so he ended up stopping treatment. He used to be a straight-A student, but his motivation had disappeared and his grades fell. He had no more drive.

Feeling helpless, George had made several suicide attempts. At its worst, his OCD was so severe he couldn't continue with normal tasks until he did things like repeating fifty different chants to himself. His mother—with their already strained relationship—threatened to commit him to a mental institution, and when he told her how awful he was feeling, she said something along the lines of "Go and shoot yourself."

Sadly, this was a push too far for George and he did exactly that. He was nineteen years old at this point and shot himself in the mouth with a .22 caliber rifle.

Miraculously, he survived and when doctors examined him, they found the bullet had lodged itself into his premotor cortex in the left frontal lobe, and fragments of the bullet were scattered throughout. He was left impaired when it came to motor skills on his right side, and his speech was affected. But something else had happened. As soon as three weeks after surgery to remove the bullet, his OCD had lessened dramatically.

George used to spend four hours doing bathroom rituals. That was now down to just thirty minutes. All these OCD behaviors eventually went all the way down to fifteen minutes. After two weeks, he considered himself "mostly cheerful." He was still a neat freak, but almost all his over-the-top OCD behavior had gone away. What's more, he found motivation in his life again and was able to complete high school. His grades were great again and he was described as calm and cheerful. His test scores improved and looking at the data, Dr. Solyum concluded that there was no other explanation for the sudden behavior change than the altering of the frontal lobe. He had essentially conducted a leucotomy, which as far as I can tell is another word for lobotomy to his left frontal lobe.

In a way, it was sort of a reversal of the case of Phineas Gage. George wanted to die, and in attempting to carry that out, he appears to have cured himself of the very thing that pushed him to those extreme measures.

This was a bizarre and extremely rare case. If you're feeling suicidal, please talk to somebody. It's important to know that there's no other record of this freak type of incident happening—it's not a cure. In fact, these types of injury studies have helped provide information to doctors about the function of the frontal lobe and basal ganglia and in very, very rare cases, surgical procedures are still carried out to sever the connections in small parts of the brain. Long gone are the days of rough and often unsuccessful lobotomies. These types of surgeries are only carried out between 10-30 times a year in the United States. And not all of them are successful in their goal of behavioral change. This particular case was like a crude accidental version of this type of lobotomy. It's a bizarre case—like Phineas Gage the railroad foreman.

Nobody knows exactly what happened to George. His identity has remained anonymous. But his story has lived on. The Internet Says It's True.

Al Capone's Altruism and Spoiled Milk

Sometimes horrible people do good things.

Saddam Hussein gave free education and free healthcare to the citizens of Iraq.

Hitler passed a bunch of animal advocacy laws.

Ted Bundy worked at a suicide hotline.

These men are still monsters. They're just awful people who did some good things. And by pointing out a story about something good they did doesn't mean I'm trying to revitalize their image or excuse their vile acts. Sometimes it's just interesting to see this strange juxtaposition. And that's what today's story is about.

There are a lot of facts about Al Capone that can't be 100 percent proven. One of the earliest has to do with how he got his infamous nickname: Scarface. Capone hated the name because he hated the scar. Almost all the photos you'll ever see of him have him turning his head to hide the scars on the left side. He had three large scars across his cheek and above his neck, and thus became known as Scarface. His close friends called him "Snorky," which apparently was some sort of reference to him dressing well. But to this day, no one knows for sure how he got those scars. We know that his early years were spent working in New York City for a bunch of different gangs like the Five Points Gang, the Bowery Boys, The Brooklyn Rippers and the Junior Forty Thieves. The most popular theory of how he got the scars places the story somewhere around 1918 and involves fellow gangster Frank Gallucio. That story involved Capone insulting either Gallucio's sister or girlfriend. But this story was never told until decades later, once Capone was in prison. Capone would tell people he earned the scars while fighting in the military in France during the war. No one has ever uncovered any evidence that Capone was in the military, so that one is decidedly false. There's a *Brooklyn Times* article that may have the true story: that he received the scar in December of 1917 by two random criminals on the street. I tell this story to stress that many things about this guy we just can't pin down. Capone is a legendary figure, so the stories about him get spread far and wide, regardless of their truth. There have been more than a dozen major films about the life of Capone and hundreds of books, so over the course of a century, the line between fact and fiction has become blurred. Even contemporaneous accounts from the early 1900s tend to contradict one another.

There are some things we know for sure. Capone left New York for Chicago in 1919 and started his career there as a bouncer for a brothel run by the Chicago mob. A lot of his legendary status as a ruthless mob boss begins in Chicago. Capone basically ran the underground crime world in Chicago through the 1920s and early 1930s. Prostitution, gambling, bootlegging, bribery, drug trafficking, robberies, protection rackets, and murder were all attributed to Scarface. He had been invited to Chicago by mob boss Johnny Torrio. But after Torrio was seriously wounded in an assassination attempt in 1925, Capone became the boss. Once Capone was in charge, all the rival gangs were completely eliminated. He is thought to have orchestrated the famous 1929 "St. Valentine's Day Massacre" in which seven members of a rival gang were all assassinated by mobsters posing as police.

I could go on to list the many, many crimes that have been attributed to Capone, but this story isn't about Al Capone the crime boss. It's about Al Capone the altruistic upstanding member of society. Or at least his attempt at being that.

The economic outlook for everyday Chicagoans in 1930 was bleak. Something like 40 percent of the workforce in Chicago found themselves unemployed after the crash of 1929. So for Thanksgiving in 1930, one Chicago soup kitchen had a line of five thousand hungry, out-of-work Chicagoans. And the proprietor of that soup kitchen was none other than the infamous Alphonse Capone.

By that point in his career, he had already become known as the most ruthless gangster alive. He had left a wake of death and destruction behind him as he took revenge on anyone who got in the way of his many illegitimate business interests. But for poor Chicagoans, some saw him as a man of the people. During prohibition, when they couldn't get alcohol, he was the man credited with bootlegging the liquor for them. He was the one bribing local law enforcement to look the other way—a man of the people! After all, it wasn't those innocent people who were being gunned down by Capone; his only beef was with mafia competitors and people who got in the way of his business.

But as ruthless as the man was, he had also started to pay for his crimes. The 1925 attack on Torrio had also injured Capone and shaken him up. He had seen friends and colleagues gunned down in the line of work, like fellow mobster Hymie Weiss and even Capone's personal driver who had been kidnapped, tortured and killed. Capone himself often traveled away from the city to stay safe. He was always careful to keep distance between himself and the crimes that were ordered on his behalf such as the gruesome St. Valentine's Day Massacre.

Capone apparently had told people close to him that he wanted to "go straight" and get out of the crime game. He had enough pull within the city to get things done and thought that the people would support him. He thought of himself as a sort of Robin Hood figure. In addition to helping support local widows and orphans, he ran projects like the soup kitchen.

There was also the fact that prohibition had ended, and he needed more revenue streams to replace the hundred-million-dollar bootlegging business.

One of his legitimate businesses was a milk bottling plant. He found that the markup on milk was even greater than the alcohol he'd been peddling. This is where the story may get closer to legend.

There's a quote that I found in multiple places, none of them with any sort of attribution. It's supposedly Al Capone talking to his brother.

"I've got to get out, Ralph. I've got enough money. I don't need this insanity. Weiss, Moran, and [the members of the other gangs] are idiots. You can't do business with crazy people. I've been shot at, almost poisoned with prussic acid, and there is an offer of $50,000 to any gunman who can kill me. They don't understand that there's enough for all of us. [. . .] They're [mad] because I run a better business. I make more money than they do. [. . .] I run my outfit like a business. It is a business."

Because this book is about actual true facts, it's important that I preface this next part with a warning that it's never actually been verified. But the story has lasted and it makes sense when you consider the place and time, and the businesses that Capone was in.

The story goes like this: sometime in the late 1920s, one of Capone's relatives became seriously ill after drinking expired milk. And as Capone was in this phase of his life where he was interested in rehabilitating his image from gangster to philanthropist, he lobbied Chicago City Council to start requiring a stamp on milk bottles that would list the expiration date. Of course, refrigerators weren't available to the public yet, and the shelf life of milk was short. So while he was lobbying Chicago politicians to enact this law, he was busy buying up all the equipment that would be necessary to stamp glass milk bottles.

The story continues that his plan ran into a snag because the milkmen were unionized and therefore only teamsters could deliver milk, not Capone's men. He tried to work out a deal with the Teamsters and it failed, so he had the Milk Teamsters President kidnapped and held for $50,000 ransom. The ransom was paid and that gave Capone enough money to buy Meadowmoore Dairy, a huge milk processing business.

As this was all happening, something else was happening in Chicago. The Feds were busy working on a tax-evasion case against the mobster. In 1931, Capone was charged with tax evasion and sentenced to eleven years in prison. So we never really got to see Al Capone the milk magnate. He went to prison from 1932-1939 and was released due to his failing health. He had developed Syphilis—likely from his time working as a bouncer at the brothel—and was in very poor health. He ended up dying in 1947 at the age of forty-eight.

Again, the milk stamping legend could be just that. But nevertheless, the story has been told so long and so often that it's often referred to as fact. The fact being that Al Capone, the most notorious gangster in history, is the reason that to this day we have expirations on containers of milk. It may not be—but at least The Internet Says It's True.

Peter the Eagle: The U.S. Mint's Unofficial Pet Bird

There's a longstanding myth about Benjamin Franklin. Over time, this story developed about Ben Franklin and America's National Bird, the bald eagle. The story goes that Franklin fought for the national bird to be the turkey instead of the eagle. And while there's never record of him ever fighting to change the national bird, we know exactly where it came from.

In a letter to his daughter, Franklin once criticized a depiction of the eagle. He didn't like the way the eagle looked on the Great Seal of the United States. Franklin and John Adams were on a committee whose job it was to come up with the Great Seal, and in 1782 a man named Charles Thomson, who was the Secretary of the Continental Congress, came up with the design that we know and use today: a bald eagle holding arrows in one claw and an olive branch in the other. In a letter to his daughter, Benjamin Franklin criticized the artwork of the seal, particularly as it pertained to the depiction of the eagle. This was a letter to his daughter Sara Bache on

January 26, 1784. He wrote to her that people thought the eagle on the Seal looked more like a turkey than an eagle. And he went on to criticize eagles themselves. He wrote, "Bald Eagle...is a bird of bad moral character. He does not get his living honestly...[he] is too lazy to fish for himself." Later in the letter, he continues, "the turkey is a much more respectable bird, and... a true original Native of America...He is besides, though a little vain & silly, a bird of courage."

That's the extent of Franklin's recorded thoughts on the matter. On top of that, scholars at the National Archives say that the letter was never actually sent. It was written while he was in France, and was never sent home to Philadelphia. Instead, it was given to André Morrellet, a French contemporary of Franklin, to translate into French. He did so, and advised Franklin about ever making the letter public—not because of the eagle/turkey situation, but because the letter was written as a satire and the entire thing was supposedly a joke. So this letter was never read until after Franklin's death by anyone other than his grandsons, to whom he showed the writing.

That's a lot of insider info to say that no, Ben Franklin never actually fought for the eagle to be replaced by the turkey. Not in any official capacity outside of a satirical letter that was never sent.

The bald eagle was chosen as the national bird because they often patterned themselves after the Roman Empire. In the Roman Empire, eagle imagery was common; in that case, usually the golden eagle. With the creation of the Great Seal in 1782, the eagle became the symbol we see today. And since then, it's been seen on seals, symbols, and currency, including countless coins.

At this point in the story, we skip forward fifty years.

Fifty years after Franklin wrote that letter in Paris, the U.S. Mint was humming in Philadelphia. It had been producing the nation's coins for thirty-eight years and it was now 1830. The President was Andrew Jackson and the U.S. had grown into a country of almost thirteen million people.

Bald eagles still inhabited the Philadelphia area back then. In the 1800s, there were around 400,000 bald eagles in the United States. For contrast, by the 1950s, this had been reduced to only 412 breeding pairs. But when eagles were rampant, even in a large city like Philadelphia, one particular eagle started flying around the Mint near 7th and Arch Streets. He would fly in during the evening and stay. This same eagle came around so often that the employees of the Mint gave it a name.

In 1830, the same eagle kept visiting the corner of 7th and Arch Streets in Philadelphia at night. The eagle would often perch on the building and come morning when employees would come in to work, he would be chased away. It would fish in the Delaware river during the day and return the next night.

We don't know why he kept returning to this area. The Mint was just a few blocks west of the Delaware River, but it's likely that a local business had some good food scraps. After a while, the employees at the Mint named the eagle. They called him Peter.

Now for some reason, they started letting Peter fly inside the windows of the Mint and he could soon be found perched inside the building almost all the time. Peter became sort of an unofficial mascot of the Mint—which is funny, considering he was basically the official mascot of the country and his species had already been depicted on numerous coins. He was considered an "exemplary employee of the U.S. Mint." On any given day, Peter could be found literally perched on the large coin presses and other machinery. Everyone knew and loved the bird. They would feed him scraps and take care of him. And this went on for six years!

In 1836, Peter was perched on the flywheel of a coining press and the press operator didn't see him. He started up the machine and the eagle's wing became caught in the wheel. The wing was broken and he was cared for the best they could, but he couldn't be saved. Sadly, their six-year employee Peter died.

If you ever take a look at a silver dollar—the Gobrecht Dollar—issued between 1836 and 1839, the design of the eagle is supposedly based on Peter. The same is true of the Flying Eagle cent of 1857 and 1858. It was a way to pay homage to this bird they had become close to.

There's another way they honored their friend. After he died, employees gave Peter's body to a taxidermist to be stuffed, and he was put on display with outstretched wings in the lobby of the U.S. Mint. This tradition has been continued to this day. Every time Philadelphia built a new Mint, the stuffed eagle was put on display in the lobby. You can still see Peter the Eagle today in the lobby of the Mint, over 150 years later. The Internet Says It's True.

Malicious Compliance: The Car Company That Sabotaged the Nazis

In the strange world of wartime obedience, there's a concept that feels almost like a practical joke, but it's deadly serious: malicious compliance. That's when someone follows an order to the letter, knowing full well that it will cause chaos. Imagine being a caterer hired to prepare sandwiches for an invading army and making them with so much salt that no one can eat them. It's passive aggression with high stakes. But in wartime, this becomes a subtle and powerful form of resistance.

In today's story, we'll eventually explore one of the most brilliant examples of this, carried out by the French automobile company Citroën during the Nazi occupation of France. But first, let's take a little tour of malicious compliance throughout wartime history. This kind of sabotage didn't always involve explosions. Sometimes, it just involved being very, *very* helpful.

Let's go to Poland during World War II. In the small town of Nowy Sącz, the Nazis had taken control of the local rail network. Trains were vital to the Nazi war effort—delivering weapons, troops, and horrifyingly, people to concentration camps. The Germans relied on Poland's extensive rail system, and they issued strict orders to keep the trains running on time.

The Polish railway workers complied. They did what they were told. They followed all the rules. But somehow, nothing seemed to work quite right. Trains were constantly delayed. Cargo shipments were misplaced. Deliveries missed their marks.

Why? Because the railway workers were deliberately screwing things up... carefully. They would reroute trains just slightly off course, causing delays of hours or even days. They'd switch out paperwork so that shipments ended up at the wrong destination. And they were masters of claiming "technical difficulties"—everything from broken brakes to faulty switches, all carefully engineered to create bottlenecks.

What made it so effective was that they weren't breaking the rules. They were following them—in a way that exposed every flaw in the system.

In one documented case, a supply train was delayed for two full days due to what was described as a "signal failure" near Krakow. The failure? A signal lever had been intentionally set at an incorrect angle, but only by a few degrees. It was enough to confuse incoming engineers and require an inspection, but not enough to be immediately flagged as sabotage.

Across the border in the Netherlands, Dutch civil servants pulled off a different kind of sabotage. When the Nazis demanded that Dutch officials identify Jewish citizens in government registries, many of the clerks... got sloppy. Entire filing systems were "lost" in office relocations. Ink was spilled—accidentally, of course—across critical pages. The names were there, but spelled just wrong enough to make tracking difficult. Officials claimed administrative overload and chronic filing errors. They complied—but their compliance was full of speed bumps.

Even in German-occupied Norway, bureaucratic compliance became a shield for resistance. Clerks dragged their feet, refiled paperwork, and used outdated forms. Permits were delayed. Approvals were bounced from one desk to another. The Nazis couldn't prove anything was being done wrong—but they also couldn't get anything done.

In all these cases, the resistance wasn't armed. It didn't require explosives or secret radio transmissions. It required knowing how a system works—and helping it fail from the inside.

Now, let's shift our attention back to France.

When the Nazis invaded France in 1940, the country fell in just six weeks. Paris was occupied. The Vichy regime took power in the south, and the German military took control of factories, railroads, and communication systems. If you were a factory owner, you had two options: collaborate, or resist. Many resisted. And one of the most famous resisters did it from inside a car factory.

The Citroën automobile company was already well-known by the time of the war. Founded in 1919 by André Citroën, the company was famous for engineering innovation. They were the first to mass-produce front-wheel-drive cars, and they had a reputation for sleek, modern designs. But by

1940, Citroën was no longer just a car company—it was a Nazi asset. German officers took over the factory and demanded trucks. Lots of trucks.

The man in charge of Citroën at the time was Pierre-Jules Boulanger. Boulanger had been running the company after André Citroën's death and was known for his quiet, calculating leadership. He didn't shout. He didn't make speeches. But he was absolutely determined not to help the Nazis.

Boulanger understood the stakes. His factory was under German supervision. He and his workers were being watched. Any obvious sabotage would result in imprisonment or worse. So he chose a different path.

And this is where the story of Citroën's malicious compliance begins.

So how do you sabotage a vehicle without touching the engine, breaking the brakes, or raising any suspicion? Citroën's engineers had an idea. A brilliant, subtle idea. They changed the oil dipsticks.

That's right. You know the dipstick—the thin metal rod that shows how much oil is in your engine? Citroën engineers lowered the "full" line on those dipsticks. So when Nazi mechanics checked the oil, they filled it up to that line—thinking it was correct.

But it wasn't. The engines were running low on oil. Not empty. Not enough to immediately notice. Just enough to slowly, inevitably destroy themselves.

Over time, the trucks began to fail. Engines seized. Vehicles stalled on supply runs. The German army couldn't figure out why their brand-new Citroën trucks were breaking down. And all the while, the French engineers at the factory just kept nodding along and saying, "We're doing our best."

It was a masterclass in quiet sabotage. And it wasn't the only trick up their sleeve.

Boulanger reportedly hung warning signs around the plant in German—signs that looked helpful but directed German soldiers away from sensitive areas. When the Nazis demanded production updates, the Citroën office delivered fake spreadsheets showing over-inflated numbers. The trucks didn't exist. The numbers did.

Factory workers created fake breakdowns on the line. They claimed parts were missing. Or they reassembled components just slightly out of alignment. One former employee later recalled that "accidents" on the factory floor were staged so frequently, they had to rotate who got fake-injured just to keep it looking organic.

And yet, no one was arrested. The Gestapo suspected Boulanger, but they couldn't pin anything on him. He was nearly executed several times, and he spent periods of the occupation in hiding. But he survived.

After the war, Boulanger was hailed as a hero. He helped relaunch Citroën as a postwar brand, and one of his first major projects was the Citroën 2CV—a small, durable car designed to mobilize rural France. It became a symbol of independence and renewal. The car that helped rebuild France had been designed by the same team that, years earlier, quietly wrecked German supply chains.

When people talk about resistance during wartime, they often think of spies and soldiers. But resistance comes in many forms. Sometimes, it comes in the form of a factory manager who says, "Yes, sir," while quietly tanking your war effort. In the end, it turns out you don't always need firepower to fight tyranny. Sometimes, all you need is a dipstick. The Internet Says It's True.

Cobra Invasion: The Springfield Snake Scare of 1953

The Indian Cobra is a highly venomous snake. The bite from this snake delivers between 150 and 250 milligrams of venom. For reference, it only takes about 20 milligrams to kill a human. It causes paralysis, respiratory failure, and death if not quickly treated. And when our story takes place—in the 1950s—the concept of providing healthcare facilities with anti-venom was a brand-new idea. And that's considering hospitals are carrying anti-venom to treat snakebites from species that naturally occur in an area. There's nowhere in the United States where Indian cobras are native.

With all of that said, getting bit by a cobra is a very rare thing. They're not aggressive toward humans and would rather shy away from a person than attack. It would take them getting stepped on or handled to be bitten.

There are more than thirty species of cobra. The most famous one, the king cobra, isn't actually a cobra at all, but gets lumped in because it has the same look and a hood that can flare out like a cobra. The Indian cobra is slightly smaller and is typically found in India, Pakistan, Nepal, Bangladesh and Sri Lanka. Just like other cobras, when it's threatened, it stands upright, hisses, and flares its hood thanks to special ribs. Its front fangs contain the neurotoxin and you don't want to be anywhere near them.

Today, many states outlaw the ownership of cobras and many others require a special permit. One of these is the state of Missouri, where the Missouri Department of Conservation requires a permit in addition to permission from local law enforcement. As far as the city of Springfield, the ownership of venomous snakes is outlawed unless you're something like a zoo or research facility. But back in 1953, these regulations didn't exist. Through almost all of America, the laws on owning exotic animals including venomous snakes were very lax. Some larger cities had laws against exotic animals or venomous snakes, but Springfield did not.

Even so, it was bizarre that Roland Parrish discovered an Indian cobra in his lawn on August 15, 1953. The snake rose upright, flared its hood and struck out at Parrish. It missed, and Roland, who was equipped with a garden hoe, killed the snake. It was one of what would amount to at least eleven encounters with cobras in Springfield in the coming months.

After Roland Parrish killed an Indian cobra in his lawn in 1953, he reported it to the police. It was a strange encounter for sure, but at the time, they probably just thought someone's pet had gotten loose.

But one week later, Roland's neighbor across the street, Wesley Rose, found another one. This time it was his pet bulldog who alerted him by barking. When he looked out the window, the dog was wrestling with the four-and-a-half-foot cobra. He ran out of the house and killed the snake with a garden hoe—apparently this was the designated tool to kill cobras. Now I was wondering the same thing you were and no, there's no record of the dog dying. I think the bulldog was fine. But the cobra wasn't. He paralyzed it with the first strike and killed it with the second. Now that we were talking about two Indian cobras, people became concerned. Rose brought this second snake to the police office, and that's where they brought together a group to examine it. It included Springfield Police Officers Raymond Sanders and Gabe Newman, a Zoo Director Bill Swinea, a college science instructor J.M. Parson, and a high school science teacher Herbert Condray. They confirmed the snake was indeed an Indian cobra, a snake not native to the Americas and incredibly deadly to humans.

Now that there was a clear pattern, the people in the neighborhood had one culprit in mind. Less than a block away was the Mowrer Pet Shop, owned by a man named Leo Mowrer. When police confronted him, he told them there was no way the snakes came from him. All his snakes were accounted for. That said, the pet shop *did* carry exotic animals including water moccasins, rare birds, and even an orangutan. His statement to the local paper wasn't "We've never lost any of our snakes." It was, and this is a direct quote, "We haven't had a cobra loose in months…We have them on hand all the time, but we haven't had any get away." Apparently this wasn't enough of a denial for panicked residents of Springfield. After the reports of these snake encounters hit the newspapers, Mowrer started receiving death threats. Cops started investigating him, but by the point they really started looking into his snake handling practices, he had secretly moved the rest of his snakes out of the city to a barn.

Snake number three was found eight days later by Ralph Moore, who shot it. Just kidding, he used a garden hoe. That same night, a seventeen-year-old kid found one in the road. Apparently thinking out of the box, he killed it with a car jack (apparently he didn't get the memo about using a garden hoe).

In September, a six-year-old little girl told her parents she had seen a snake slither into their garage. They were sure she was just scared from the reports of snakes in town. But sure enough, they looked in the garage and found a cobra. That's where Howard McCoy killed it with a garden hoe.

It's safe to say by this part—after five deadly Indian cobras in just a few weeks—people in Springfield were freaking out. The hospital got its hands on anti-venom just in case someone got bit. The fact that no one had been bitten yet is a testament to how unlikely it is to be bitten by these snakes. Like I said earlier, they would much rather flee from humans than strike out unless they absolutely need to.

The next snake was found by Reo Mowrer himself, who found one in the bushes outside of his shop and took it inside before police arrived.

The next encounter is probably the scariest. It's from a source that I found called "UndergroundOzarks.com." This is nuts.

This is Cobra Encounter #7: "Later that day, across the street from Mowrer's shop, L.H. Stockton saw a snake coming out of his garden. Stockton threw a rock at it but missed his target and he watched in horror as the 4-foot-long snake crawled through an opening in the foundation of his house and disappeared. The police were called, and Chief Frank Pike tried to use a 10-foot pole with a rope noose underneath the house to snare the snake but failed. Stockton and his landlord gave the police permission to bombard the crawlspace with tear gas. A gas grenade was set off underneath the house and the cobra came out. Officer Jack Strope aimed a shotgun at the snake but the weapon jammed. Strope grabbed the pistol from his holster and shot the snake five times; however, the snake still managed to raise its hooded head. Chief Pike used his 'snake catcher' pole to capture the snake with the rope, and the snake was killed with another hoe. By now, the entire town of Springfield was in an uproar."

So once again that was from UndergroundOzarks.com and I won't go into detail on each one of these, but it added up to eleven snakes in all—those are the ones they found anyway. At one point, the City Health Director Del Caywood commandeered a truck equipped with a public address system and drove around the neighborhood playing a record of "Indian snake-charming music" and blasting it from the truck's roof-mounted loudspeakers. Absolutely crazy.

In October, one of the snakes was actually captured alive. One of the snakes is still around. You can see it, preserved in a jar of formaldehyde at Drury University. The snake scare lasted from August 15th to October 25th.

After October, no other snakes were found. They couldn't find a culprit and couldn't prove that Mowrer had anything to do with it, even though he was the guy that sold exotic snakes to carnivals. He always denied it—denied it to the grave. The police discovered the barn where he was storing his snakes on the outskirts of town and forced him to move them out of the county. In December, the city enacted an ordinance banning the ownership of dangerous snakes.

Springfield's Cobra Scare of 1953 was so surprising and unusual that *Life Magazine* and *Newsweek* both ran stories about it. It became such an interesting story that was associated with the city that they put a cobra on their official city seal. Well, the truth of that one is that the seal already had a snake, and they changed the head on the snake to make it look like a cobra.

The origin of the snakes remained a mystery for thirty-five years. It took that long for the real culprit to come forward. This was eleven years after the death of Reo Mowrer. It was an exclusive interview that the *Springfield News-Leader* ran in the June 26th, 1988 edition of the paper where a man named Carl Barnett finally admitted the truth. His exact words were "I'm the one that done it." At this point, Carl was forty-nine years old, making him just fourteen in 1953. He told the whole story to the paper. He had bought a fish from a pet store. It was an exotic fish and the fish died. He went back to return it and get his money back and the store owner wouldn't give him a refund. So as he was leaving out the back door of the pet shop, he noticed a crate full of snakes and opened it up before running away. He didn't know they were cobras. He said if he had known that they were deadly, he wouldn't have done it. He was just trying to get back at the pet shop owner. Any guesses as to who that was? That's right, it was Reo Mowrer. Mowrer's pet shop was the source of the cobras after all, and he never knew how the snakes got out. But now thanks to the guilty conscious of a man who held it in for more than three decades, we know the truth.

The Internet Says It's True.

Why Are Pencils Yellow?

I love pencils. Any chance I get, I'd much rather use a pencil than a pen. I don't know why, but there's something that's really cool about writing on paper with a pencil. It's like I'm using a rock to scrawl on a tree. It's archaic. And I also remember growing up in the 1980s, they'd tell you not to put the tip of a pencil in your mouth or you might get lead poisoning. Do you remember hearing that?

Well, the truth is, pencils haven't contained lead since— well they've really never contained lead. There are reports that some of the ancient Romans and Egyptians used lead to write on papyrus, but not in the form of what we now know as a pencil. Pencils have never contained lead. And that's one of those things that sounds like I'm making it up, but it's true. I always thought, like a lot of you that "no, pencils don't contain lead now, but they used to at one point, kinda like Coca-Cola used to contain cocaine." But it's true. The wooden pencil that we know and use never contained lead.

The reason people started calling the dark inner part of the pencil lead was because that's what they mistakenly thought it was made from. What we call lead in a pencil has always been graphite based. Originally, they were all supplied from the same source: a single huge deposit of graphite that was found in Cumbria, England. It was discovered in the first part of the 1500s and this vein that was discovered was the purest and most solid ever recorded. They called it "plumbago," which was the Latin word for lead ore, because even the people who discovered it mistook it for a type of lead. As they mined the graphite, they found that it could easily be shaped into sticks and those were commonly used for marking sheep in those early days. Eventually, they started mixing the graphite with clay and other substances to try to find the best writing tip.

It wasn't until around 1812 when a cabinetmaker named William Munroe in Concord, Massachusetts invented what we know as the pencil. That has also been attributed to Henry David Thoreau, who strangely enough was also in Concord at that same time. There's also a claim that an Italian couple named Simonio and Lyndiana Bernacotti came up with the idea in the 16th century. Their pencil was more similar to the flatter carpentry pencils. None of these people patented it, so Eberhard Faber did and started mass producing them in a factory in New York in 1861. They were using graphite found in New Hampshire in 1821, but for the most part, as pencils became popular around the globe, England had a monopoly on producing them because of the Cumbria graphite vein. And that monopoly lasted until the graphite there ran out in the 1860s. In the late 1800s there was a pencil boom in the U.S. with factories producing them with names you've heard of, like Faber and Joseph Dixon of Dixon Ticonderoga. Every day in the U.S., Americans were using a quarter of a million pencils.

If you're interested in this stuff like I am, you'll be interested in a piece written by economist Milton Friedman back in 1980. He delivered it on a PBS series called "Free to Choose" about the free-market economy. And whether or not you agree with Milton Friedman's economic principles, this is certainly interesting. It puts forth the idea that no single person can make a pencil.

"The wood from which it [the pencil] is made, for all I know, comes from a tree that was cut down in the state of Washington. To cut down that tree, it took a saw. To make the saw, it took steel. To make steel, it took iron ore. This black center—we call it lead but it's really graphite, compressed graphite—I'm not sure where it comes from, but I think it comes from some mines in South America. This red top up here, this eraser, a bit of rubber, probably comes from Malaya, where the rubber tree isn't even native! It was imported from South America by some businessmen with the help of the British government. This brass ferrule? I haven't the slightest idea where it came from. Or the yellow paint! Or the paint that made the black lines. Or the glue that holds it together. Literally thousands of people co-operated to make this pencil..."

It's a wonderful little piece to analogize their free-market ideas. It's not original, he stole it without credit from a writer named Leonard Read, who came up with the idea in 1958. Maybe Friedman sees stealing the work of others as part of the free market too. But none of this answers the question that I had. Why is the stereotypical pencil yellow? If you google image search the word *pencil*, or look at clipart of a pencil, you'll see one that's school-bus yellow. The famous yellow pencil. Why?

When pencils started being used around the world in the mid 1800s, most of them were just natural wood colored. Nicer pencils would have a lacquer on them, and pencils with lower-quality wood would be painted darker colors like purple, red, maroon, navy blue, and black. This would help disguise the imperfections in the wood grain, which was usually cedar wood. Then, toward the end of the 1800s, at the World's Fair in Paris, this all changed.

The 1889 World's Fair in Paris—the Exposition Universelle—is famously remembered for its shining new marvel: the Eiffel Tower. There were lots of things that were famous about this World's Fair. It was the hundredth anniversary of the French Revolution. Lots of cutting-edge technology was shown to the people like cinema, electricity, and mechanical wonders. Annie Oakley put on a shooting demonstration.

The Hardtmuth Company from the area that's now known as the Czech Republic launched a rebrand of their pencils as the Koh-i-Noor Hardtmuth Pencil. Koh-i-Noor is Persian for "Mountain of Light." At the time, people knew that word because the largest diamond in the world, which was part of England's Crown Jewels, was called the Koh-i-Noor diamond. So they used this word that had a connotation of royalty and elegance to brand their new pencils, which they called "luxury pencils." According to Duke University Professor Henry Petroski, who wrote a book called *The Pencil: A History of Design and Circumstance,* the best graphite in the world had come from England, but eventually that supply ran out, and a newer and far superior supply was found in Siberia, near the border between Russia and China. And so for these new luxury pencils, Hardtmuth was using this newer, better graphite supply so they could advertise their pencils as the best in the world.

There was something else different about them. They were bright yellow. Nearby to the Siberian graphite mine, the Empire of China used the color yellow to represent royalty. The Yellow Emperor was a mythical cultural hero that had been revered for centuries and modern-day royalty in China were the only ones permitted to wear the color. In China, yellow represented glory, happiness, and wisdom along with being high-class. In addition to bright yellow paint, the Hardtmuth Company even dipped some of them in twenty-four-karat gold. The cost of these pencils was something like seven times the cost of a normal pencil. They did everything they could to make these pencils stand out from the other ones on the market. People loved it. The Koh-i-Noor pencil was so popular that the company actually changed their name to the Koh-i-Noor Hardtmuth Pencil Company.

It wasn't long that the word of these pencils reached the U.S. and other companies followed suit. Faber and Dixon Ticonderoga started painting their pencils yellow and even went so far as to give some of their pencils Asian-sounding names. Their pencils were inferior to the ones using the real Siberian graphite, but by this point, people didn't care. There's even a crazy story about Faber—they did a field test of the popularity of their pencil colors. They gave half the test subjects yellow pencils and half of them dark green pencils. The pencils were identical in every other aspect. The people who got the green pencils hated them and returned them because they said they were bad quality.

This pattern can be seen with retail markets all throughout time. One company creates a luxury product, they create a demand and other companies try to cash in on it. I had some shoes when I was a kid. They were L.A. Gear, which was like a cheap knock-off brand of shoe. But they had these little clear rubber windows in the heel. They were trying to knock off the popularity of Nike's Air Max, who had manufactured a premium shoe with a bubble of air in the heel. The L.A. Gears I had didn't have a bubble of air, but they were making a cheaper product that was meant to sort of look the same. That's what all these companies were doing with pencils. It stopped being about the actual quality and more about the appearance. Yellow pencils became the most popular.

In modern times, there are only a few companies—in fact only three companies in the U.S.—who still manufacture wooden pencils. And while pencils are made in all different colors and the royal luxury stigma associated with the color yellow is probably completely gone, yellow pencils are still what come to mind when you think of a pencil. It's like the fact that magicians haven't worn a top hat and tux for centuries, but if you google image search a magician, that's what you're gonna get. It's just stuck in time that *that* is what this thing looks like. And in the case of the yellow pencil, it's all because of the human desire for nice things. We all wanted luxury. So we got yellow. The Internet Says It's True.

The Immovable Ladder and the Status Quo

In Glasgow, Scotland, there's a statue of the Duke of Wellington on a horse. It depicts Arthur Wellesley, the first Duke of Wellington, outside the Gallery of Modern Art. And if you look up a picture of the statue, chances are you won't be able to see the Duke's face. That's because the statue almost always has a traffic cone on its head. Even though the statue was erected in 1844, the traffic cone tradition only started in the 1980s. It began as a bit of vandalism, just some locals having fun. But the image was so funny to the public that once it was removed by the city, another cone went on. City Council hated it. They put the statue on a higher pedestal. It didn't matter. The cone kept appearing. And soon, the image of the statue with the cone carried more cultural relevance to the people of Glasgow than the Duke of Wellington himself. It was a way for them to express the city's sense of humor. The city removes the cone a hundred times a year and it doesn't matter. By all accounts, it seems like the traffic cone is now a permanent object. That's because the people want it there.

On the eastern coast of Scotland, there's a stone called the Stone of Destiny (also called the Stone of Scone) that is considered a permanent, immovable object. It was supposedly used to coronate Scottish Monarchs dating back to the first century. Traditionally, Scottish kings were crowned while seated above the stone, believed to confer divine approval and authority. After it was taken by Edward I in 1296, it was built into the English coronation throne, where British monarchs have been crowned above it ever since. It has a long and storied history of being taken and used by different groups, political and religious, but was most recently seen in 2023 during the coronation of King Charles.

A lot of these immovable or permanent objects are that way because of a deep meaning, usually religious. And while today's story is about religion, it's not about an object that has any deep religious meaning.

If you visit the Church of the Holy Sepulchre in Jerusalem, there's a ledge on the wall of the Armenia Apostolic Church. Above that ledge there's a window, and leading up to the window there's a small, five-rung wooden ladder. And that ladder has been there since at least the early 1700s.

Just to go into a brief background of the Church of the Holy Sepulchre—this is the site that's largely agreed upon as the place where Jesus of Nazareth was supposedly crucified and resurrected. And because of that, it's one of the most revered places in the world for believers. But it's also a place that's incredibly fragile. Throughout history, many different groups have laid claim to the site. Since the 4th century, people have been claiming control and dominance over the Church of the Holy Sepulchre. Think about all the different sects of Christianity—they all have slightly different thoughts on tradition and history and all want to control the site slightly differently. And then you've got the Muslim groups in the area as well, and the whole thing becomes incredibly complicated. It's actually been destroyed and rebuilt several times. With religious sites being commonly destroyed throughout history, it's amazing that this place exists today.

Control of the Church has been taken through blackmail, bribery, and outright fights throughout history and currently, it's resting on a delicate balance of an insanely complicated set of rules—we're talking like American income-tax-policy level of complications. The Church of the Holy Sepulchre is currently cared for by the Greek Orthodox, Armenian Apostolic, and Roman Catholic Church, along with Coptic, Ethiopian, and Syriac Orthodox churches. Each group has different duties and areas of care, and the entire thing is incredibly fragile and complicated. Not all of it has been completely agreed upon. There are some areas of the holy site that cause arguments even today.

In 2008, Armenian Monks and Greek Monks got into a huge fight over a chair. Apparently there's a place where a chair is placed for a Coptic Monk to sit on the roof. It was a hot day and he moved the chair something like eight inches to the right so he could be in the shade. This was seen as a huge affront and caused a literal fistfight. And since it was in the 2000s, there were videos of it that got spread around the world. Something like eleven people were hospitalized.

So imagine now that this building has something that needs to be repaired. How do they decide who is responsible? Since it's so complicated, it's a huge task to do the tiniest amounts of work. They must maintain the centuries-old agreements, which are referred to as the "Status Quo."

We see every day on the news the precarious situation in the Middle East. In Jerusalem, you've got a very small piece of earth that many, many different religious groups lay claim to. It's not just Jewish people and Muslims. So as a result, there are nine different religious sites in Jerusalem that are subject to an agreement called the "Status Quo," which dates back to the Firman of Ottoman sultan Osman in 1757. It basically splits up the responsibilities of ownership and care of these sites between six different religious communities, and says that no one can make any changes to these places without consensus among all the groups. The Status Quo is old and has gone through a bunch of iterations, but it was most recently formalized in the 1949 UN Conciliation Commission, which was a response to the 1947-1949 Palestine War.

The most famous symbol of the Status Quo is a single ladder. It's a small, five-rung wooden ladder in the Church of the Holy Sepulchre, one of the six Status Quo sites. And this ladder rests against a window of the Armenia Apostolic Church. The ladder has been there since at least 1728, which is the first time we see a reference to it in print, but it's likely been there long before that. It's known as "The Immovable Ladder," but some refer to it as "Jacob's Ladder," which is a Biblical reference that has nothing to do with this particular ladder.

The ladder was originally used for who knows what. There are a ton of theories as to what the ladder was used for and there's really no way to know which is the truth. It could have been a ladder to help monks get a breath of fresh air. It could have been a ladder used by a mason to work on the stones of the building. We just don't know.

The use of the ladder isn't important. The reason the ladder is significant is because of what it represents symbolically. It's a symbol of the agreement for all these different people, with different beliefs—strong beliefs—to come together and respect each other's use of this space.

It was removed once by Pope Paul the Sixth in 1964. He didn't like that the ladder reminded people of the divisions within the church. So he had someone pull it in through the window and hide it. A week later, it was returned and this time, a steel grate was installed in the window so it couldn't be pulled in again. I guess we're just lucky this one didn't result in a huge fistfight like the battle over the chair.

The immovable ladder is now seen as an important piece of the history of that region—it represents the Status Quo and the agreement between a lot of people who don't always agree. So next time there's a mess in your house and you can't decide whose job it is to clean it up, maybe just think of it as a symbol of agreement (or lack thereof) and leave it….and tell them the Internet Says It's True.

Puffin Patrol: Throwing Puffins off a Cliff

There aren't many places you can go to see Puffins. Some people call them the "Clown of the Sea" because of the colorful markings on their beak. They're a black-and-white bird with bright orange webbed feet and beautiful colorful markings on their beak. Where I live in North America, if you want to see them without leaving the continent, your options are basically either Nova Scotia, where they inhabit a few tiny islands near Cape Breton, Newfoundland, or a couple islands off the coast of Maine. We're talking about the Atlantic Puffin and most of them live in the cold northern waters of Greenland, Scotland, Wales, Ireland, Norway, the Faroe Islands and the largest population in Iceland. And that's where our story centers. Because in Iceland, people are throwing young puffins off a cliff.

Occasionally humans who have encroached on an animal's habitat will really disrupt the behavior and threaten their ability to thrive. And in some of those instances, measures have been taken to sort of reverse this damage.

For example, in Florida, North Carolina, and a few other places on the American East coast, human activity—namely, city lights—have confused hatching sea turtles. The natural behavior of these turtle hatchlings is, once they're born, to crawl toward the moonlight bouncing off the ocean. But in human-populated areas, they can crawl the wrong way. To offset this, there are light restrictions near known hatching areas, shades that keep the light from leaking onto the beach, and human walls, where local people will line either side of the turtle's pathway to the beach to help guide them. This has led to a huge improvement in the number of disoriented and lost turtles.

In Alaska, Caribou migration routes have been severely impacted by roads and oil pipelines. As a mitigation measure, engineers designed specifically designated Caribou corridors and crossings that allow the caribou to travel safely between feeding and calving areas. Some of these are even highway overpasses that are simply grass-covered bridges for wildlife only.

There are tons of examples of these. There's a section of Reddit called "humans being bros" that often includes stories like these. Some are indirect engineering feats like the caribou corridors in Alaska and similar corridors like the ones created for the pronghorn of Yellowstone. It also includes things like salmon ladders to help salmon travel upstream, where their migration routes have been interrupted by hydroelectric dams and road construction. But some are more like the sea turtle helpers or people who help rescue beached whales and dolphins—actual people intervening to help out our animal friends. And THAT is why people are throwing puffins off cliffs in Iceland.

Iceland has the largest population of puffins in the world. 60 percent of worldwide puffin breeding happens in Iceland, most of it in the Westman Islands off the southwest coast. Somewhere between 8-10 million puffins live there. Most people will go their whole lives without seeing a puffin, but for people in Iceland, they're common. Even so, they're classified as a vulnerable species because climate change and human encroachment have threatened their habitat. On top of that, overfishing has lessened their available food sources. And speaking of food sources, there are still populations in Iceland and in the Faroe Islands where it's a cultural tradition to hunt puffins. For these people, puffins are a food source. This happens primarily in coastal communities, but in some areas puffin meat is considered a delicacy. They also used to be hunted for their feathers, but this is pretty rare in modern times.

Because of this and a slowly dwindling population, hunting bans are starting to be put into place in locations where the puffin numbers are dropping significantly, like Iceland's Westman Islands, where they're experiencing a 70 percent decline in population since the 1990s. This is a huge red flag. Puffins mate for life and only produce one egg per season, so rebuilding the population can be slow work. One of the culprits of the declining population is the city lights.

We mentioned earlier that human light pollution has disrupted the hatching behavior of sea turtles. After they're born on shore, it's innate for them to crawl toward the moonlight on the sea. The same is true for the Atlantic Puffin. Once a puffin hatchling—referred to as the adorable name puffling—is able to fly, they join their colony by following the moonlight, which leads them to the sea. City lights, like the lights of Vestmannaeyjaaer in the Westman Islands, have confused the pufflings and caused them to become lost from their colonies.

This is where humans have stepped in to help. In a practice that occurs between late August and the end of September, residents of the Westman Islands and a few other places in Iceland go on the hunt for baby puffins in order to help them on their journey to the sea. People will venture out in the middle of the night to find the pufflings (they can usually only be found between 9 p.m. and 3 a.m.) and grab them, putting them in a cardboard box until the morning. The residents have been instructed to visit a website where they can enter the size and weight of the pufflings for tracking. This puffin-napping seems cruel at first, but it's for the good of the young birds. These are pufflings that they're finding in the city, already lost. As the city lights have confused them, people were seeing lost pufflings wander the opposite direction of their colonies because their instincts were completely hijacked. It's important that the young birds find the water, so in the morning, these captured baby puffins are taken to the tall cliffs of the Westman Islands overlooking the Atlantic Ocean.

It's there on the cliffs that they're chucked out off the edge, certain to be able to see the water and fly away to meet their colonies. It's become an honored tradition during what they call "puffling season" every year, and during those two months in the fall, it's common to see adults and children alike walking around with flashlights and cardboard boxes on this unusual but wholesome mission. People on a "Puffling Patrol" are told to wear gloves to protect from human skin oils and to protect themselves from avian flu. They'll put a little bit of grass in the bottom of the box to make the bird comfortable and to help keep the box and the rescuer clean from feces. Then in the morning, they're brought to the top of the cliff, and while some people just place the birds on the ground for them to take off on their own, most people enjoy throwing the birds in the air and watching them fly out over the ocean. By the time a young puffin is a puffling—we're talking six to eight weeks old—they can already fly, and this practice of throwing them off a cliff is completely safe. In fact, it's helping to restore the shrinking puffin population. Thanks to these dedicated locals and volunteers, hundreds of lost pufflings are safely rescued and released back to sea each year, ensuring Iceland's beloved puffin population continues to thrive. The Internet Says It's True.

William Rankin: The Man Who Fell through a Cloud

William Henry Rankin was born in 1920. He joined the military after school and fought in World War II and the Korean War as a Marine Pilot. By the 1950s, he had reached the rank of Lieutenant Colonel and was flying F-8U Crusaders off aircraft carriers during the Cold War effort as the Commander of VMF-122, a Marine Fighter Attack Squadron. His home base was in Beaufort, South Carolina, and Rankin along with Lt. Herbert Nolan were traveling from Naval Air Station South Weymouth, Massachusetts, back to their base in Beaufort, South Carolina. They were flying their two F-8U Crusaders and were somewhere over Virginia when disaster struck.

If you're unfamiliar with the F-8U aircraft, this is a supersonic single-engine jet aircraft designed to operate from aircraft carriers. It was developed in 1952 and had a relatively short production life - the last one was manufactured in 1964. It's often referred to as "the last of the gunfighters" because as aircraft were being designed with their primary weapons as missiles and bombs, the

F-8U's primary weapon was the 20mm cannon, which is a huge round—not as big as the A-10 Thunderbolt's 30mm rounds, but they wanted this aircraft to have something larger than the 50-caliber guns that had proven insufficient during the Korean War. It was also a super-fast aircraft, the first American jet fighter to reach a thousand miles per hour. It had a variable incidence wing, which is a system to change the angle of the wings; that's different than sweep wings, but it also had the ability to fold the wings up at the end, which helped to make more space on-board the carriers. It was equipped with a ram air turbine, which was a common backup system. Basically, if the engine stopped while the aircraft was in motion in the air, the ram air turbine could use incoming air to restart the engine. This will be important to remember in William Rankin's case. The F-8U had a ceiling of about 52,000 feet, and was often used for reconnaissance and spy missions.

It was a difficult plane to fly, and the technology was fairly new. In 1959 alone, thirty-two F-8U crusaders crashed. Now fortunately, only three of those crashes ended in pilot fatalities, but it was July 26th and fourteen of these crashes had already occurred.

For Rankin, this was just a flight home to South Carolina from Massachusetts. He and his flight partner were flying under the call sign *Tiger Two* and were expecting the trip to take around 70 minutes to span the 800 miles. It was a pretty routine flight and the two were just wearing light summer flight suits. As they entered the area over Norfolk, Virginia, they approached a huge thunderstorm, with thunder clouds extending up to 44,000 feet.

To avoid the storm, the pair ascended to 48,000 feet. And that's when Lt. Col. Rankin heard a thump and then grinding noises coming from the jet's single engine. Then another thump and a warning light in the cockpit before he heard the engine seize up and cut out completely.

Immediately the experienced pilot thought of the failsafe in place for this very type of emergency. But as Rankin pulled the lever to deploy the backup ram air turbine system, the lever broke off in his hand. He had run out of options. At 47,000 feet, and still traveling hundreds of miles per hour, he pulled the lever to eject from the aircraft. It was around 6 p.m. in the evening. When Lt. Herbert Nolan looked out the window of his jet, he saw Lt. Col. Rankin spinning wildly with all his limbs outstretched before he disappeared into the thunderstorm below.

Ejecting from a jet fighter is never routine. But through the years, engineers have developed all kinds of ways to make it survivable. In the case of the F-8U-1, the early variant that Lt. Col. William Rankin was flying, it was equipped with a Vought Ejection seat. When he pulled the ejection lever at 6 p.m. on July 26th, 1959, the seat operated as expected. But that wasn't the problem.

The problem was that he was at 47,000 feet. Humans don't have enough oxygen to breathe above around 26,000 feet and the ambient static pressure is only about 13 percent of the air pressure that we experience at ground level. To put it simply, it's basically lethal to remain at that altitude wearing nothing but a thin flight suit and no pressure suit. Rankin was falling quickly and was instantly hit with rapid onset frostbite to his extremities. His abdomen swelled several times its normal size and he began bleeding from his eyes, ears, nose, and mouth.

The temperature change William Rankin experienced was going from 75 degrees Fahrenheit inside the cockpit to an instant -70 degrees Fahrenheit in the sky. The spin that he fell into pulled his limbs outward and the centrifugal force from spinning was too strong to even move his arms or legs. His oxygen mask had been knocked free from his face, so his first order of business was trying to get that back to his mouth and nose to breath from his bail-out oxygen tank. He fell into the storm cloud below and his spinning slowed down enough to reach the oxygen mask, which was the only thing that kept him from experiencing brain-death from lack of oxygen.

He was freefalling into the violent storm, but still alive. The next test would be for him to deploy his chute. The chute deployment worked on barometric pressure and would automatically deploy when Rankin hit 10,000 feet. But he was in a giant cumulonimbus cloud. The barometric pressure was all messed up. So, at somewhere between 15,000 and 20,000 feet, the parachute deployed prematurely. It was good that the chute expanded above him and slowed his descent, but the fact that he was still so high in the air meant that he was subject to the violent storm conditions and winds inside the cloud. And the movement was violent. Instead of falling, the parachute suddenly carried him upward thousands of feet.

Rankin's body had been through so much already, and now he found himself vomiting from all the trauma. He was being violently pelted by baseball-sized hailstones at one point, and at another the rain was so thick he found himself needing to hold his breath just in order to keep from drowning. Lightning began surrounding him. The bolts appeared as bright blue columns of light several feet in diameter. The accompanying thunder shook his body to its core. One lightning bolt was so close, he thought he had been struck and had died.

Finally, Rankin could see the dark ground approaching below him and landed in the forest in North Carolina. He didn't know it yet, but he had landed in Ahoskie, North Carolina, more than 65 miles from Norfolk, Virginia, where he had bailed out. His aircraft crashed in Scotland Neck, North Carolina, 30 miles from where he landed. Bruised, badly frostbitten and covered in welts from hail, Lt. Col. Rankin looked at his watch. It was 6:40 p.m. In clear conditions, he would have landed somewhere around 5 minutes after he ejected. Rankin had been falling for 40 minutes.

William Rankin made a full recovery from his harrowing ordeal and went on to continue his successful aviation career. He died in 2009 at the age of eighty-nine. His story was written in an autobiography he penned in 1960 called *The Man Who Wrote the Thunder.* To this day, he's only one of two people to survive falling through a cumulonimbus thunder cloud. The Internet Says It's True.

Self-Surgery: Leonid Rogozov Removed His Own Appendix

Imagine the moment that you're holding a blade above your skin, about to cut into it in order to save your own life.

There are only a few circumstances where someone would be drawn to perform surgery on themself: the first one would be some sort of rare psychological disorder that would cause someone to mutilate themselves. We're talking about something very different than cutting or self-harm. In the case of the very rare body integrity disorder, people have been known to actually want to amputate their own limbs...some have even carried through with it.

But then there's the case of medically necessary surgery. The only situation you'd ever want to do it to yourself is in a dire circumstance in which getting to a hospital isn't an option. Or perhaps someone might choose to do so to avoid medical expenses, or laws. In all these cases, self-surgery is an extreme last resort and incredibly rare.

Our story today is about one such case: the story of Leonid Rogozov. His story is probably the most popular of all the tales we have about people doing surgery on themselves.

There's a story from 1920 in which a German doctor had heard about the idea of reaching a horse heart through a jugular vein, known as catheterization. It hadn't been done on a human, so he did it to himself. The funny story here is that he wanted to do it to a patient. The chief of surgery said no, so he asked if he could do it to himself. The chief still said no, so he secretly recruited an operating-room nurse to help him do it anyway. He needed her permission to use the room. She volunteered to be the patient, but he still wanted to do it on himself. So he said yes to her, just so he could use the room. He anesthetized her and told her she would be the patient. Then he just did it to himself. He was successful in reaching the heart with the catheter and became the first to do so.

Sometimes the person doing the surgery isn't a surgeon, but has to do it in order to survive. This was the case with hiker Aron Ralston. In 2003, he was exploring a canyon and a boulder above him came lose, trapping him to the rock wall by his right arm. He had no way to contact anyone for help because his phone didn't have a signal down in the canyon. He knew that if he didn't free himself, he would die of starvation. So he reached his left arm into his pocket and retrieved a pocketknife. The rest of the story is told in the Danny Boyle film *127 Hours*, but you can imagine what he did. He had to cut through the skin, muscle and tendons, twisting and breaking his own bones with no anesthesia. He was able to amputate his own arm and climb the remaining sixty-five feet to safety.

And in the case of today's story, the story of Leonid Rogozov, it's a combination of surgical know-how and survival. Because in 1961, he found himself in a dangerous situation.

Leonid Rogozov was trained in pediatrics and became licensed in the Soviet Union as a General Practitioner in 1959. It was then that he began to study for what he really wanted to do—surgery. So at the age of twenty-five, he started his clinical surgery training, but only got a year into it before an opportunity for work showed up.

In 1960, at the age of twenty-six, he was asked to join the sixth Soviet Antarctic Expedition as their doctor. He had his general practitioner training and that was enough to be more than able to serve as the expeditionary doctor for a team of thirteen researchers on their trip.

Their mission was to head to the Novolazarevskaya Station in Antarctica, 5,500 miles from where he graduated medical school in Saint Petersburg, Russia. They would leave as the polar winter came over Antarctica in 1961. The remote research station had only just been established in February and the job of this group was to reach the station and see it through the harsh winter months. The harsh weather wouldn't allow for a flight, so the group had to travel to Antarctica by sea. It took the group thirty-six days to get to Novolazarevskaya. Once there, they would be a thousand miles from the next nearest Soviet research station. It was truly a remote location, but the researchers made it successfully.

Everything was going smoothly until late April of 1961. On the morning of April 29, Leonid Rogozov woke up with a stinging pain in his abdomen that moved toward the lower right side. That symptom, along with the weakness, nausea, and fatigue he was experiencing made it clear to the medically educated man what was happening. He was suffering from peritonitis, most likely from an appendix that had either ruptured, or was about to rupture at any minute.

Rogozov hadn't ruled out more conservative options. He considered them, but he knew that none of them would have helped. There was already infection happening inside his body and the appendix absolutely had to be removed if he wanted to survive. The crew began contacting other research stations run by other countries, but no one had an aircraft available, and even if they did, the weather conditions outside would have prevented safe flying. The nearest Soviet station was Mirny, which was a thousand miles away. The ship that had brought them wouldn't be back for another year. He was out of options. It was remove the appendix, or die.

The idea of removing one's own appendix wasn't new. According to a report by the National Institute of Health, it was first attempted in 1912 by American Surgeon Bertram Alden, who was forced to end the procedure when his assistant threatened to leave. It was successfully accomplished by another American surgeon, Evan O'Neil Kane, in 1921. After his successful self-surgery, Kane boldly wrote "I wish to emphasize my statement that any surgeons, if not obese, can, with perfect ease and even comfort, self-operate in cases such as mine."

Whether or not Leonid Rogozov had researched these cases or not remains unknown, but he made the decision to move forward with the surgery on May 1st. Thanks to a journal he kept, we know what he was thinking at the time. Rogozov wrote the following:

"I did not sleep at all last night. It hurts like the devil! A snow storm whipping through my soul, wailing like 100 jackals…Still no obvious symptoms that perforation is imminent, but an oppressive feeling of foreboding hangs over me… This is it… I have to think through the only possible way out - to operate on myself... It's almost impossible... but I can't just fold my arms and give up."

Before going forward with the surgery, it was important that the entire thing be approved by their commander in Moscow. This was 1961, a time when tensions between Russia and the West were at a high, and every little news story about failure could cause national embarrassment for the Soviets. The decision was made that the surgery would happen.

Rogozov recruited two of his fellow expeditioners to help him out. The team's driver and meteorologist. They would aid in handing him instruments, holding a lamp and a mirror. Another member stood watch in the room in case anyone passed out or additional hands were needed. The tools were sterilized by putting them outside in the freezing cold, with lethal temperatures, well below zero.

Rogozov had to find the right reclining posture to be able to be most effective. What he decided was that if he were in a semi-reclining position, with the upper half of his body upright and tilted slightly to his left, he would have the best opportunity to see what he was doing. His only anesthesia was a 0.5 percent solution of Novocain injected into the abdominal wall. The helpers watched as Rogozov cut an incision into his abdomen. Not being able to see properly, he accidentally cut too far and cut into his intestine, which he had to suture before continuing. Once the repair was done, he finally was able to see the appendix. He reported it as having a dark stain at its base and concluded that it wasn't ruptured, but would have within the next day. He felt bad for his assistants. In his journal, he wrote, "My poor assistants! At the last minute I looked over at them. They stood there in their surgical whites, whiter than white themselves. I was scared too. But when I picked up the needle with the Novocain and gave myself the first injection, somehow I automatically switched into operating mode, and from that point on I didn't notice anything else."

The idea of using a mirror was a good one, but it threw him off with everything being mirror image. So he decided instead to work by feel alone, removing his gloves. As the surgery went on, Rogozov grew weak and dizzy and began needing to take twenty-minute breaks just to keep himself from passing out. The bleeding was heavy. After two hours, the surgery was done. The appendix had been successfully removed and he sewed the final stitches in his abdomen. He wouldn't know if it had been a success until he fully recovered over the next days. And this part is amazing. After five days, his symptoms were gone. No more fever. After seven days, he removed his stitches. Two weeks later, Rogozov was back on his feet, resuming his normal duties tending to the needs of the other researchers.

This was groundbreaking, and one of the reasons it became so widely known is because of Rogozov's meticulous journal entries, detailing every step. There's also the fact that his fellow expeditioners took photos of the entire process. We have a very detailed and accurate account of everything that took place. Again, this was a time in which exhibitions of toughness and ingenuity went a long way to capture the imagination of the Soviet Union and was viewed on a world stage.

Later that year, Rogozov was recognized for his courage and awarded the Order of the Red Banner of Labour, which was at the time the third-highest award that a Soviet civilian could be given. The surgery also resulted in a change to policy on long expeditions like these. Future researchers would undergo medical testing to ensure their fitness before undertaking long expeditions.

Leonid Rogozov lived until 2000, dying at the age of sixty-six from lung cancer. His story of resilience, self-reliance, and fortitude lives on. The Internet Says It's True.

The Amazing Story behind the Bluetooth Logo

The country of Denmark is named Denmark because it's an old Norse word for "The Marches of the Danes." Originally it was known as "Danmark," and common folklore tells a story about it being named after "King Dan," who was sort of a mythological first king of the area. But there's no one real person that we can point to who was "King Dan."

But Denmark as a nation was a unification of a bunch of different lands in the area, including what we now know as Norway and Sweden. The unification of the country saw its first official unified King somewhere in the 10th century by a Viking king, Gorm the Old, and then by his son Harald. Harald is the Viking king of Denmark that's credited with really uniting the lands as well as introducing Christianity to Denmark. He ruled from 958 to 986.

We have a great reminder of these Danish Kings. If you visit the railway town of Jelling, Denmark, you'll find the earliest written mention of the name of the country: two large stones known as the Jelling Rune Stones. These stones were placed by Gore the Old and his son Harald and they are covered with inscriptions of ancient Norse runes, including the name "Danmark." The stones are absolutely huge, considering they were placed there in the 10th century. The larger of the two stones was placed by Harald and has an inscription: "King Harald bade this monument be made in memory of Gorm his father and Thyra his mother, that Harald who won for himself all Danmark and Norway and made the Danes Christians."

And it was the joining of nations, the joining of Denmark with Christianity, that Harald is known for. As it turns out, we still say his name every day. Because Harald's last name, as inscribed in the Jelling Rune Stones, was Bluetooth. Harald Bluetooth.

What we know of Harald comes from the Rune Stones, but also from several contemporary accounts of his reign as the first Christian king of Denmark. One source called him "remarkable by the force of his mind and faith," but other sources from the time called him "deprived of wisdom," or "without great intelligence." His last name was Gormsson— he was the son of Gorm—but he was known throughout his life with the nickname name Blåtand, which translates to "Blue Tooth." Harald, it's believed, had a "dead tooth" that appeared black or blue in his mouth. Other legends describe his love for eating berries, staining his teeth blue. Whichever story is true, his nickname became his last name, and Harald Bluetooth the Viking became known as the first Christian king of Denmark and the man who united the country.

So how did a Viking king of Denmark end up being immortalized a thousand years later and linked to technology he could have never dreamed of?

For this part of the story, we're going to forget the ancient Danes for a minute and skip forward a thousand years.

In 1994, Ericsson Mobile, the Swedish tech company, was working on an idea for a wireless headset to work with their phones. They were building off a couple earlier patents from Johan Ullman and a team consisting of Nils Rydbeck, Todd Wingren, Jaap Haartsen, Sven Mattison, and Örjan Johansson. They teamed up with the other major mobile technology companies; IBM, Nokia, Toshiba and Intel all joined Ericsson in working on this project. The goal was to unite the PC and cellular industries in creating a sort of "short-link radio" signal to help devices talk to each other within a small area.

They considered several possible names for the technology: Biz-RF, MC-Link, Low-Power RF, and the project name that was most commonly used: Personal Area Networking (PAN). The resulting technology allowed a device within ten feet of the primary unit to receive and send communication signals over radio frequency. Of course, this has since expanded to somewhere around a hundred feet, but the original signal could only travel around ten feet.

When it was time to market this new technology that could allow things like headsets to wirelessly pair with mobile phones, they didn't like the name PAN because it seemed way too broad and difficult to patent and market. That's where Jim Kardach comes in.

Kardach was an Intel Engineer and thought that a challenge they were all facing presented an interesting story to tell. The major problem was that all these communication technology companies were using different standards for cell phone connectivity. Kardach ran the group that brought together engineers from all these different companies—at the time they called it "SIG" for "Special Interest Group." It was Kardach that had heard the legend of how Harald Bluetooth had united the different lands to form Denmark and thought that unification was exactly what was needed here. So he lightly started calling his group "Bluetooth SIG" and later just "Bluetooth." It was a project name - just a name to be used internally to describe the project. But it stuck.

Just like Harald Bluetooth had joined together different people with different customs, this special interest group developed a technology that could converge not only PC tech with networking and communication, but also multiple different telecom companies, countries, and standards into a tool that could be used widely by all of them. So when the first products to include it were released, the Ericsson R520M and T39 phones, they were able to be paired using the technology they released with the name "Bluetooth." Soon, wireless earpieces started showing up on shelves like Nokia's HDW-1 in 1997 and HDW-2 in 2003.

But what about that logo? The Bluetooth logo is something that we all see just about every day, whether it be on our computers, gaming systems, phones, or TVs. It looks like an alien symbol. And it comes from the very place where the name Bluetooth was taken: the rune stones in Jelling, Denmark. Harald Bluetooth's initials, HB, are used on that stone in the Futhark rune language; the H appearing as a symbol that looks like a line with a small X through the middle, and the B looking like what we know as a lower-case b, but without any curves. If you stick those two runes together, using the left half of the H and sticking it to the side of the B, you get what we now know as the Bluetooth logo.

Today, Jim Kardach, one of the founders and the namer of Bluetooth, is semi-retired. He has taught at Cal State, but also works part time with a few other tech companies. He left Intel as Chief Power Architect in 2012. And as you know, any wireless communication device now carries the initials of this ancient Danish Viking king. It sounds made up, but it's true. Bluetooth is named after Harald Bluetooth. The Internet Says It's True.

London Bridge is Falling Down (and Coming to America)

When I first started learning about this story, I made the same mistake that a lot of non-British people probably make. I thought the iconic bridge that we see associated with downtown London was known as London Bridge. But no. That's Tower Bridge and a completely different thing. Tower Bridge, the appropriately named bridge connecting to East London across the River Thames, was built in 1894, and is an icon that will forever be associated with London. It's the one with the towers that you've seen. It raises with a bascule in the middle.

And while our story doesn't focus on Tower Bridge, I did find a separate fun story about it.

Back in 1952 this guy named Albert Gunter was doing what he did every day: drive the Number 78 Bus in London. He was headed toward Shoreditch and driving over Tower Bridge and didn't realize the bridge was opening. And just like that scene in the Blues Brothers movie where they jump the car over the open bridge, Albert had no choice but to gun it. He was too far and made the decision that the only way out of this situation was forward. So Albert slams on the gas and JUMPS a city bus through the air over the gap in the opening bridge. The reports I read said that the bus was only going twelve miles an hour, which seems WAY too slow. But however fast he was going, he got his bus—with all twenty passengers—across the bridge safely. He was the only one injured when he broke his leg. And yes, it was a double-decker bus.

So that's Tower Bridge. London Bridge, however, is a completely different bridge. This is the next bridge to the West of Tower Bridge. It's the oldest Thames crossing in London and if you go back, there were a series of "London Bridges," going all the way to Roman times and 50 AD. The bridges back then were made of Timber and before that there's some evidence that there was an even more simplistic pontoon bridge. But in 1209, they built what's known as "Old London Bridge," which is the bridge that they were singing about in the popular children's song, "London Bridge is Falling Down." And we know that because Old London Bridge was in use until 1831 and that song started showing up in the late 1600s and was first published in the 1700s.

The origin of the song, otherwise known as "My Fair Lady," has multiple stories. There are some weird ones, like the belief that the bridge would collapse unless humans were sacrificed and put into the foundations of the bridge. This is probably linked to some alternate lyrics that were used over the years in which different types of fixes to the bridge are presented and then excused for different reasons. With that said, I've never seen a verse with lyrics that say "kill a guy to please the gods, please the gods, please the gods." There's also an alternate origin story for the song about Vikings sacking the town and stealing the gold.

The most likely origin for the song is that the bridge was literally breaking down. This was a bridge 926 feet long supported by 19 piers and arches and a wooden drawbridge. And it was in use for more than 600 years. During that time, there were two collapses of the bridge, neither one of them destroying the whole bridge. There were also several fires. This version of the bridge had houses and shops on it. It had waterwheels for power at the bottom and decapitated heads on top. The heads of traitors were dipped in tar and placed on spikes on top of the bridge. At one point, there were more than 30 heads on top of Old London Bridge. Toward the end of this bridge's life, they removed the houses and widened the roadway, but it was in need of total replacement.

In 1799, they held a competition for designs of the new bridge. The winning design was by John Rennie and included five stone arches spanning the River Thames. The foundation was laid in 1824 and was built in the same place as the Old London Bridge. This would be the final project of Rennie's career, a career that had made Rennie well-known for designing bridges and canals. The New London Bridge, as it was being called at the time, cost £2.5 million, the equivalent of about £320 million today. A huge part of that cost was tied up in remaking the approach roads to the bridge, which cost something like three times the cost of the bridge itself. This new Victorian stone arch bridge opened in 1831 and became one of the busiest spots in London. At the height of its use, it saw the traffic of 8,000 pedestrians and 900 vehicles every hour. But this was the 19th century. It was created just before a time when the definition of "vehicle" was about to change dramatically. It was handling more and more weight every year. And it began to sink.

The New London Bridge was getting old. And by old, I mean it was 137 years old. Nothing like the age of the Old London Bridge. And by global standards, there were much older bridges. But that 137 years had seen a huge change in the way people traveled over it. The difference between 1831 and 1968 was huge.

London Bridge was literally falling down, sinking an eighth of an inch every year. And it wasn't sinking equally on each side. In 1924, it was reported that the east side of the bridge had sunk about four inches more than the west side. This combined with the overall state of the bridge and the fact that it was never designed for modern automobiles meant that the New London Bridge would have to be replaced.

In most cities, this would mean that they scrap the bridge while building the new one. But a member of the Common Council of the City of London, Ivan Luckin, had an idea that they should sell the bridge. The city of London put the bridge up for sale in 1968, and that April, it was purchased.

The new owner of the London Bridge was an American. An Oil Entrepreneur from Missouri by the name of Robert P. McCulloch had made a fortune with his company McCulloch Oil and by selling chainsaws. He also had success in selling motors and superchargers. He purchased London Bridge for $2,460,000. You may be asking: when you buy a bridge, how do you then get it to America? The answer is that you take it apart, brick by brick.

They disassembled London Bridge while carefully marking each brick so it could later be reassembled. That applied to the granite facing blocks, anyway—a lot of the blocks from the bridge were sent to a quarry in Devon. The rest were put on a cargo ship and sent through the Panama

Canal to California. The blocks were then put on trucks and shipped to Robert P. McCulloch's new home: Lake Havasu, Arizona.

At Lake Havasu, a popular vacation spot South of Las Vegas, right on the California-Arizona Border, the blocks arrived and were ready to be reassembled. This time, they'd be placed on a hollow-steel core frame that McCulloch had arranged to be pre-built for the granite blocks. It would span the Bridgewater Channel, which is a manmade waterway running through Lake Havasu City. It was completed and dedicated on October 10th, 1971, and when the project was finished, it looked just like the bridge looked when it spanned the River Thames.

While this was going on, a *new* New London Bridge was being built in London. It's known as the Modern London Bridge and is the bridge that exists there today.

In the city of Lake Havasu, Arizona, you can go and see London Bridge today. In many respects, it's THE London Bridge, the one that was built because London Bridge was falling down. It's the bridge that stood through two World Wars in Europe. It stood through five kings and two queens. It saw the world develop during the Industrial Age. And I don't think many people know about it. That makes it a great story for this book. The Internet Says It's True.

Running Out of Bullets: Greeks and Turks

Back in 2015, I had this crazy nine-hour layover in the Athens airport in Greece. I had been to Crete for some shows and was on my way on to the next stop, but I wasn't about to stay in the airport for an entire day, so I checked my luggage and paid a cab driver extra money to show me around Athens for the day. I got to see the original Olympic stadium, the Changing of the Guard at the Presidential Mansion, Lycabettus Mountain, the Acropolis, and the Parthenon. Today's story revolves around the Parthenon.

When I visited ten years ago, the Parthenon was under a decades-long reconstruction project. People working on this thing were spending their entire careers studying the missing blocks in the marble and using 3D imaging to recreate the blocks. They're attempting to restore it to its original condition. So, fwhat was this thing first built for?

It was built in 432 BC, or 2,456 years ago, as a temple to the goddess Athena as a sort of celebratory monument for the Hellenic victory over Persian invaders during the Greco-Persian Wars. It was also used as the treasury. Later, it was converted to a Christian church, then after the Ottoman conquest, was a mosque. The Ottomans were using it as a munitions dump and it when it was attacked by the Venetians, it destroyed a lot of the original structure. Over the years, the story of the Parthenon continues like this. Seven different times, the Parthenon was attacked and completely transformed. During one of these times, a huge forty-foot shining bronze statue of Athena was stolen and never recovered. At one point, many of the important pieces of marble were shipped to Britain for study and never returned.

From 1821 to 1830, the Greeks fought for their Independence from the Ottoman Turks. This war is now known as the Greek War of Independence and the Greek victory resulted in the formation of what we now know as modern-day Greece. It's the beginning of this eight-and-a-half-year war where today's story takes place.

The Greeks had been fighting for their independence from Ottoman rule for literally centuries. None of the rebellions had been particularly successful. But in March of 1821, a large organized Greek uprising began. And they instantly took back all of Athens—except the Acropolis. The Acropolis is the area around the Parthenon, a giant hill in the middle of the city that almost acts as its own town. In fact, the Ottomans had built many houses and store houses around the Parthenon. It was their military fort and their armory. If you see a photo of the Acropolis, you'll understand why. It's an easily defensible position, rising above the city of Athens below, so they had high ground. But they also were leveraging the fact that they didn't think the Greeks would attack their own sacred Parthenon. So that's one of the reasons they used it to store munitions and powder.

Despite this belief, the Greeks were attacking to take it back. The force was made up of around six hundred Athenians, but reinforced to a size of about three thousand attackers with the help of Aeginan, Hydras, Cephallonians and Keas. The Ottomans also called in reinforcements and soon took back the surrounding city of Athens for a short time. In 1822, a second siege by Greeks once again had the Ottomans surrounded at the Acropolis, and that's when the Ottoman Turks began running out of bullets for their flintlock muskets. They started looking to the marble stones of the sacred Parthenon to make more bullets. That's when the Greeks said "NO" and came up with another idea.

The Turks of the Ottoman Empire fought with several types of weapons in the Greek War for Independence. Ottoman flintlock muskets were smoothbore muzzle-loaders, mostly of Ottoman build, but they also fought with imported weapons from Europe like the British Brown Bess and the French Charleville musket. Officers commonly carried pistols made in both the Ottoman Empire and by the Balkans. They also used artillery like cast-iron and bronze cannons.

In 1822, the Greeks were making their second attempt to lay siege to the Acropolis. During this time, the Turks started running low on bullets. Lead had been used in the joints of the stones to build the ancient structure, and, as the Turks needed lead, they started actually dismantling the Parthenon to make more bullets. They had already removed around five hundred stones. This was in the area that still stood after the horrible explosion that blew apart much of the structure two hundred years earlier when the Venetians attacked. This area of the Parthenon was now being destroyed and the Greeks watched and fought back.

A young historian named Kyriakos Pittakis becomes very important to the story at this point. He was an important Greek Historian, but he was also part of an underground resistance movement against the Ottoman Turks and likely fought in the 1822 siege at the Acropolis. He saw, before his very eyes, the Parthenon being destroyed so the Turks could make more bullets, and he went to give a speech at the Academy of Athens, pleading for an unusual solution. He asked Odysseus Androutsos, a military leader of the time, for bullets. Why? Pittakis's plan was to actually give bullets to the Turks—their enemies—in the hope that they stop dismantling the Parthenon. And they did! The Turks fought with the newly supplied bullets and left the rest of the Parthenon standing.

They actually sent bullets up the mountain to the Acropolis, so that they would stop removing stones from the ancient temple. This one man and his connection to the history and preservation of the landmark actually saved part of this beautiful structure as the battle continued.

By June of that year, the Turks surrendered the Acropolis after a year-long siege. The terms of surrender were that the Ottomans would be given free passage out of the country on foreign ships not aligned with Greece, and the Turks who wanted to stay in Athens would be given amnesty to stay without being harassed.

Eventually, the Russians, the British and the French all came to the aid of the Greeks, and by 1829, they won victory over the Ottoman Empire and regained their independence after centuries of Ottoman rule. And today, the Parthenon still stands.

Nine years ago, when I visited the Parthenon, some of what I was seeing had been restored and rebuilt, but much of it was original—and only preserved because one man cared about their ancient heritage enough to come up with an incredibly unusual tactic. The Internet Says It's True.

Tarrare: The Man Who Ate Everything

Joey Chestnut is 6 feet tall and 229 pounds. In 2021, he ate 76 hot dogs in 10 minutes. The last record holders before him were Matt Stonie and Takeru Kobayashi who ate 70 and 66, respectively. While Chestnut is known for the Nathan's Hot Dog Eating Contest, he's also broken competitive eating records by swallowing ridiculous amounts of matzo balls, steaks, chicken, pizza, and just about anything else.

While he's a natural at competitive eating, Joey Chestnut has to train to be able to do what he does. He exercises his mouth and jaw, which he says usually start to fatigue about seven minutes into the contest. He also goes through cleanses, diets, and practice rounds. He says that when he eats the hot dogs every year, it's the equivalent to around sixteen pounds of food, so he needs to keep his body in shape in order to be able to process that amount with his mouth and jaw. After a competition, it takes him about two days to feel normal again.

Today's story is about a man who never needed to work out to eat ridiculous amounts. It just came naturally to Tarrare.

Tarrare was a man from Lyon, France. He was born in 1772, and it's unknown if Tarrare was the man's real name, or simply a nickname taken from the French saying "bom-bom-tarrare," which basically translates to "Boom goes the dynamite."

From a very young age, the boy had an insatiable appetite. So much so that he was abandoned by his parents, who couldn't afford to keep him fed. How much was this kid eating? Well as a young kid, he would regularly eat one quarter of a cow—more than his own body weight. And he would do so and never gain weight. He was always a skinny kid. So his parents, out of self-preservation, kicked him out.

He roamed the streets as a teen, eating anything he could. Even garbage. He eventually found his way into a band of prostitutes and thieves. He would travel around with them, and during the day would perform on the streets, eating ridiculous amounts for the amazement of onlookers. While he was always described as being thin as a rail, his mouth was said to be freakishly large. For the crowd of people, he would swallow corks, rocks, and anything people would point to, and eat them without a problem. This included entire baskets of apples and, sadly, cats and dogs. A contemporaneous account from an eyewitness used these exact words: "he seized a live cat with his teeth, eventrated it, sucked its blood, and ate it, leaving the bare skeleton only. In about thirty minutes he rejected the hairs in the manner of birds of prey and carnivorous animals."

At one point, it was reported that he bit the head off an eel, then swallowed the eel whole. One bite. Similarly, it was said that he preferred snakes, lizards, and other reptiles. At one point, there's an account of Tarrare attending a dinner for fifteen people. He ate all the food and drink for all fifteen people. And being a skinny guy, when he would do this, it would change his physical appearance.

After eating, his abdomen would blow up like a balloon. And while we're talking about his physical characteristics—the guy was disgusting. Not just his eating habits. He was said to be constantly covered in sweat, horribly smelly, and unclean. It was said you could smell him so strongly you couldn't stand within twenty paces of the man. I already mentioned his abnormally large mouth, but inside that mouth, his teeth were dark and permanently stained. And due to the constant shrinking and growing of his abdomen, he was reported to have skin that would hang loosely from his body. After he ate, his eyes would be bloodshot and the smell would get worse. And the guy was constantly farting. Some have said that's the origin of the use of the phrase "Bom-bom tarrare" to describe him. Boom goes the dynamite.

Tarrare was sort of a vagrant. He didn't have anywhere to go, and was literally only motivated to eat. In the 1790s, The War of the First Coalition broke out within France. He joined up with the French Revolutionary Army. Finally he had found purpose. But if you think modern Army rations wouldn't be enough to satisfy your hunger, try being Tarrare. He found himself trading all sorts of duties and jobs just to be able to eat the rations of his fellow soldiers. This still wasn't enough. He would eat everything he could find, including inside dumpsters and trash heaps and all of the gauze for wounds he could find, and he was still malnourished and ended up in the hospital. Doctors were stumped. No one had any explanation for the strange eating habits or the fact that he couldn't put on weight. The man was constantly malnourished.

At one point, the military had an idea to put Tarrare's unusual ability to their use. They would turn him into a spy. He would swallow military documents, travel in plain clothes through enemy lines, and deliver plans to people who needed them. In other words, someone had to rummage through his droppings to retrieve the plans. At this point, we're talking about the Army of the Rhine, which was a group trying to bring the French Revolution to the Prussians. The generals put him to a test. They put documents inside a wooden box and wrapped it in paper, then gave it to Tarrare to eat. He ate the box, no problem, so they rewarded him with thirty pounds of random cuttings from a cow.

So once he'd proven himself, they gave him his first official assignment. A French colonel had been imprisoned in Prussia and the Army of the Rhine needed to deliver important plans to him. They gave these plans to Tarrare to swallow. What he didn't know was this was just another test. The plans he was carrying were nothing but a note to confirm that the colonel had in fact gotten the message from Tarrare. But he didn't know this at the time, so he dressed like a German peasant and headed toward Landau, where the man was being held captive. Heck, he already smelled like a peasant. But when locals discovered that he didn't speak their language, it sent up red flags and, before long, he found himself in front of a Prussian commander, who was now accusing him of being a spy.

Now the man who ate everything was facing the gallows. History didn't record how, but somehow the Prussian commander changed his mind, didn't hang Tarrare, and just had his soldiers beat the crap out of the man instead.

Tarrare returned to France and promptly decided he was sick of this military stuff. So he decided that he needed to go back into the hospital and figure out what was wrong with him. At this point in his life, he suffered from constant horrible diarrhea. Doctors were still confused. They had never seen a case like this.

But there's a story that often gets included with tales of Tarrare that really caught my eye. Is it true that Tarrare once ate a living toddler?

Much of what we know about Tarrare comes from the accounts of his doctor, Pierre Francois Percy. Percy was the Surgeon in Chief at the military hospital. But some of the rumors about Tarrare came from other people at the time. And one of them was about a toddler.

At the same time Tarrare was in this hospital, a fourteen-month-old boy disappeared. Many people nearby suspected that the boy was eaten by the insatiable Tarrare. But there was never any proof of that and he was never formally accused. So, we don't have any evidence at all that this was true, but there is THIS fact. He was known to sneak into the hospital's blood storage and would drink the blood. He also was accused of sneaking into the morgue and feasting on the bodies of the dead. So maybe it's not that much of a stretch to believe this guy ate a kid. We'll never know. But while he wasn't formally accused, the hospital, including his doctor, Percy, believed he ate the kid. So they made him leave the hospital.

Four years later, Percy got word that Tarrare wanted to see him. He reluctantly visited Tarrare, who was now in a hospital in Versailles, and found him bedridden, ill, and still experiencing constant gastric distress. The diarrhea had never stopped and to make matters worse, he told Percy he had swallowed a golden fork a few years earlier that was causing him horrible pain. Percy had tried everything with no success. And he now recognized that Tarrare was suffering from another ailment—an advanced case of tuberculosis. It killed Tarrare within days of Percy's arrival.

The details about his autopsy are pretty gruesome. They talk about how quickly the body decayed, how it was rotten on the inside and filled with pus and ulcers. They never found a golden fork. They also never finished the autopsy because the smell was so bad. So sadly we'll never really know exactly what made him this way.

The word for what he experienced throughout his life is polyphagia, an abnormal appetite that just never goes away. But that's generally a symptom, not a cause. The cause could be a lot of different things. Parasites, blood-sugar issues, or brain chemistry problems are just a few of the possible causes. But next time you eat so much you don't think you could possibly eat another bite, go ahead and load up that fork and do it for Tarrare.

Swindled in Wichita Falls: The World's Littlest Skyscraper

There's a legend about the Viking Erik the Red. When he was exiled from Iceland, he ended up in Greenland, but at the time, it wasn't called that. He was there with his ships, family and servants, but he wanted to entice other Norse settlers to come from Iceland. The legend goes that he named it Greenland so it would be enticing to the settlers despite more than 80 percent of the island being covered in ice. It worked, and thousands of new settlers came to Greenland on twenty-five ships. Only eleven of the ships actually made it and when the Norse settlers got there, they saw that there was no green land to farm. They got scammed, but somehow were able to establish a couple settlements anyway. It's really one of the first recorded cases of real estate fraud in history.

Then there's the story of the man named George C. Parker. He was a famous con man who would go around selling public landmarks to his victims. At different points in his life, he supposedly fraudulently sold Grant's Tomb, the Statue of Liberty, the Metropolitan Museum of Art, and Madison Square Garden. Famously, Parker sold the Brooklyn Bridge several times to multiple people. The folks thought they had bought control of the access to the bridge. At one point, someone even got arrested after trying to erect a toll booth on their newly purchased Brooklyn Bridge. And if you're wondering, yes: that's where we get the expression "if you believe that, I've got a bridge to sell you."

You've heard of a Ponzi scheme. The original Ponzi was a conman who devised all kinds of schemes to defraud people out of their money, but one of the most famous scams was in 1925 when he bought a bunch of Florida swampland outside of Jacksonville and sold lots to investors as "Prime Florida Land." Investors bought the land and couldn't do anything with it.

Our story today deals with a case of fraud just like these. And to be specific, it deals with a scheme to defraud people investing in a piece of property: the Newby-McMahon Building. It's known better as "The World's Littlest Skyscraper."

When the building was completed, it was reportedly a complete embarrassment to the residents of Wichita Falls, Texas.

Witchita Falls, Texas is a small to midsize city with a population of about 104,000. It's home to Sheppard Air Force Base, which is notable because it's the largest Air Force training base.

The town was founded on the site of a large Choctaw settlement by cattle ranchers and people who were drawn to the waterfall on the Wichita River. It became a city built on different industries, including food processing and retailing, flour milling, railroads, cattle, banking, and oil. A petroleum reservoir had been discovered just North of the city in 1912, and a sort of boom happened with 20,000 new settlers moving in over the next 6 years. Between 1910 and 1920, the population went from 8,000 to 40,000. Some of them were becoming instant millionaires from the oil boom. In addition to new homes going up everywhere, there was a severe need for office space. There were reportedly people setting up tables and chairs on the sidewalk and doing business deals on street corners.

One of the offices in the downtown area was the Newby building, built by Augustus Newby decades earlier. It was across the street from the popular St. James hotel and nearby the city's rail station. This is where we meet our conman, J.D. McMahon.

J.D. McMahon was an oil man and promoter who had his own oil rig construction company. He recognized the town's need for office buildings and saw it as an opportunity. So going into 1918, he started looking for investors for a brand-new addition to the Newby building. It would be a skyscraper, which was incredibly special and rare for the time. The world's tallest structure at the time was the Eiffel Tower at 984 feet. The tallest building at the time was the Woolworth Building in New York City, which was 792 feet. There were only five buildings in the world that were taller than 500 feet—all in the United States.

McMahon's skyscraper would be 480 feet, making it the sixth-tallest building in the world. That plot of land at the corner of 7th Street and LaSalle in downtown Wichita Falls would be a true wonder of the time and people would come from far and wide just to see it, let alone rent an office. Everyone was eager to invest. They needed the office space, they had the money, and soon McMahon had collected $200,000 in investments as startup capital for the project. That's the equivalent to something like $3.4

million in today's money. Investors were shown the plans for the high-rise building and signed off on them.

Then the construction began. McMahon used his own construction crews and equipment to build it. It's a neoclassical-style red-brick and cast-stone building that looked very similar to the original plans the investors saw —

with one major difference. When it was completed, the skyscraper wasn't 480 feet. It was 40 feet, just four floors. There were a few legal issues. Firstly, apparently McMahon hadn't gotten permission from the owner of the lot to even build there. But the issue that everyone was talking about were all these investors who got conned. They had given money for a skyscraper, not a small office building. Or had they? The court case revealed the con that McMahon had run. Remember how I told you the investors signed off on the building plans before giving their money? McMahon was able to show the judge that the building plans listed the building not as 480 feet, but 480 *inches*.

The lawsuits from investors began immediately.

The investors lost the case, and their savings, save for a little bit of money they won back from the elevator company, who had refused to build one once they saw that it wouldn't fit in the building. In fact, the tiny new building, known as the "Newby-McMahon Building," didn't have an elevator OR stairs. The only way to get to the upper three floors was with a ladder. When they installed staircases, they took up 25 percent of the building's interior. The bottom floor had room for just six desks, or one desk for each of the six companies that would be the building's original tenants. But four of those companies moved out. Through the next decade, the building only had two tenants using it.

Locals were embarrassed by the tiny office building, but someone from out of town took note. Robert Ripley, who had made his name with his famous "Ripley's Believe It or Not" publications wrote about the debacle, and called the Newby-McMahon Building "The World's Littlest Skyscraper." The name stuck.

Soon after the building was erected, the Texas Oil Boom ended, and people stopped moving to Wichita Falls. The population didn't decrease, but it slowed dramatically, and there was much less need for all the office space. The Newby-McMahon building was boarded up and became vacant for years. It survived a fire, multiple tornados, and even survived part of its wall caving in. None of the tenants had a long stay in the run-down tiny office building.

Today, the Newby-McMahon building still stands tall—forty feet tall—in Wichita Falls. It's changed hands multiple times and has been bought and sold for much less than the money that was raised to erect it. It's been restored as recently as 2005 and it now houses a used furniture and decor store called Hello Again. The World's Littlest Skyscraper is listed on the National Register of Historic Places and has been declared an official Texas Historic Landmark.

So, what happened to J.D. McMahon? Well, after he won his court case against the investors, he disappeared and was nowhere to be found. His con was a success and its legacy lives on in the form of a curious roadside oddity: the World's Littlest Skyscraper. The Internet Says It's True.

The Explosion at Black Tom Island

You may have heard about the Mandela Effect: the idea that somehow a large group of people misremember something collectively. One Mandela Effect that's related to this story is about the Statue of Liberty. There are a ton of people alive today who claim to remember visiting the Statue of Liberty and climbing the stairs all the way up to the torch, where they looked out over the New York Harbor. But it's doubtful that anyone currently living has been up to the torch of the statue. Because while the statue was built for the torch to be accessed by tourists, it's been closed from visitors since 1916.

And the reason it was closed? It was irreparably damaged in a massive explosion only 3,000 feet away.

World War One was raging in Europe. The deadly Battle of the Somme had just begun in France and would last for five more months, producing more than one million casualties. And during the Great War, there were at least ten instances of attempted terrorist attacks in America by Germany.

For instance, Germany had sponsored a program the previous year to sabotage the American cattle industry. America didn't join the fight in Europe until early 1917, but Germany was nervous about America's supply of materials to France and Britain, including cattle. Anton Dilger was an American who sympathized with Germany after studying there. He returned to the United States with anthrax and glanders with the intention of infecting and killing livestock. While it's not thought that he was incredibly successful, he was discovered by the FBI and fled to Mexico.

That same year, a German agent entered the U.S., planted a bomb in the Senate reception room at the U.S. Capitol, and set it to detonate at midnight. It didn't kill anyone, but the saboteur's plot was to send a message for America to stay out of war profiteering. One of the largest profiteers was J.P. Morgan and the same German agent, Eric Muenter, broke into the home of Morgan and shot him twice. J.P. Morgan survived, but Muenter died soon after — most likely from suicide.

The deadliest of these acts of German-sponsored terrorism happened on July 30, 1916, just 3,000 feet from the Statue of Liberty. It was the middle of the night and the summer night on New York Harbor was calm. Just southwest of Liberty Island, which used to be known as Bedloe's Island, there was a munitions depot called Black Tom Island. Just outside of Jersey City, the island was a manmade rectangle of land, mostly built up from refuse and rocks in the New York Harbor. It had a reputation as an environmental hazard, and people in New York hated that it was so close to the city. A lot of this criticism came because of an 1875 accidental explosion on the island that killed four people.

The island was the location of two million pounds of small arms and artillery ammunition. They were being stored on rail cars sitting on barges, ready to be shipped to Russia to assist them in the war effort.

That night, around midnight several small fires were discovered on the pier near the barges. Employees on the island started frantically trying to fight the fires, and eventually called the Jersey City Fire Department for help. Some simply ran away, thinking there was no way these fires were going to be contained. They were right. Two hours later, at 2:08 in the morning, a huge explosion rocked the island.

This explosion was so large that it was heard all the way in Philadelphia. It blew the windows out of every high-rise building in lower Manhattan. One of the barges was loaded with fifty tons of TNT. It had 417 cases of detonating fuses. According to an article at *Firefighter Nation*, the blast wave traveled at 24,000 feet per second and tore firefighters from their boots, throwing them in the air. With shredded clothes, bleeding ears, and faces full of soot and dirt, the Jersey City Fire Department continued to fight the fire. They couldn't get to a second barge with another fire burning. At 2:40 a.m., another explosion—this one slightly smaller—rocked the island. The explosions that went off that night would have registered high on the Richter Scale. For reference, when the World Trade Center's North Tower collapsed in 2001, it registered a 2.3 on the Richter Scale. It's thought that, had the Richter Scale existed, the Black Tom Island explosions would have registered somewhere around a 5.5.

It wasn't until the next morning that most of the city saw the devastation. The Statue of Liberty was pelted with shrapnel. The rivets popped out of the right arm and the arm holding the torch was pushed up against the statue's crown. The island was temporarily closed. Nearby Ellis Island was evacuated. Throughout the city, office buildings were missing windows. Nearer to Black Tom Island, blackened, twisted metal and debris covered an area several city blocks wide. A giant crater extended below sea level near the pier and filled with debris and water. James Doherty, a police officer from Jersey City, was killed in the explosion. So was Cornelius Leyden, the Lehigh Valley Railroad Chief of Police. One of the barge captains was also killed. A ten-week-old baby lost its life as well, being thrown from his crib in Jersey City. A total of seven people were killed as a result of the series of explosions.

And what did the public think caused the explosions? As reported in many of the newspapers in the aftermath, they thought it was negligence. Remember, this was an island with a history of being filled with rubbish and explosives with little protection from accidents and without the proper safety measures. So, everyone just thought it was another accident like the one that had happened in 1875. And that was partly true. There wasn't nearly enough water supply to the island to fight the fires. One of the things that was blamed was the lighting of smudge pots to keep mosquitos away. Railroad officials, warehouse owners, and barge operators were immediately arrested. Edgar Clark, a Commissioner with the Interstate Commerce Commission, immediately began working on a report to President Woodrow Wilson, and found that there was no violation of federal laws governing the packing and transportation of explosives. The men that were initially arrested were freed. They knew a fire had started the chain of events. But they hadn't yet discovered the sinister truth. They had been the victim of what's thought to be one of the first foreign terrorist attacks in the United States.

At this point in the war, mid-1916, America was neutral, meaning that the munitions being stored at Black Tom

Island could have been sold to the highest bidder, whether that be Germany, France, Austria, or Great Britain. But there was a blockade of Germany in place by the Royal Navy, so America was only supplying munitions to the Allies. This was one of the major reasons that Germany was sending saboteurs to disrupt the supply chain from America.

But in the aftermath of the catastrophic explosions on Black Tom Island, the agencies investigating sort of preemptively decided it wasn't the work of foreign saboteurs. The FBI was in its infancy. The CIA wouldn't be established until after World War II. And they couldn't imagine that Germans would have done this. America was full of hard-working Germans looking for the American dream, and with all the safety issues on Black Tom Island, it's like they weren't even looking for a saboteur.

The truth was much darker. Captain Franz von Rintelen had arrived in the U.S. the previous year. He was a German Naval Intelligence officer and a master spy. Even the other agents from the German military didn't know about his secret orders. Von Rintelen entered the U.S. with huge sums of money and direct orders from Berlin. He wanted to try to buy off some of the people in charge of the storing of ammunition to see if he could get some rerouted to Berlin. He bribed officials, which included some of the security men responsible for guarding the pier at Black Tom Island. He had worked with a chemist to perfect a particular type of tiny bomb with a time-delayed incendiary device, and he told Admiral von Tripitz back in Berlin, "I'll buy what I can and blow up what I can't."

Well it was option B on July 30th, 1916. He was responsible for setting the fires that led to the explosions. Von Rintelen and his ring of helpers were fairly successful in their efforts. In New York alone, there had been 70 pier fires and 139 fires on board ships. The Black Tom event was the largest and the deadliest.

We know all of this now, but without any sort of unified investigative body in 1916, this info took years to uncover. There simply wasn't any sort of federal body with the ability or the authority to deal with foreign saboteurs.

It wasn't until several decades later that Germany was declared officially responsible and was sued. It was 1939 and Germany had other plans happening at the time. The Nazi Party in control of the government refused to pay. It wasn't until 1953 when the Federal Republic of Germany agreed to settle the matter and paid the United States $95 million in damages. That money continued to be paid until 1979, sixty-three years after the attack.

If you visit what's left of Black Tom Island today, there's a historical marker that tells this story. It starts, "You are standing on a site which saw one of the worst acts of sabotage in American history!"

If you ever run across someone who claims they've been up to the Statue of Liberty's torch, now you know why they haven't. They've likely been up to the crown, which is open to the public, but the public hasn't visited the torch since 1916. And now you can tell them why.

Nub City: The Worst Kind of Insurance Fraud

In 2010, a federal jury convicted four women in California of wire fraud, mail fraud, and other charges for a scheme to claim $1.2 million from two different insurance companies. Here's what they tried to do: They invented a man—and they were real inventive with his name. They called him "Jim Davis." They must have just looked at the Sunday comics and said, "Should we call him Garfield? No that's too weird. Odie? No, that's too conspicuous. How about Jim Davis!? Yeah! That'll be our fake victim."

Somehow, they were able to apply for insurance policies on this fake person and then they killed him. They forged a fake death certificate and purchased a casket and buried it. This part didn't make much sense to me. It may have been that they were thinking that the authorities were on to them, so they exhumed the fake casket, and filled it with cow parts and pieces of a mannequin. Then they took it to a mortuary and had the thing cremated. How did they get access to the mortuary? One of the women in the scheme worked there. They also advertised the death of Jim Davis in the obituaries and people showed up to the funeral. They even paid a crooked doctor $50,000 to forge medical records to support the fake death certificate. The insurance companies weren't fooled and when they did some digging, of course all four women were caught and charged—really stupid criminals.

In January of 2011, Jeffrey Stenroos was working his normal patrol as a police officer in Los Angeles when a man with a ponytail and a bomber jacket shot him in the chest and fled. Stenroos ended up serving a couple years in prison. Why?

The idiot shot himself. He made up the story about the ponytailed man. The motive is pretty unclear, but he had to pay hundreds of thousands in restitution and was charged with insurance fraud. It was pretty expensive restitution, because when he called it in, it triggered a huge manhunt with over 500 police officers canvasing the area. Of course, they never found the ponytailed man, and the cops were skeptical. It didn't help that Stenroos confided in one of his fellow officers that he staged the whole thing.

In South Carolina in 2008—this guy's a real piece of work—

Gerald Hardin needed a new truck and couldn't afford rent. His buddy David Player cooked up a scheme to scam the insurance company. They took a pole saw—that's a saw that's used for cutting off tree branches—and convinced a person that they knew who had an intellectual disability to let them cut his hand off. The guy went by the name "Porkchop." So Gerald—who was addicted to crack at the time—cuts Porkchop's hand off with the plan that they'll collect insurance claims. The mentally disabled man received almost $700,000 after he let Gerald remove his hand, then Gerald paid his rent and bought a truck with the money. David Player got fifteen years, and Gerald got three. They had to pay restitution in the amount of $671,000 and doctors were unable to reattach Porkchop's hand.

That brings us to Vernon, Florida, the deep South. Vernon is a horribly impoverished community, and has never had a population more than around 700 people. There are two stoplights and a few stores, but not much else. It's in the middle of Florida panhandle swampland between Panama City and Dothan, Alabama.

A man named John Healy worked for a company called Continental National American Insurance Group. He was an investigator for the insurance firm, so his job was examining claims that seemed dubious. They started getting a lot of insurance claims from around Vernon, Florida—all in the same small area. And besides the unusually high concentration of claims in one area, there were a few clues that something was up, so he traveled to Vernon, Florida, to find out.

The first case that happened in Vernon actually may have been an accident rather than self-mutilation. Nobody knows for sure, but it happened sometime in the late 1950s. A farmer had a hunting accident and lost a limb to a shotgun. He collected a modest amount of money, but enough that the poor citizens of Vernon took note.

Vernon was a really depressed area. The Holmes Creek which runs through the town used to be an important shipping lane to the Gulf of Mexico, but had been abandoned, probably due to that traffic using the larger Apalachicola River. You've likely never heard of either, and that's how remote this place is. But when the traffic on Holmes Creek went away, so did the chance at any commerce for this five-square-mile town.

In a poor town, when one guy comes into some money, people talk. Everyone knew. And it wasn't long before someone else accidentally blew a limb off and collected some insurance money. According to a 1982 *Saint Petersburg Times* article by Peter Gallagher and Claire Martin, a rash of these stories started popping up in the late 1950s and early 60s.

For instance, there was the Vernon farmer that took out policies with at least thirty different insurance companies and lost his foot. This guy wasn't even one of the town's poorest. But there were a ton of clues as to why his collection of almost $1 million in insurance money smelled rotten. Firstly, he had a tourniquet with him. They asked him why and he said "snakes." Secondly, there was the clue that the premiums he was paying for these thirty-pllus insurance plans were more than his annual income. The most interesting clue, however, was that he lost his left foot. Which was tough for the man because he drove a stick shift and needed that left foot for the clutch. But on the day of the accident, he drove his wife's car, which was an automatic.

Or there was the guy that blew his arm off in the backyard and immediately yelled to his wife to call the sheriff but first find the insurance policy. And it was his left arm—the man was right-handed.

A lot of these cases involved people's nondominant hand, or their non-driving foot. Some of them were double amputees, missing an arm and a leg from opposite sides—

which was done on purpose so they could still walk with a crutch.

One man who worked as an oiler for a construction company asked an insurance agent about what he would get paid if he lost a limb. The next day, he stuck his hand in the wench of a crane.

The rash of bizarre amputations even extended to nearby cities like Panama City Beach, where a man at a Sawmill accidentally lost some fingers pushing wood through a saw. The insurance company wouldn't pay up, so when he got back to work, he pushed his whole hand through and collected a measly $1,000 in claims.

In total, as many as 60 to 75 people in the Vernon, Florida area got payments because of freak amputations of limbs. Seventy-five people out of 700. John Healy noticed that of all the dismemberment claims in America in those years, around 70 percent of them came from the region around Vernon, Florida. And they were almost all nondominant limbs. People started calling it "Nub City," because if you visited the town, it was almost impossible to not see someone who was missing a limb.

Over a period of four or five years, people received payments from a few hundred up to a few million dollars. And insurance companies, thanks to the work of investigators like Healy, showed up to put a stop to it. But no one in the early 1960s could ever believe that someone would do this to themselves. There was really no great proof that they had done it to themselves. So, no one in Vernon was ever convicted of fraud. The investigations did however really put an end to the phenomenon. Also, because the insurance companies started paying so little, it wasn't worth it--even to the poor residents of Vernon— to self-mutilate.

The town came back into focus when filmmaker Errol Morris heard about the story and traveled to Vernon in 1980 to create a documentary called *Nub City.* As he interviewed Vernon locals and had them telling their stories, the word got out about his film, the subject, and the title, and the residents of the town didn't appreciate it. He started getting death threats and at one point was beat up by a man who objected to the film's title. It had been a couple decades since the rash of incidents and Vernon was still known as "Nub City"—a nickname they were trying hard to shake. In those few days that Morris was in Vernon, he became frustrated and realized he was hitting a brick wall. He quickly changed the title of the film from *Nub City* to *Vernon, Florida,* and made it about some of the more interesting people in the town, like a turkey hunter who, if you watch with closed captioning on, you can almost understand what he's saying. Also, there's a scene with a preacher who delivers one of the weirdest sermons I've ever heard about how he set out on a journey to learn the meaning of the word "therefore." You can find the whole thing for free online if you want to see it, but there's not a single mention of the thing for which Vernon was known best.

As someone who works with his hands for a living, and I know most of you do too, I can't imagine doing that to myself just for a little money. But maybe the story here is a snapshot of the late 1950s in a depressed rural town. And desperate times called for desperate measures. It's a story about why insurance plans cost so much in the first place, but also on what our economy does to us when the system fails people in these types of places. It's also a story about stupid contagion, like the people who danced themselves to death in the 16th century, or the wealthy people who walked with a limp to be popular. Human beings do stupid stuff. The Internet Says That's True.

The Awful Reason There Aren't More Mummies

There's an 1815 painting by Martin Drolling that hangs in the Louvre. It's an interior painting of two women and a child sitting in the light of an open window. The women are painting and the child is on the tiled floor, playing. The painting, called *Interior of a Kitchen,* is filled with dull earth tones, browns and reds. And one of the notable colors in the painting is called "mummy brown." It's a particular shade of brown that was very desirable at the time, and very difficult to come by. Because it wasn't just the color of mummies. It was made *from* mummies.

Mummy brown had a certain transparency and shine to it that was popular for depicting windows and shadows. And it was sold all the way up until 1930. The pigment used ground flesh of actual mummies, mixed with other chemicals, to create a paint that was known to all artists of the time. In addition to mummy brown, it's even rumored that Drolling used the blood from the hearts of monarchs to create some of the red hues in the painting, but that fact is disputed.

For this story, we're mostly going to talk about mummies and why there aren't more of them. When this topic comes up, there's usually an exaggerated statement like "there would be way more mummies if people in Victorian England didn't eat them." The title of this chapter even uses this little bit of hyperbole. It's not really true. There's no evidence that the total number of mummies would be huge if it weren't for this particular type of desecration, but yes—people ate mummies.

As early as 5000 B.C., humans were deliberately mummifying their dead. And while scientists have discovered naturally mummified human remains throughout history, we're talking specifically about people that were deliberately mummified, which is most commonly associated with Egypt. Mummification was a part of normal life and death in Egypt, for both rich and poor Egyptians.

There's something about the way that people were mummified that was interesting to scientists and doctors in Victorian England. The flesh of the mummies was dark, almost black. Put a pin in that and we'll come back to it in a minute.

A little backstory: ancient scholars and medicine men used a substance called bitumen to treat a whole assortment of ailments and to protect plants from insects. It was a dark, sappy, tarlike substance that formed in the Middle East from decayed plant and animals. In Persia, it was called Mumia, from the word "mum," meaning wax. And they referred to this bitumen tar as mummia when they used it for medicinal purposes. Even Pliny the Elder, the famous Roman author and naturalist, mentions using bitumen to treat coughs and dysentery. Scientists later discovered that there is indeed some antimicrobial properties to bitumen, and it contains sulfur, which is a biocidal agent. So it makes sense that when preserved Egyptian remains were discovered and appeared to be covered in this dark waxy substance, they believed it to be bitumen. And because bitumen was known as mummia, that's where we get the word "mummies." There's some dispute as to whether any of the flesh of the mummies actually contained any bitumen. Some of it may have been, but not all of it. Most of the waxy black surface of mummified flesh was just the result of the mummification process and wasn't bitumen at all.

Just like any natural resource, naturally occurring bitumen from the ground was becoming more and more rare. And, even if they were mistaken, the people who found these mummies had found a possible new source.

It was around this same time, that the actual definition of mummia began to change to include not only naturally occurring decayed material, but that taken from an embalmed body. I think it's probably easy to see at this point where this is going.

Along with heroin for cough syrup, tobacco for headaches, and mercury for STDs, people started to believe that eating small bits of ground mummy flesh could be beneficial to their health.

It was a very strange and disconnected form of what's known as medical cannibalism. There was a time when King Charles II of England sipped what he called the "King's Drops." It was his own personal tincture and was made up of ground human skull suspended in alcohol. In the 1600s, a scientist named Thomas Willis believed that if you ground up a human skull and mixed it with chocolate, you could cure apoplexy. In Germany, doctors used human fat, soaked into bandages, to treat wounds.

In Victorian England, consuming blood and tinctures made from ground human bone were up to date with the science and the beliefs of the time. It wasn't considered some sort of strange medicine. It's interesting to think about the fact that, at this very same time, Protestants were persecuting Catholics for their belief in transubstantiation and thought it was outrageous that Catholics believed they were drinking the blood and eating the flesh of Jesus. And here at the same time, people were consuming blood, fat, skull, and flesh of the dead for their health.

Some of the health benefits that they believed consuming mummy powder would provide was vitality, protection against illness of the liver and spleen, curing paralysis, and the list goes on. It was like a snake oil of the time.

So where did these mummies come from? It turns out the mummy trade was big business. English, Spanish, French, and Germans began working in the mummy importing and exporting business. Sometimes they'd buy and sell complete bodies. Sometimes it would just be fragmented pieces of mummified flesh. But as soon as this business arose, that meant that Egyptian tombs were also raided. Some were raided and stolen for display as oddities in museums. But many were raided and ground into powder for medicine and paint.

There's this idea that we would have a TON more mummies if the Victorians didn't eat them. I've seen that argued, but I've also seen it argued that it's not necessarily true. Dr. Sarah Parcak is an Egyptologist and author, and she says in a Twitter thread:

"Mummies are NOT rare b/c people ate them. A) Mummies are found all the time. See all media of mummies found B) Mummies were used for paint + as medicine in 19th c *but* there is a huge mythology around them. Countless mummies were lost to unethical mummy wrappings AND were used as fertilizer. How many mummies were used for mummia? We cannot quantify. Only a small percentage of mummies lost compared to other reasons. Also if mummies are so rare how come my colleagues & I keep finding them?"

And then she added a TL;DR: "Mummies are cool but learn about them from experts."

The practice of using mummies for medicine led to something even more sinister: the selling of fake mummies. People began robbing graves and selling corpses as Egyptian mummies. After all, mummies themself were an extremely limited resource. Eventually, science proved that there was little benefit to the practice, medically speaking.

So, it's partially true. If you're ever asked by a child why there aren't mummies anymore, you can look them in the eye and say with a serious face: "It's because we ate them."

The Boston Molasses Flood

It was January of 1919. Just two months earlier, World War One was officially over, though the Treaty of Versailles had yet to be signed. America was suffering from the Pandemic of 1918, often referred to as the Spanish Flu, which killed 675,000 Americans. The Boston Red Sox had won the 15th World Series the previous year and the United States was getting ready to enter into Prohibition.

In Boston, the temperature on January 15th was a sunny forty degrees Fahrenheit at the Purity Distilling Company. This sounds cold, but it was a nice warm relief from the freezing temperatures the weeks before. Along Keany Square, the Purity Distilling Company had a giant 2.3-million-gallon tank of molasses. At 12:30 p.m., people in the North End neighborhood heard a tremendous crash. To many, it sounded like thunder. To people close to the tank, they immediately saw what happened. The tank seemed to explode into pieces, behind the power of a giant tsunami-like wave of dark, thick molasses. A nearby truck was hurled into the harbor. The wave of molasses reached twenty-five feet tall at its peak, tall enough to slam the steel of the tank against the elevated railroad structures nearby. The heavy molasses—40 percent more dense than water—traveled at thirty-five miles per hour away from the tank. Nearby buildings were lifted off their foundations and crushed. Horses were stuck. People were drowned. The next morning, the *Boston Post* ran, in giant letters, the headline:

"HUGE MOLASSES TANK EXPLODES IN NORTH END: 11 Dead, 50 hurt."

The article goes on to describe "Horses blown about like chips, houses torn asunder, and the heavy section of the elevated railroad structure smashed like an eggshell."

A police patrolman, Frank McManus, is quoted in the article. McManus was a hundred feet from the tank and he said he felt some wet, sticky substance strike him on the shoulders. He thought it was mud, but then saw the entire tank fall.

The *Boston Post* continued, "Ensnaring in its sticky flood more than 100 men, women and children, crushing buildings, teams, automobiles and street cars - everything in its path - the black reeking mass slapped against the side of buildings footing Copp's Hill and then swished back toward the harbor."

By the time the scene was fully cleared and examined, 21 people would be dead and as many as 150 would be injured. Horses would be killed, buildings, cars, and trucks destroyed—absolute terror. For years, authorities argued about why.

In the period leading up to what became known as the Great Molasses Flood of Boston, molasses had become hugely popular as a sweetener. It was an alternative to white sugar and it was the main ingredient in brown sugar.

It also created byproducts that could be sold like rum and alcohol. When fermented, molasses could create a type of alcohol that at that point was important for making munitions like the ones that had been used in Europe in WWI.

At the Purity Distilling Company in the North End neighborhood, which was a subsidiary of the United States Industrial Alcohol Company, they had used a giant steel tank to store molasses as it was offloaded from ships in Boston Harbor. The tank itself was designed to hold up to 2.5 million gallons. On January 14th, 1919, a ship from Puerto Rico filled the tank to 2.3 million gallons—almost completely full. There are a couple theories that have been put forth about what happened.

In 2014, an analysis by structural engineer Ronald Mayville found that the structure wasn't properly built to hold molasses. It may have been okay with water, but the thickness of the tank walls (an average of half an inch thick) just wasn't enough to hold molasses. As I said earlier, molasses is 40 percent more dense than water and weighs about 12 pounds a gallon. Another issue experts have pointed out was a flawed rivet design. And while the tank had been filled 29 times, the way it was filled the day before this disaster was only the fourth time it had been filled to capacity.

There were also warning signs. Neighborhood kids were known to have visited the tank prior to the disaster. They would bring cups to fill with molasses that would leak out between cracks in the steel. The tank was known to make groaning noises. One employee actually brought a piece of broken steel from the tank into his boss's office. He was dismissed and nothing was done.

But what made the steel so brittle may have been that there wasn't enough manganese mixed into the steel. This would make the walls of the tank very unstable and brittle with temperature changes. And a temperature change is what took place before the tank ruptured.

As I stated earlier, the weather in Boston had been cold. That week, the temperature rose to forty degrees, which was warmer. The ship filled the tank to the 2.3-gallon mark, and they would heat the molasses during the pumping process to make it flow more smoothly.

One of the deadliest factors of the flowing molasses after the catastrophic collapse of the tank was that the warm molasses flowed quickly and then cooled when it hit the streets and the air, making it much more thick and sticky.

The Boston Police, the Red Cross, the Army, the Navy, and 116 Cadets from the USS Nantucket helped by wading through knee-deep molasses to locate victims. They set up a makeshift hospital in a nearby building that hadn't been destroyed. And for the next four days straight, working day and night, they located the flood's victims one by one. Twenty-one people in all, including two ten-year-old children. Ships sprayed the harbor's salt water onto the streets to clean off the molasses and it wasn't until then that workers could cut apart giant plates of steel to find victims underneath. Some of them had been swept into the harbor by the flood and weren't found until the spring.

After a class action lawsuit against the United States Industrial Alcohol Company, the company had to shell out $628,000 in damages, or just over $9 million in today's money, and families of those who were killed received $7,000 settlements. The court case went on for years and to this day is talked about as one of the pioneer cases in arguing for government regulation of corporate practices.

One of the most interesting parts of this story is one of the strange consequences. For decades after the disaster, the North End of Boston had a recognizable reminder of the lives lost on that tragic day. For twenty years, it was said the North End neighborhood had a sweet smell in the air—the smell of molasses.

Thirteen Months: The Kodak Calendar Experiment

Imagine having an extra month between June and July. Sounds pretty great to me! In the International Fixed Calendar, that's what would happen. Thirteen months. Extra month of summer. I'm here for it.

Our story begins in the 1920s, but in order to give this idea proper credit, we really have to go all the way back to 1849 and a guy named Augustus Comte.

Comte was a Positivist. Positivism is basically a sort of way of looking at everything in the world from a measurable, scientific method. No theology, intuition, or metaphysics—
everything must be positively measurable and calculated. And to someone who believes in looking at the world that way, the Gregorian calendar—the one used around the world even today—just feels like chaos. Comte was one of the first people to vocally call for calendar reform.

In Comte's Positivist Calendar, the year was broken up

evenly into thirteen months, each consisting of twenty-eight days. For those of you who are awesome at math and just did the calculation in your head, you're right. That's only 364 days. Comte had an idea to make that extra day a festival day to commemorate the dead. It wouldn't have a number, a month, or even a day. It wasn't a Monday or a Friday—it was just the celebration day. As for the months, they would be named after famous figures of history. Moses, Homer, Aristotle, Archimedes, Caesar, Saint Paul, Charlemagne, Dante, Gutenberg, Shakespeare, Descartes, Frederick, and Bichat. Super easy to remember, right? "We'll just schedule that meeting for the 14th of Archimedes." It's no wonder that the Positivist Calendar didn't catch on—after all, at this point we had been using the Gregorian calendar for more than 250 years, since 1582. No one was persuaded.

A quick history on the Gregorian calendar that we use today: It was introduced by Pope Gregory the 13th as an update to the Julian calendar. The Julian calendar came from the Roman calendar, and all Pope Gregory the 13th did was account for leap years by adding in an extra day every few years to keep the year aligned with the astronomical year. The problem was that, because the solar year is slightly longer than 365 days, Easter was falling further and further from the spring equinox. So the addition of Leap Year fixed this. We've stuck with this Gregorian calendar since 1582 and at this point I can't imagine changing it. But I'm not George Eastman.

George Eastman founded the Eastman Kodak Company. He brought the idea of the roll of film to the masses and "Kodak Camera" became a household name. The company was started in 1892 and still exists today. It was a leading manufacturer of film, then of cameras, and today they still make chemicals and products to support the print film industry. And from 1928 to 1989, they operated on their own calendar—the International Fixed Calendar.

Where did George Eastman get the idea of creating his own calendar for Kodak?

After Augustus Comte invented the Positivist Calendar in 1849 and the idea wasn't widely adopted, the idea sort of died for seventy-some years until a British accountant named Moses Cotsworth brought it back. In addition to having one of the most British-sounding names ever, Cotsworth developed the International Fixed Calendar while working for a railroad company. As you know, railroads rely heavily on timetables and schedules. And the idea that monthly accounts at the railroad couldn't be evenly and fairly compared with one another really bothered him. Let me give you an example that was laid out in *The Outlook*, a popular New York periodical in the 1920s:

"A hotel that did a business of $10,000 per week in room sales found that its receipts from room sales were less in May than those in April. It looked as if the business was dropping off. May was one day longer than April and yet its room sales were less. The figures, however, proved to be very misleading. As a matter of fact business was actually better in May than in April—ten dollars a day better—but the monthly comparison seemed to show that it was worse."

Cotsworth had figured this out and, in 1907, formed the International Fixed Calendar League, an organization to gain support for the idea of a fixed calendar internationally. Here's what his calendar looked like:

The months were the same as the Gregorian calendar currently being used, except every month was shortened to 28 days. An extra month was added between June and July and it would be called "Sol," S-O-L, named after the sun and because the summer solstice would fall in this month. Now again: if you multiply 28 times 4, you're still a day short, so a day was added at the end of the year. That day wouldn't fall within one of the months, or one of the weeks. It wouldn't have a weekday name—it was simply called "Year Day" and could be a day of celebration. Leap years would still be observed by adding one of these weekless, monthless days between the months of June and Sol.

Here's what that does. The calendar still lines up with the Gregorian calendar in most respects. Some holidays would have to be moved slightly, but January 1st would still be January 1st. But most importantly, it makes every month the exact same amount of time. Business results could be measured evenly. Every quarter was exactly 91 days, and so there was an apples-to-apples comparison on a ledger. And furthermore, the 28-day month is perfectly divided into four even weeks, starting on Sunday the 1st and ending on Saturday the 28th. Every month, the 1st would be a Sunday, the 10th would be a Tuesday, and so on. Unfortunately for those who are superstitious, every month would have a Friday the 13th.

You know how you don't really know what day of the week you were born on without either a) knowing from what your mother told you or b) looking it up on the internet? Well with this calendar you'd instantly know. Because every month, that numbered day would always fall on the exact same day of the week.

In the 1920s, the idea was being spread in publications around the world. Cotsworth placed articles explaining the benefits of the idea in newspapers and magazines. And he made a compelling case, arguing how his new calendar, the International Fixed Calendar, was better for business and better for simplifying the understanding of the dates of the year. He laid out all the reasons, with many newspapers publishing a graphic of what the calendar would look like.

In 1922, a convention was held in Washington to consider the calendar. It was also presented in front of the United States Chamber of Commerce. Cotsworth met with business and labor leaders around the world. He gained the support of George Eastman of the Eastman Kodak Company. Together, they sent letters to more than a thousand businesses, trying to persuade them to change to the new calendar.

Even the United State House of Representatives took up the matter when a Minnesota legislator, Tom Schall, brought it to them in 1919. In their version of the International Calendar, however, the extra month was called "Vern" because of the Vernal Equinox. The idea never made it out of committee. By the way, can you imagine telling people your birthday is Vern 12th?

Unfortunately for the supporters of this radical idea, something like a calendar isn't easy to change unless EVERYBODY changes. After all, if your business is on the new Fixed Calendar and ships a product to someone on the old Gregorian Calendar, how do you tell them when it will get there? It forces you to convert the date any time you communicate with someone else, which then forces you to first find out which calendar they're using. It's similar to the headache of asking someone what time zone they're in before you schedule a meeting.

There were also religious objections to the calendar. If you're celebrating a day of rest on the seventh day of the week, whether it be Saturday or Sunday, what do you do with the Free Day? Do you just pretend it didn't happen? If you don't, the next year's day of rest will be off by a day, and it will be another six years after that before it gets back to the day where it used to be.

These were serious issues for people, and were the reason that almost nobody adopted the calendar. It's like when video tried to shift from VHS to Laserdisc. It's cool, but now you have to have both players, because you already own your collection on VHS. Now you have to buy everything again. Compatibility is a serious concern.

Despite no one else adopting the calendar, George Eastman said, "I'm doing it anyway," and in 1928, adopted the International Fixed Calendar for the Eastman Kodak Company. And he continued advocating for the adoption of the calendar, even addressing the League of Nations, who twice took up the idea. In both instances, it was religious leaders who organized to put an end to the idea.

For Eastman, it was a matter of fiscal tidiness and predictability. In a letter to businessmen, Eastman argued, "Nobody is ever sure until he has looked it up whether the first of the month falls in the beginning or the end of the week."

After the adjustment period, employees actually enjoyed the predictability of the calendar, which was just used internally at the company. Every employee had a pocket-sized calendar with them all the time. Every company boardroom had a large poster of the fixed calendar. And this system worked so well for the company, that they continued to use it for sixty-one years.

George Eastman's health started to decline dramatically in 1930. He lived with constant pain in his spine and suffered from horrible depression because of the pain. He took his own life in 1932, but his company lived on—as did their fixed calendar, which they continued to use all the way until 1989.

So, the Internet Says It's True. The Kodak Company operated under their own thirteen-month calendar for sixty-one years. And it could be argued that it's a better calendar! But if that were a good reason to make a worldwide change, we'd probably be using the metric system.

Abraham Lincoln Invented the Chokeslam

The chokeslam is a move in professional wrestling where one person grabs the throat of another person, lifts them into the air, and then slams them to the ground.

In professional wrestling, this is accomplished by grabbing the defender at the top of the chest, just under the jaw. The defender grabs the attacker's arm and then the attacker will put the defender's right arm over his shoulder. Then they'll usually grab the waist or back to help support the weight as they lift the defender into the air. The defender then falls and straightens out at the last minute to help spread out the impact of the fall. Now, that's a very simplified and summarized version of the move, and you definitely shouldn't try it unless you've had a professional teach you the proper way to do it. If you don't know the ins and outs of these wrestling moves you could get seriously hurt.

In case I have to say it, a chokeslam doesn't involve actual real-life choking. But it's a popular finishing move for wrestlers like the Undertaker, Kane, the Big Show, and more. They'll sometimes make it even more exciting by slamming their opponent out of the ring and through tables, or from inside the ring to outside on the floor. There are something like ten variations on the move, each with their own specific name based on the positions, but we don't need to get into that. What's important is that it's a move so popular, even non-wrestling fans know what it is. If I say chokeslam, you have a basic idea of what I'm talking about.

You'll only see it in professional wrestling or backyard brawls. It's not technically legal in UFC or MMA fighting because you can't grasp the throat. You could maybe do a version of it if you could execute a legal hold around someone's neck first, but it's not really a useful move in those sports anyway. It's mostly just for show.

In professional wrestling, there's a claim that it was first performed by the wrestler 911 in the mid 1990s and was invented by his promoter/manager Paul Heyman. And we know that 911 frequently used it as a finishing move—even chokeslamming a referee in one match.

But I did some searching and it seems it's pretty clear that neither Paul Heyman nor 911 brought the chokeslam to professional wrestling. The earliest I can find is from a Japanese wrestler, Akira Taue, who wrestled starting in the late 1980s. His popular finishing move was the chokeslam.

The move itself has an origin much older than the 1980s. I'm sure there were hundreds of street fights where people used the move, but for the purpose of this story, we're looking for the first time it was actually described in writing, the first time we can prove someone chokeslammed someone else. It goes all the way back to the summer of 1831 and a lanky six-foot-four general-store employee in Illinois.

If you visit the National Wrestling Hall of Fame and Museum in Stillwater, Oklahoma, you'll find that Abraham Lincoln is immortalized there, honored with their "Outstanding American" award. There is a display about Lincoln and other Presidents who enjoyed wrestling and a large mural of Lincoln wrestling with a man named Armstrong. It's the very match that we're interested in.

There are so many legends and tall tales about Lincoln's wresting career that it's hard to separate fact from fiction. We know that he enjoyed the sport and was known for his wrestling ability as a young man. One of the legends is that he wrestled three hundred men and was only beaten once. Of course, in the rough and tumble prairie of Lincoln's youth, wrestling wasn't so much an organized sport as it was just fighting.

There are a few of Lincoln's bouts that are well-documented. In the recollected works of Abraham Lincoln by Don and Virginia Fehrenbacher, Lincoln tells a story on the campaign trail about his wrestling days. In 1860, he told a college professor named Risdon Moore that he was undefeated until he was thrown twice by a man named Lorenzo Dow Thompson, a man who, according to Lincoln, "could throw a grizzly bear."

Another one of the well-documented matches is the one with a man named Jack Armstrong. Armstrong was the young leader of a group of tough guys. I don't know if you'd call them a gang, but they were a group of ruffians that lived in the next settlement over from where a twenty-two-year-old Abe Lincoln worked in a general store. Lincoln was in New Salem, Illinois, and these guys were from Clary's Grove. The Clary's Grove Boys would come into New Salem to drink, gossip, trade, and play.

The store owner where Lincoln worked, Denton Offutt, used to brag on how tough Abraham was. He would claim that Lincoln was faster and tougher than anyone around. Well Bill Clary, whose family founded Clary's Grove, didn't believe him. He bet Denton Offutt ten dollars that Lincoln couldn't beat Jack Armstrong in a wrestling match. When Lincoln reluctantly agreed, a whole crowd of people gathered in front of the general store in New Salem.

There are differing accounts here on what happened. Some say Armstrong won. Others say Lincoln won. But what we know for sure is that someone cheated and the match got ugly. It's thought that maybe Armstrong attempted to foul Lincoln with some sort of dirty move and Lincoln got mad. Abe grabbed Armstrong by the throat, lifted him off the ground with his enormous height, and shook him out like a wet rag before dropping him to the ground.

From there, it sounds like the rest of the Clary's Grove Boys jumped on Lincoln, beating and kicking him as he laughed. I have to say, picturing this now, it kinda makes Lincoln sound like a psychopath. In any case, what we know is that Lincoln and Armstrong ended the match by shaking hands and being friendly. And believe it or not, this match gained Lincoln entry with the group of boys and made him welcome anywhere in town. Later, Jack Armstrong called Lincoln "the best fellow who ever broke into camp."

Lincoln later became great friends with Armstrong and his wife. After the passing of Jack Armstrong, their son Duff was arrested for murder, and none other than Abraham Lincoln represented him in court. He taught Duff how to read while in prison, and Duff Armstrong's defense became Lincoln's most well-known court case. The eyewitness described seeing Armstrong murder a man named James Metzker one night by the light of the full moon. When it was Lincoln's turn to cross-examine the witness, he proved with an almanac that there was no full moon that night. Duff Armstrong was found not guilty.

Despite his client being found not guilty, do you know who is guilty? Abraham Lincoln, of officially being the first recorded account of chokeslamming a guy during a wrestling match. So yes: the Internet Says It's True. And while he never jumped off a turnbuckle or donned a championship belt, Abraham Lincoln, the Great Emancipator and 16th President of these United States, officially invented the chokeslam.

About the Author

Michael Kent is a professional comedian and magician who, as of the printing of this book, has toured 49 states (c'mon Wyoming!) and 19 different countries performing live for audiences. He's appeared on the hit television show *Penn & Teller Fool Us* and is the host of the livestream talk show *Joke/Story/Trick*.

He started *The Internet Says It's True* podcast as a 2020 pandemic project (then called *Tell Me What to Google*) and, when people listened, decided to continue it as an ongoing project.

Michael is originally from Urbana, OH, and resides in Columbus, OH.

www.ingramcontent.com/pod-product-compliance
Lightning Source LLC
Chambersburg PA
CBHW020532030426
42337CB00013B/813